DONALD TRUMP

Repeal, Replace, Impeach

Compiled and Written by

Dwight C. Douglas

ISBN-13: 978-1975779030

ISBN-10: 1975779037

DEDICATION

To all my ancestors who came to this land 333 years ago. I will do what I must to protect the original idea of America for you. And to all those who gave their lives fighting for freedom and truth.

1. WHY I WROTE THIS BOOK
You Must Put America First

The first President I remember was Dwight D. Eisenhower. My first name was given to me in his honor. I was told that General Eisenhower was my father's General during World War II. I didn't realize until I was a bit older that Dwight D. was not only my father's General, but the top dog for the whole army.

I can recall Eisenhower's baldness, his five stars and my parents' unquestioning loyalty to him. Not only was he a war hero, he was the "Commander-in-Chief" of the Armed Services of the United States of America.

My family on my father's side came to this land through the James River settlement 333 years ago. We are American and you cannot find anyone in my family who isn't totally proud of being so.

The eight years of the Eisenhower era were the "wonder bread" years when everybody was working and buying houses while playing and watching baseball. Fifteen dollars would get you six large grocery bags full of food. We never went to bed hungry.

I didn't think that much about politics, because it had no effect on me. In 1960 my Pittsburgh Pirates beat the New York Yankees in the World Series and I started to believe that anything was possible in our country. I walked with an extra bounce in my step. Finally, my hometown wasn't a punchline in a joke.

Then, something happened. Everyone started to talk about who would be the next president. Everyone had to take a side. I was rather confused why this became such a big topic.

My family, being loyal to Eisenhower, were Republicans. Eisenhower's Vice President was Richard Nixon, therefore, following the party line, my parents wanted Nixon to be the next president. I never had any affection for Richard M. Nixon, but I wasn't quite sure why.

It was during this debate about who should be the next president that a disturbing opinion surfaced in my family. My family felt that John F. Kennedy would not be a good president because, as they claimed, he would have to take orders from Rome. I thought, "What a strange concept." Then it was explained to me on the street, playing baseball with friends, Kennedy was a Catholic.

Now I was aware that the Pope oversaw the church, lots of my friends were Catholic, but why would the Pope have anything to do with our country? Growing up in a Presbyterian home I was aware of the disdain for Catholics, but I never quite understood why. They are Americans too.

Kennedy seemed smarter than Nixon and unquestionably was a more likable person. I remember the morning after the election when JFK had won. My parents were a bit speechless and obviously in a little shock. I would remember their faces and feelings. I liked Kennedy and was glad he won.

After the election, I got a paper route, which meant that I would be delivering Pittsburgh Press newspapers to my one-hundred customers for the next eight years. One of the great things about being a newspaper delivery boy was being able to read the newspaper every day.

Politics usually landed on the front page and seemed complicated. The more fun stuff for me was on the sports pages. Politics didn't add up like a box score or a batting average. I did learn from an early age, however, that what happened around the world had a major effect on my country.

When I got to high school, my civics class taught me a little bit about how our country functioned. Do they even teach civics anymore? I think they dressed it up as Social Studies, and then Western Civilization.

What puzzled me most was the fact my family seemed to have a different view of politics than what I would have assumed. My father was a milkman and my mother was mostly a housewife, but she also worked for a while as a secretary at the elementary school. My father was a union member, a Teamster, because he drove a truck in his work. I never understood why they were Republicans rather than pro-labor Democrats.

I viewed Republicans as the party of the owner class and even saw some of their actions at times to be anti-union. I remember asking my father about the union and what he thought when they went on strike. He seemed to view the union as a necessary evil rather than fighting for him. He felt sorry for the owner when the drivers went on strike. My first lesson in politics was that feeling of division, a divide between the owners and workers, the distance between the Republicans and the Democrats and the overreaching separation of religious houses.

Kennedy was a very charismatic leader and my family slowly warmed to him. Things were going well economically, even as my parents added additional offspring. We all felt JFK's crafty negotiation with the lunatic Nikita Khrushchev saved the world. We were schooled by Eisenhower and Kennedy about the evil communists. Knowing they were protecting us from the enemy was more important than whether Kennedy was Catholic. And, of course, everyone loved Jackie Kennedy.

The day that Kennedy was assassinated in Dallas in 1963, my patriotic family was very disturbed by this tragedy. I could see a bit of fear in their eyes. We weren't a family that would have ever had a president's picture up on the wall, but we always had an American flag to wave.

The transition to Lyndon B. Johnson stabilized the country in many ways, but also put a giant magnifying glass on the Vietnam war. While the newspaper headlines were not that good for old LBJ, he seemed to keep us in the loop. When he decided to not run for a second term, the specter of a Richard Nixon presidency reared its head. Of course, my parents fell right into line. My mother even said she loved Richard Nixon. They believed Spiro Agnew's ongoing negatives about the "evil" media and that somehow, he and Nixon represented the views of middle-class America.

Hubert Humphrey didn't have a chance against Nixon and all his men. I could see it in the newspaper every day. There were anti-war protests, which divided the nation and drove a wedge between my father and me. There was a general sense in the south that Johnson had given too much freedom to African-Americans and something had to be done. More people moved over to the "law and order" Republican side. The Southern Democrats were on the march.

By the time I got to college in 1967, I had long hair and a bad attitude about government. I knew that this great political divide in my family was happening in many homes. The seeds were being planted, not by some outside agitator conspiracy or communist infiltration, but by the fact the younger generation was reading, learning and knowing that our government wasn't telling the truth.

We knew that Johnson had lied about Cambodia. We knew that Nixon had lied about Watergate. We also knew that a free press helped the country. We "baby-boomers" read more than our older siblings and became politically aware. Our friends were being sent halfway around the world and coming back in boxes. We didn't understand why this was happening.

Thus, began my on-again, off-again obsession with politics and government. I hated that Gerald Ford pardoned Richard Nixon, but knew he was right about the healing part. Jimmy Carter was a nice guy who thought he could change the world. Nothing changed and little got done.

Ronald Reagan was not thegod" that most conservatives believed him to be. He was a smart politician and a great actor who landed the greatest role of his life. Yes, things got better and we saw that wall torn down in Berlin, but America probably would have done just as well with another four years of Carter.

George H.W. Bush, Reagan's Vice President, was wired into the global power structure of the world. He served as Chief of the U.S. Liaison Office to the People's Republic of China and also the Director of the CIA before he became Vice President. Bush 41, became even friendlier with Saudi Arabia after he left office.

Bill Clinton, one of the smarter Presidents, did the dumbest things. He continues to amaze me with stupid behavior, but as President, he made America better. He got our finances in order and kept the Republicans from turning the clock back to 1950. It's too bad he got into so much hot water with his other head. His actions drove the remaining old line southern Democrats over to the RNC.

Now, I love America, but we do crazy things. Really, we elected George H.W. Bush's son as President? Who wrote this script? George W. Bush, who I now find intriguing and acceptable on many levels, seemed to be in the grasp of Dick Cheney, who had been Daddy Bush's Secretary of Defense. Dick, aptly named, was one of those hawks who probably wanted the first Iraq War to end differently. So, he started another one.

George W. Bush is a good man and didn't ask for 9-11 on his watch. He had to deal with lots of terrible things. We can look back now and see that he gave it his best, but in the end, he almost bankrupted our country on bad banking laws and costly nation building. Oh yeah, and a lot of people died and millions were physically, mentally and emotionally injured for life. That is the dark and real side of political decisions. You want to be the decider, you better be right.

Then, out of nowhere, we got this guy from Chicago, who was really from Hawaii. He spoke like a man who understood just what America needed, and he just happened to be African-American. Now, I know my friends have yelled at me about this claim, but I did see the same thing that I saw with my parents about Kennedy. That hushed whisper, "He can't be President, he's a Catholic." Only this time, you can change the word "Catholic" to "Black."

Barack Obama was a very smart president and understood how to motivate African-Americans, Hispanics and Democrats to make a difference. We were aiming for change and what we got was constipation. I totally blame Next Gingrich for his involvement in the Republican party in 2008, and he can be specifically blamed for all the Obama failures in Congress. Sure, Obama didn't wine and dine the Republicans; why should he when they announced their number one goal was to make sure he didn't get a second term?

In 2013, Barbra Bush said on CNN, "I think it's a great country. There are a lot of great families, and it's not just four families or whatever. There are other people out there that are very qualified and we've had enough Bushes." (or Clintons).

She was suggesting we needed someone else for President, but she didn't use those words.

And that is what we got: Someone else. And that brings me to answering the question "Why did I write this book?"

This is my country and this is your country. We will disagree on the details of this great nation, but we probably don't disagree with the proposition that it is our duty to stand up and say what we think. I would like to advance that to mean that if we make a mistake in one of our elections, it is up to us, the people, to fix it. As Colin Powell said, *"If you break it, you have to buy it."*

I marched against the Vietnam war because I thought it was wrong. I thought Nixon should have been put in jail, not because I wanted to inflict pain, but to make sure that everyone who came after him knew that **if you lie when you are in office you will be removed** and judged just like any other criminal. There must be a sense of honesty and justice in this land.

For all the bullshit that we have heard about how bad Obama was from the Red side of the country, he wasn't bad at all. Sure, he made mistakes, but the demonizing was over the top and brushed right against the very fiber of racism and bigotry. That same fiber that Donald Trump has been rubbing, I must point out, since the first day he announced his run for the office.

I wrote this book because if I can get one person to read it and understand how harmful Donald Trump is to this country, I will have accomplished something.

The chapters of this book are the daily posts from my blog called WhyWait4Years.com, which I started right after the election. This book covers the first 200 days of the Trump invasion.

The idea of the blog was to say, hey, don't be involved only every four years, start today, start now, get this lunatic out of power. Activism in America takes a lot of energy. The Democrats failed to harness the Bernie Sanders energy to win. They preferred to go with the assumption rather than the crazy old screaming other guy.

We must stop those who make laws that take away our freedom or poison the water we drink. Don't be fooled by how they gold-plate what they say will help you. No one ever made the middle class stronger with trickledown economics. Don't believe the fork-tongued devils.

We need to vote them out of office, and if you can't wait for an election, recall them. Replace them and, yes, even impeach them. That is what I really think we need to do about Donald Trump. Now.

2. THE INAGURAL SPEECH
The Day He Lost Me

I was going to include all the text of the January 20, 2017 Inaugural speech of President Trump, but as we got further away from that "grand" day, I knew that most people reading this book would have no desire to read what the man said.

I'm old enough to remember some of the great inaugural speeches that have taken place in our history. I was only three-years old when Dwight Eisenhower was sworn in and I don't remember if we even had a TV at that point, but I remember reading his inspired words.

I do remember Kennedy's Inauguration. The breath of Robert Frost reading his poem "The Gift Outright" and the wonderful line from JFK, "And so, my fellow Americans: ask not what your country can do for you— ask what you can do for your country." Now that was a great president and a great speech. Not too many people have topped it, although Obama and Clinton came close. There was only one John Kennedy.

When I sat down to hear the new President's address, I, like many people, was expecting a pivot from the campaign rhetoric, perhaps something that a smart business man would give to the board of directors about the upcoming plans for the corporation known as USA. I thought perhaps that the Donald would let his reality TV persona fade away and that his pep talk would be more presidential and positive.

What I heard, turned my stomach. These were not the words of someone who wanted to unite a nation, this was the same egomaniacal farce we saw during the campaign, parading around the country in his big jet casting negative energy, racism whispers and flippant comments and digs.

It was at that moment, I heard the screaming voice of George Orwell's Big Brother. The speech revealed the true Donald J. Trump. I realized that a less than majority of voters had just made the biggest mistake we, as a nation, could have ever made.

Before he finished his tirade, I said to myself, "You must do something." It was a call to action that other presidents never brought out of me for the right reasons. This call was for all the wrong reasons.

Rather than regurgitate Trump's horrible speech word for word, let me bring you the most painful parts and offer some real American insight into what I think he was saying. I will put his words in italics, as I will throughout this book.

The Big Opening

Today's ceremony, however, has very special meaning. Because today we are not merely transferring power from one Administration to another, or from one party to another — but we are transferring power from Washington, D.C. and giving it back to you, the American People. For too long, a small group in our nation's Capital has reaped the rewards of government while the people have borne the cost. Washington flourished — but the people did not share in its wealth. Politicians prospered — but the jobs left, and the factories closed. The establishment protected itself, but not the citizens of our country. Their victories have not been your victories; their triumphs have not been your triumphs; and while they celebrated in our nation's Capital, there was little to celebrate for struggling families across our land.

There are a lot of people working in Washington, just doing their jobs and trying to get by, like any other "working stiffs" in the country. Trump begins by condemning everyone in Washington and accusing them of making money while factories closed. Yes, there is some truth that the rules have been changed so that people who do very little can make a ton of money, like Newt Gingrich, but Trump's over simplification was disheartening for those who work within the system. He opened by condemning them all as guilty, even the ones whose support he will soon need to get things done.

The Pledge

The forgotten men and women of our country will be forgotten no longer. Everyone is listening to you now. You came by the tens of millions to become part of a historic movement the likes of which the world has never seen before. At the center of this movement is a crucial conviction: that a nation exists to serve its citizens.

The idea of "forgotten" people is not new, but it sets the table for an agenda that can be forced on people who think they are being heard, rather than just "used" by this demagogue.

We can all agree that a government exists to serve all citizens, not just the people who have bought into this historic movement. Not all historic movements are positive events, like when planes crashed into the World Trade Center, the Pentagon and a field in Pennsylvania. We must remember that it's rare that the subject of the event declares it "historic." The over use of that word by this President should be alarming to historians.

The wealth of our middle class has been ripped from their homes and then redistributed across the entire world. But that is the past. And now we are looking only to the future. We assembled here today are issuing a new decree to be heard in every city, in every foreign capital, and in every hall of power. From this day forward, a new vision will govern our land. From this moment on, it's going to be America First.

Here is the core of the populist propaganda, that somehow all our jobs and all our money has been "redistributed" by some evil deep state. Trump cries out to every "foreign capital" that he is the new sheriff, not realizing they didn't ask for him.

Trump is the guy with the big gold badge who has been making his ties and shirts in those very capitals. Yes, America first, unless it's a hotel he wants to build in those foreign lands, and then, he will take their money. He used Asian steel in his buildings in the US, but that doesn't matter now, because things are going to be different.

The Biblical Con

We do not seek to impose our way of life on anyone, but rather to let it shine as an example for everyone to follow. We will reinforce old alliances and form new ones – and unite the civilized world against Radical Islamic Terrorism, which we will eradicate completely from the face of the Earth. At the bedrock of our politics will be a total allegiance to the United States of America, and through our loyalty to our country, we will rediscover our loyalty to each other. When you open your heart to patriotism, there is no room for prejudice. The Bible tells us, "how good and pleasant it is when God's people live together in unity."

I always love when someone tells me we don't want to impose our way of life on anyone and then declares a ban on certain people of a certain religious belief from coming into our country, while determining that people who believe what we believe will be treated differently, as far as travel visas go. The line that still burns me today is "… we will rediscover our loyalty to each other." What a crock of shit. He says it right there, patriotism pushes out prejudice? Nationalism by its very nature creates an US and THEM mentality. Let me quote the Old Testament Psalm 133:1, *A Song of Ascents, of David. Behold, how good and how pleasant it is for brothers to dwell together in unity! 2, It is like the precious oil upon the head, Coming down upon the beard, Even Aaron's beard, Coming down upon the edge of his robes….* Did he realize his reference was about the anointment of chosen people, while in the same paragraph pitches for the "civilized world" to unite against *Radical Islamic Terrorism*? I wonder if that is an expression he will use when he stands on Islamic soil?

The straw that broke the camel's back

The line that produced my strongest ill feeling was our new President listing all the terrible things that people must endure daily. He said, *"But for too many of our citizens, a different reality exists: Mothers and children trapped in poverty in our inner cities; rusted-out factories scattered like tombstones across the landscape of our nation; an education system, flush with cash, but which leaves our young and beautiful students deprived of knowledge; and the crime and gangs and drugs that have stolen too many lives and robbed our country of so much unrealized potential.*

I was thinking, okay, where does he go from here? After you tell someone how bad you have it, what do you say to make them feel better? What do you say next, you say this: *This American carnage stops right here and stops right now."*

For as long as I live, I will never forget this man put the words, "American" and "carnage" in the same breath. Lest we forget, **Carnage** means the killing of many people. Perhaps he could have saved himself if he would have simply laid out how he could make it better. It's like calling Mexicans rapists. Once you say it, you can't take it back. You have said that most or all Mexicans are criminals. To put the American educational system in a league with gangs and drugs and then say they are American carnage, is a slap in the face of every hard-working teacher and educator in the nation. Boy, he really brought us together with that one.

Now I know that Donald Trump didn't write that speech. Stephen Miller and Steve Bannon were the voices behind this negative view of our beloved country. Don't get me wrong, I know there are lots of problems in America, but I also realized that this new president doesn't care about everyone.

He cares about himself and his family. He cares about pleasing those who give him total loyalty, love and affection. Those who disagree with him are simply the enemy, no matter what country is on their passport. If this speech was the only thing that bothered me, I would not have created the blog and written so much about him. But read on and you will see a real-timeline analysis of who Donald Trump really is and why he must not be president.

3. THE PROPOSITION: IMPEACHMENT
What the Rules Say
Posted: 2-11-2017

The Constitution, Article II, Section 4:

The President, Vice President and all civil Officers of the United States, shall be removed from Office on Impeachment for, and Conviction of, Treason, Bribery, or other high Crimes and Misdemeanors.

The Constitution, Article I, Section 3:

The Senate shall have the sole Power to try all Impeachments. When sitting for that Purpose, they shall be on Oath or Affirmation. When the President of the United States is tried, the Chief Justice shall preside: And no Person shall be convicted without the Concurrence of two thirds of the Members present. Judgment in Cases of Impeachments shall not extend further than to removal from Office, and disqualification to hold and enjoy any Office of honor, Trust, or Profit under the United States, but the Party convicted shall nevertheless be liable and subject to Indictment, Trial, Judgment, and Punishment, according to Law.

4. STEVE, STEPHEN & AGENT ORANGE
The Brains Behind the Curtain
Posted: 2-13-2017

We now know the source of poison that leaks out of the windows and the doors of the White House. Every president has had people who whisper into their ear. Some objective observers have said that these aids are not just advisors, but they actually control the leader of the free world.

George W. Bush had Dick Cheney who, like his father, had roots and connections in the C.I.A. There are those who say that Cheney misled and manipulated the younger President Bush and gave him justification to re-enter Iraq and finish the job that his father failed to accomplish.

Richard Nixon had John Ehrlichman and H. R. Haldeman, who historians believe were pulling the strings of the soon-to-be broken president during the Watergate scandal. Haldeman was an experienced advertising man who used his talents to sell Nixon to the American public. Ehrlichman was an attorney who believed the President had unlimited powers and could not be held accountable for dirty deeds.

Trump has Steve Bannon and Stephen Miller as puppet masters, writing up executive orders based on their ideology and political beliefs. It is obvious that their efforts are not filtered or tested through any analysis of *who this helps* and *will it hurt anyone?* They simply don't care about people; they care about creating a world they believe is right.

While Stephen Miller read his answers to the questions from all the Sunday morning talk shows, one could feel the defensiveness and witness the deflection laced vitriol. The non-fact of voter fraud was repeated, covering the fib of the President and showing that, he too, bought into the lie. Or did he create the lie?

Mr. Miller's pronouncement that Federal judges didn't have the authority to stop the President's travel ban was nothing more than an attempt to argue his position to the media, that same media they claim is so dishonest and terrible. Judges judge, presidents lead.

Mr. Miller and Mr. Bannon should remember that both Haldeman and Ehrlichman were convicted of conspiracy, obstruction of justice and perjury and both served time in prison. Steve and Stephen should focus on the phrase "obstruction of justice" as they carry on the business of President Trump.

The key to keeping America safe from terrorism starts with keeping America safe from tyranny. Let Democracy win first and the rest will be fine. Who is the puppet and who are the puppeteers? Time will tell whether the pitch-man is reading a well-prepared script, or is true to his convictions.

5. ST. VALENTINE'S MASSACRE
Trump Exposed by General Flynn
Posted: 2-14-2017

One of the great things about a free press is that they don't stop doing their job when they are attacked. Those who work in the press have learned the craft of journalism. The fourth estate, and now the fifth estate, have a purpose in Democracy. That purpose was codified by the founding fathers.

Retired Lt. General Michael Flynn exposed President Trump as a slow moving, unaware and non-detailed oriented "learning on the job" leader. Flynn violated the Logan Act and the President learned of this on January 26 yet he waited twenty-days to act. Trump's spokespeople seem to be bumping into their own claims. At this point, Sean Spicer is nothing more than a visual pun and Kellyanne Conway has no credibility. Thanks to the Washington Post for doing their job.

While this "shit storm" is happening in the administration, Trump wastes his valuable time with Twitter, adding layers of uninformed chatter and tacky vague innuendo. The President's legal advisors may think they are there to protect the POTUS from unnecessary legal actions, but what they fail to do is to inform their client of the most important part of this mess. TWEETS are legal documents and can be used in court against the President and will likely damage relations with other nations. Trump has been exposed as a feckless leader with a monumental lack of perspective or knowledge of how basic governance works. Flynn liked Trump, Trump likes people who like him. The General was a tough-rogue general who Colin Powell described as "right-wing nutty." But Trump thinks tough style and great nicknames are the only substance he needs to put people into his administration.

It's time for President Donald J. Trump to start his "extreme vetting" in his own house first. How can he claim to love this country so much, but continue to appoint and nominate such mediocre and un-empathic characters to the departments and councils they are predisposed to not like? You have been exposed by your actions, Mr. President. The confusion and the disparate positions that are sprouting from your many spokespeople make it seem like you are out of touch with your own people.

6. UNBELIEVABLY DECISIVE?
Follow the Vodka
Posted: 2-15-2017

Sean Spicer, the White House Press Secretary, has a responsibility to back his boss and protect him from the 'evil' media. We get that, but when people speak English they use words, and words have meanings. It's clearly unbelievable that Spicer claims President Donald Trump was decisive with the Ret. General Michael Flynn fiasco.

Why does the president even need Spicer? Why does Trump need Kellyanne Conway? He kept saying during the campaign that only he knows how to fix things, but when given the opportunity to fix things fast with Flynn, he was frozen with inaction and waited for the damage to go away. Just like a typical politician.

Once again, Trump's latest legal document, his tweet of 2-15-2017, sets the tone of the administration-always looking backward, always comparing itself to Obama, shoveling crap on Hillary Clinton hoping to divert the attention away from his own inadequacies.

Why don't the American people know what Trump owes to Russia? Why can't the 'all powerful' legislative body we call Congress get to the bottom of Mr. Trump's financial entanglements with Russia? While Nikki Haley talks tough at the U.N., Trump undermines her positions with his tweets and talks. While the Senate hawks harbor suspicion with this bizarre bromance between Trump and Putin, the Congress has failed to demand an answer.

In the 2004 novel by Philip Roth, *The Plot Against America*, the scenario he presented was the manipulation of the US election so a pro-Nazi candidate, Charles Lindbergh, could use his fame and nationalist viewpoint to take power and then pal with Adolf Hitler. Clearly, if Donald Trump's administration was in cahoots with the Kremlin during the election, that was a real plot against America.

There will be a list of those people who spoke up. And there will also be a list of those people who remained silent while America was shamed and devalued by this egoist puppet of Putin.

7. JARGON, JEWS & THE JUGGERNAUT
Does Trump Have Classic German Guilt?
Posted: 2-16-2017

While reading, the Jewish Telegraphic Agency's TELEGRAPH this morning, I couldn't help but notice the story about how President Donald Trump answered one specific question during the joint press conference with Israel's Prime Minister Netanyahu in Washington yesterday.

An Israeli reporter asked a question. To quote the article,

REPORTER: "Mr. President, since your election campaign and even after your victory, we've seen a sharp rise in anti-Semitic incidents across the United States. And I wonder, what do you say to those among the Jewish community in the states and in Israel and maybe around the world who believe and feel that your administration is playing with xenophobia and maybe racist tones?"

Trump then wandered around in the desert for forty-seconds talking about how he won the election and the electoral college. One might interpret his first answer to be saying, "Well, yeah, we have lots of those people in our tent, but, hey, they voted for me." Like a dog pissing on trees to mark his territory, he went out of his way to make sure everyone knew he won the election. His insecurity appears often.

Trump then promoted the fact that he has Jews around him, stopping short of the old cliché, 'Some of my best friends are Jews!" Like the phrase 'Some of my best friends are black," after an unknowing racist just told a tasteless joke.

The Telegraph summed it up nicely, urging Trump to make "a strong statement condemning anti-Semitism and a pledge to carefully monitor hate crimes and threats." Why can't he find the leadership in his soul to say that?

The flawed logic is the fact that Trump always caters to his base, not the total America electorate. 48.2% of those who voted wanted Hillary Clinton, while only 46.1% cast their ballot for the Donald. Trump continues to be sullen about the popular vote he did NOT win. He makes no attempt to talk to 48% of the country. His insecurity appears often.

The jargon that he uses when replying to questions about hate groups, anti-Semitism and the actions of vile people is inadequate. It's like the great line in the TV show *Fawlty Towers*, when two German guests are staying at the hotel, *"Don't mention the war!"* It was clearly a suggestion to help the guests deal with their German war guilt.

Could Trump have something in his past that would create an embedded need to cover some deep-rooted guilt about Jews? He advertises his proximity to Jews, perhaps to say, *"Hey, I'm cool with the Jews,"* but even in this case, his insecurity appears and the words fall short of real meaning and empathy.

Trump should talk to his son-in-law about what the Jewish Community really wants to hear from the President of the United States or, better yet, actually listen to people's questions during press conferences and answer them honestly.

8. WORST PRESS CONFERENCE EVER

"I'm really not a bad person"

Posted; 2-17-2017

In an overblown 77-minute press conference, the president of the United States took the mic away from Sean Spicer and commanded the communication himself. His opening lecture to the press belabored his quest to discredit the media.

His attempts to alienate journalists smacks of the implication of the opposite. Donald J. Trump loves the press and lives for their attention. When he says, *"The tone is such hatred"* in the reporting on his administration, he takes on a martyr complex that is seriously unattractive in any human.

His statement, *"I'm really not a bad person"* was as shallow as Richard Nixon's *"I am not a crook."* If you must tell people you aren't something, you open the door for the listener to think that you are saying the opposite. *"The roll out was perfect, there was zero chaos"* and *"the administration is running like a fine-tuned machine"* was simply not true. The rollout of the travel ban was vague and disruptive and found to be poorly written. I'm not sure the hail of executive orders is something to brag about, especially when they aren't comprehended by the very person who signed them.

The on-going reverse engineering that is taking place is atrocious. When Trump was confronted on the misinformation about his electoral vote number by NBC's Peter Alexander, the president's defense was *"I was given that information"* and then, *"Actually, I've seen that information around."* While claiming that everybody else is fake news, the lie bubbles coming out of his little round pie-hole expose his lack of truthfulness with facts and figures.

Why would any country want to deal with someone who can't get the facts right for a press conference? Any Congressional leader who isn't asking how to contain this paranoid-pathological liar posing as president has probably sipped enough of the Kool-Aid of power to no longer be thought of as a viable leader. We are talking to you Paul Ryan.

The reality TV show—referred to as the press conference—had some simple rules. Ask a tough question, you're out. Ask a question that provides a way for the host to brag about himself, you get praise. Ask a controversial question, and you will be put down with lines like, *"Quiet, quiet, quiet,"* and then, *"See he lied about — he was going to get up and ask a very straight, simple question. Okay, sit down."*

Once again, Trump treated a Jewish reporter with disrespect, going on a self-absorbed tirade about himself, rather than answering the question. To the credit of other reporters, they didn't let the president off the hook and returned to the question and pointed out the questions wasn't about him personally, it was about what was his answer to this problem. This was the worst press conference I have ever seen.

A president can be impeached if he commits a misdemeanor. This president has continually lied to the American public, to Congress and to the Judiciary. Isn't that a misdemeanor? Let's keep counting the lies for the writing of the Articles of Impeachment. If only embarrassing America was a misdemeanor.

9. PRESIDENTIAL APPRENTICE
More Divots than Pivots
Posted: 2-19-2017

I remember when the 70's mega-rock band, The Eagles were reaching saturation in the press, on the radio and on music video channels. Rather than pour on more, their cunning-larger than real life manager, Irv Azoff, decided to hide his prize property for more than eight months. This ingenious idea created a demand for information and music from the band and, when they returned, propelled them even further. It also gave them time to prepare more brilliant songs. The limelight sometimes bakes creativity out of an artist.

We have just had a super blast of Trump and I have noticed people on social media saying that they are tired of hearing his name and having the news focused on him every time they turn on the powerful "fake news" outlets. I'm sure his fans love it, but there will come a point of enough being enough.

Clearly the shock of losing the election has mobilized many non-right-wing people in America, those who didn't vote for Trump, and those Bernie people who may not have voted at all. Yeah, YOU!

Trump is accused of being smart by the over analysis that takes place on the cable news channels. Trump needs a villain in his life, so he has decided to beat up the media. This amateur wanna-be dictator doesn't realize he's attacking the First Amendment, therefore undermining the Constitution itself. That's a great way to endear yourself to the Judiciary, Mr. President. Donald Trump is the apprentice now, trying to learn the ropes while massaging his ego. Why not take some time to understand his political power and his need to lead the WHOLE country? Too busy tweeting?

Trump's quoting Thomas Jefferson as a justification for his rants on the press was, as he would say at the end of a tweet, Sad! Trump loyalists keep saying, *"Hey, give him a chance,"* or *"Why is everyone in such a panic?"* Well, we are giving him a chance. We have no other choice. People who are undocumented are alarmed and anxiety ridden. When the news showed what was really happening in Vietnam, we woke up. As the *"dishonest"* news shows America the crying children watching their parents taken away in plastic handcuffs, maybe that place called compassion will stir.

If only your core fans buy your next album, your fan base doesn't grow. If the Pew Study is correct and Donnie "boy-president" has only has 39% of us approving of what he does, then he has a lot of work to do to impress the boss. He certainly doesn't realize it, but he is NOT the boss, WE are! He says it, but does he really believe it? No one seems to know what he believes. Clarity has never been his strong suit.

He talks more about himself than the country and its people. He must not only dominate TV but he tries to impress us as well. He hasn't pivoted to a presidential position. The long sweat drenched speech in Melbourne, Florida served up colder mashed potatoes with lumpy gravy. Don't talk about what you are going to do, just do it.

10. CLARITY CREATES CONFIDENCE
Who is the Real President Here?
Posted: 2-21-2017

Donald Trump is a dreadful communicator. There is nothing in the rules that says that the President of the United States must be a good thinker or talker. George W. Bush was no statesman. Some of his more famous lines, "For every fatal shooting, there were roughly three non-fatal shootings. And, folks, this is unacceptable in America," and of course, who can forget, "I'm the decider, and I decide what is best." But one of the words most people believe he invented, Strategery, wasn't his creation, but something he quoted from of all places, a Saturday Night Live skit.

When we hear Donald Trump quote Thomas Jefferson to justify his disgracefully inaccurate denouncement of the press, poor Sally Hemings is turning in her grave. Knowing that words were driven by Good Old Jefferson's anger at the press after exposing Jefferson's long-term and fruitful affair with his favorite slave, it kind of makes Trump complicit with the attempted cover-up. Did he see this on TV?

It's okay that Trump's sixth grade vocabulary connects with the masses, but does he use his skills of "propagrandisement" for any good? He continually talks about himself, looks backward and divides us. Fox News was your source for terror in Sweden? That's how wars get started.

When you paint a whole industry, or a whole group of people, with one brush, there is a medical definition for that; it's called scapegoating. This is the process in which one applies the mechanisms of projection or displacement, focused on feelings of aggression, hostility or frustration to another individual or group; the amount of blame being unwarranted. Not all media outlets are bad, not all Mexicans are rapists and not all presidents are smart.

When Donald Trump gets a chance to make it right and hit the bull's eye with a real leadership decree, he's a deer, frozen in the headlights of his own fears, ego and need to be loved.

Mr. President, we know you aren't anti-Semitic, but we haven't heard you lead the way with your words. You daughter condemns the hate crimes and your press secretary says you don't condone those actions, but when do YOU address America? Why can't you be the leader who truly attempts to bring people together. Are you even capable of this?

George W. Bush knew what to say when crisis hit. Standing on the pile of scorched earth at Ground Zero, he grabbed a bullhorn and said, "I can hear you! The rest of the world hears you! And the people – and the people who knocked these buildings down will hear all of us soon." And indeed, his words were baked into history. Remember, bin Laden did hear from us. That is leadership Mr. President.

You are living in denial, most-likely wrought by your right-wing hooey, Mr. Bannon. You fail to see the connection between your rhetoric and the emboldened hate speakers and terrible actions such as bomb threats and grave site desecrations. A real President of our country would take to the airwaves and give the haters a piece of their mind. But then, we've already seen some of those pieces and there's not much clarity there.

11. THE LADY DOTH PROTEST TOO MUCH, METHINKS!

The Inner Voice of Lunatic
Posted: 2-22-2017

Most political and marketing experts' analysis of the presidential election of 2016 showed that Twitter played a major role. There is no question that social media is a double-edged sword.

It cuts one way when instantaneous reactions and pronouncements are transmitted to a wide number of fans and opponents. Trump has more than 38.5 million followers and has dumped 35.5 thousand 140-character bundles of wisdom our way. That may seem like a lot, but Kim Kardashian West, Kanye's wife, has 50.2 million followers.

Like a teenage bulimic, Mr. Trump must psychologically vomit once a day. He pays a price for his uncensored use of a non-secure consumer phone and exposes his lack of depth and any real desire to "bring us all together."

In his most recent tweet, Trump deflected once again, but there is some truth in what he is saying. He just doesn't see what's really happening.

Let's look at this missive. Trump is limited in his mastery of the English language and uses repetition rather than significant revelation to reveal his inner voice. Catch his use of *"so-called"* which is his code for *"not legit"*; as in *"so-called"* judges. He could have used that against Obama with a quick slap: *"so-called American."*

He uses the word *"some"* as if he isn't sure of the facts. He peppers it into his speech like, *"Some of them are good people, I guess."* Or as I might say, "Some of the things you say, Mr. President, simply aren't true."

He says, *"in numerous cases"* giving him plausible deniability for a later time when someone will accuse him of painting with too broad a brush. One phrase that is absolutely true, however, is the line, *"…planned out by liberal activists."* Yes, can you believe the opposition to your policies have a plan? Planning is a good idea, wink, wink.

If he looked a little deeper, or had someone in the White House who wasn't filling his belly with expense Beluga caviar, he would learn what those liberals are doing. They use this web site called Twitter to spread the word and organize these protests. They are simply using the other side of the knife against you, Lard Ass. Many phones against one.

Time to quote Newton's third law here: For every action, there is an equal and opposite reaction. For every tweet, you push through your illegal phone, Mr. President, there will be an opposite reaction and it will continue until you finally grow up and go back to posing as a successful business person.

And finally, Mr. Trump, for the good of the nation, would you please seek psychiatric help from a medical professional? The number of times you have declared your sadness in these legal documents called Tweets is alarming. It's downright Sad!

12. L.G.B.T.Q. F.U.
Trump Transitions to Discrimination
Posted: 2-23-2017

When Mike Pence, then Governor of Indiana, signed that state's 'religious freedom' bill, he cemented his name on the short list of those politicians who would be considered for Trump's Vice President.

The Republicans in the Indiana state government kept saying that this bill would not restrict the freedoms and liberties of the LGBTQ community, but it was certainly a way for businesses to use their religious viewpoint to restrict those who may not share their 'normal' views on gender.

Within days, Pence was challenged and backed down, *"After much reflection and in consultation with leadership in the General Assembly, I've come to the conclusion that it would be helpful to move legislation this week that makes it clear that this law does not give businesses a right to deny services to anyone."*

Proving that Pence, an astute politician, wasn't going to let valuable dollars from major national events leave his state, he moderated. Now, we find another move to thwart the rights of a 'certain kind' of person in America.

Trump revoked federal guidelines specifying that transgender students have the right to use public school restrooms that match their gender identity. His administration released the letter after the national newscasts were put to bed, but right before the Trump teams appeared at the CPAC Meetings.

Obama, while in office, cited Title IX as the basis for providing services, protection and restrooms to transgender humans in schools.

Title IX says: "No person in the United States shall, on the basis of sex, be excluded from participation in, be denied the benefits of, or be subjected to discrimination under any education program or activity receiving Federal financial assistance."

One of things that new Attorney General Jeff Sessions worries about is the difference between the words 'sex' and 'gender' and whether the title alone could make the Obama rule stick. Now we get to play an interesting little game of what words mean.

Gender means the state of being male or female (typically used with reference to social and cultural differences rather than biological ones) and sex means either of the two main categories (male and female) into which humans and many other living things are divided on the basis of their reproductive functions. Except worms.

So, if you thought Roe v. Wade was in jeopardy, you were right. Those who want to repeal Roe v. Wade are the same people pushing the agenda that tries to force LGBTQ people to kowtow to those meanings rather than reality. Lawmakers should focus on the word "typically" because, as we have learned, there is nothing typical about this situation. Typically means, "in most cases" and that does leave the door open to this not fitting all cases.

If the government gets to control what you do within your own gender-self view, could they then demand that you NOT look like the gender of your choice? It's not a far reach to be nervous that those in power could decide what every woman, or man, does with her or his own body, as in repeal of Roe v. Wade, as an example.

Gay people are already in your restrooms, Republicans. You just might not know which ones of YOU are gay. And lesbians use women's rooms because of how they view themselves, not because of any law. Bisexual people do what they want, not because of Title IX, but because they are free to be who they want to be.

NPR says there are as many as 1.4 million Americans who consider themselves Transgender. And if the United States doesn't take a stand for all citizens, then we might as well burn the United States Declaration of

Independence. All men are created equal, even when they may not want to be men, or women. Pretty clear to any thinking American, that Trump, Pence and Sessions are living in 1952.

13. CLIMATE FOR CONSTITUTIONAL CRISIS

Nixonian Activities in the Trump White House
Posted: 2-24-2017

The headline on CNN this morning (2-24-2047) read: **FBI refused White House request to knock down recent Trump-Russia stories.** What would be your greatest fear for the United States of America? Would it be terrorism; check. Would it be insane leaders of nations with nukes; check. Would it be a president who thought of himself so powerful he could attempt to change the flow of rivers of information away from the people?

In this administration's attempt to *"publicly knock down media reports of conversations between campaign loyalists and Russian operatives"* we have now entered a very dangerous era in our country.

According to CNN, White House officials had sought the help of the FBI and other agencies investigating the Russia matter to say that the reports were wrong and that there had been no contact.

The Trump gang does not care who controls the press, as long as they control the "facts." Even if the news is fake, it must be their version of fake.

The important word here is "control." When Steve Bannon spoke at CPAC he said that another top Trump priority would be the *"deconstruction of the administrative state."* What does that mean? As I have always said, if you listen to the words of a person, you will know what they are really thinking.

Well, a guy named Dwight Waldo, yes real name, wrote a book called The Administrative State in 1948. Ironically, the same year that George Orwell finished writing his book 1984. I am sure Bannon knows both books and was applying the theories accurately.

In Waldo's book, he claims that in an 'administrative state' there is a tension between democracy and bureaucracy and offers that a political administration dichotomy is false. Whatever that means? Public servants must do more than implement policy set by elected officials and ironically the book says that government cannot be run like a business.

The funny thing about what Bannon is offering here, is a real glimpse into the workings of a dark and sinister plot to destroy the way Washington works. Deconstruction would, we assume, be followed by reconstruction, you know, like after the Civil War. A person who says he is against the administrative state is obviously saying the executive branch must be all-powerful.

Attempts to use administrative offices, bureaus of law enforcement or judicial appointees to manipulate the news and rewrite the dialog about this new President is the first step in this deconstruction. Sure, all Republicans think they are right and all Democrats believe their cause is worthier than what comes out of the other side of the aisle, but someone should stand up against this ruthless squad of radical Presbyterian terrorists. Joke intended.

If you say you are going to tear down the administrative state, you are really saying that whistleblowers don't have a legal role in government. You are saying there will be no dissent. And just like tyrants from the past, they will brag about the how all the miners are going back to work and the trains are running on time. If that doesn't ring a bell in your head, go back and study how nationalism in Germany ruined lots of people's lives. No administrative state there.

14. PRESIDENT TRUMP BREAKS THE LAW

Loose Lips Sink Ships

Posted: 3-5-2017

Let our readers and followers mark down in their calendars that on March 4, 2017, the president of the United States, Donald J. Trump broke federal law by disclosing on his personal twitter account a United States Foreign Intelligence Surveillance Court secrecy order by disclosing an on-going investigation into a foreign state's interfering with our national election.

OR, he is making a false claim, that can be readily verified by the court and federal agencies, and he has the power to order those agencies make that information available to the public with no liability to him personally. In short, he has embarrassed himself, the judicial branch, the intelligence community and our beloved America.

Let's review how this works: Due to the sensitive nature of what it does, the United States Foreign Intelligence Surveillance Court (FISA Court) operates in secret with its hearings closed to the public. Records of the proceedings are kept, but they are NOT available to the public, although copies of some records with classified information redacted have been made public in the past. This is the only way that the government claims it can fight terrorism and keep us safe. Secrecy, not something our founding fathers had in mind, has been codified into law as if these covert activities are military secrets, although the actions can be domestic in nature.

Thanks to Edward Snowden, who lives in Russia, we learned how far reaching some of these warrants have been and how US communications and internet companies have bent over to give the feds more information than they claimed they ever would in their End User License Agreements (EULAs). In fact, many phone companies violate their EULAs every day and we don't even know because we didn't read that long legal document they make us sign before we click the Agree button.

But let's get back to Trump, our 'leader' or as I like to call him our Bragger-In-Chief. He is not above the law. If I disclosed the existence of a FISA warrant, I would be arrested and charged with a felony. Trump, probably is using Breitbart News as a source, and believing their "fake news" that was created by those ALT-RIGHT loonies, should make us all nervous. Imagine that Trump might use the FISA Court to spy on his enemies, then say, "Well Obama did it." The president continues to use Obama as his whipping boy, sad!

Clearly there is no filtering process, thus one could argue, we don't have a functioning administration and the executive branch is dangerously close to running off the tracks. You may be on the 'Trump Train' but be warned, the conductor is a lunatic.

Some people see the Donald more like an infallible false-prophet rather than the flawed human being he truly is. We must make a move to replace him. This is the only way to end this circus and the daily 'SHIT SHOW.

15. PARANOIA STRIKES DEEP, INTO YOUR LIFE IT WILL CREEP*

Trump Sees Boogie Man in Every Shadow

Posted: 3-6-2017

Houston, we have a problem. New York, we have a problem. Chicago, we have a problem. You get the picture. Donald Trump has decreed that his personal myopia and deep-seated need to live in alternate universes and concocted conspiracies will have a great effect on the way his United States of America will be managed.

There are three things that we suggest to enhance the stability of the union at this point. These points should motivate US citizens to write to their representatives in Congress (addresses can be found on the web at www.whywait4years.com). Suggest to these representatives they consider it vital that we have a peaceful and orderly transfer of power to someone mentally stable.

Number One: Trump, or any president, should not be allowed to use Twitter. Or, at least, the tweets should enter a queue for review by his team before they are released to the world. This is a matter of national security. We must guard that these legal documents of 140 characters not cause damage to our nation.

Number Two: Trump must release all his tax returns and a law should be enacted that states clearly that all candidates for President or Vice President must release the last four years of their tax returns within 90 days of the election. Not doing so should be grounds for disqualification.

Number Three: The Constitution should be modified to create the opportunity for a midterm vote of confidence. We have elections every four years. Why not have a midterm referendum, which would give the leader a report card of what the electorate feel about the job they are doing. You cannot claim a mandate when things change so quickly.

These are not unreasonable requests. The world has changed. I believed our government was fortified against a lunatic getting into office, but that has been proven to be false. Let's admit that the value of the Electoral College, being the safeguard against an unqualified person getting into the highest office, worked in reverse this time. We now must pursue a different path to purifying the office of President.

It would be sad to impeach Donald J. Trump and end up with Mike Pence. However, when people like Marco Rubio, John McCain and Lindsey Graham seem more reasonable, we can see clearly now that America has made a terrible mistake. Trump must go. Don't leave America, stay and fight.

*The headline for this piece was a partial lyric from the 1966 Buffalo Springfield song, "For What It's Worth" written by Steve Stills.

16. TRUMPGATE
The On-Going Abuse of Power
Posted: 3-7-2017

There is something happening in the White House that the American public needs to know about. It also happens at the King's castle in Florida; known by its very foreign sounding name Mar-a-Lago. The mainstream media fails to reveal or even follow this story. Even the Alt-Right propaganda arm of the administration avoids the subject. But we will not be involved in covering up the daily cover up of Donald J. Trump. Clearly stated, the President of the United States of America wears makeup.

When he came down his gold-plated escalator to announce that Mexicans are rapists and criminals, and oh yeah, that he was also running for president, he was wearing makeup.

When he debated all the other people on the clown bus running for President, he was wearing makeup.

When he traveled to Mexico to disrespect the president of that country by saying they discussed his infamous wall, he was wearing makeup.

Business Insider said, *"Though no one knows for sure what the source is, many makeup artists and tanning experts have a pretty good guess: a bad artificial tanner."*

Are they involved in this obvious cover-up? Trump has used so much of that tanner that makeup artists must cover his bad tan lines with pounds and pounds of makeup. And the sad thing, the U.S taxpayers are picking up the tab.

The only time Agent Orange doesn't have makeup on is early in the morning when he takes the daily Trump dump with his Android phone in hand to tweet up his unwise and reckless pronouncements.

It is clear, that our President is addicted to makeup, which helps increase his confidence greatly and chemically protects him from the 'evil rays' that Obama is sending to penetrate his thin skin. Unfortunately, one of the side-effects of always wearing makeup is having the sniffles. The president should talk to the Surgeon General, a real man who doesn't wear makeup.

We need to ask Congress to investigate this. We need to see the President without makeup. Perhaps a special prosecutor could get to the bottom of all the makeup and find out what is hiding under there. Is there a 'there' there?

To quote the Scarlet Letter: *"No man, for any considerable period, can wear one face to himself and another to the multitude, without finally getting bewildered as to which may be the true."* We think Nathaniel Hawthorne said it best.

17. LEADERSHIP AND LIES
Trump's Legislative Disconnection
Posted: 3-8-2017

We all know that most Presidents send well-deliberated messages to Congress that they would hope to eventually see in legislation. Those ideas are then whittled and worked into a proper bill, voted on by both houses and then sent back as a finished bill or act for the President to sign.

The messaging coming from this Commander-In-Hype is based on pure generalizations instead of any well-thought plan with details and the ramifications of those details.

Let's review what Trump has foamed:

"Nobody knew health care could be so complicated."

"Obamacare. We're going to repeal it, we're going to replace it, get something great. Repeal it, replace it, get something great!"

"There's many different ways, by the way. Everybody's got to be covered. This is an un-Republican thing for me to say because a lot of times they say, 'No, no, the lower 25 percent that can't afford private'… I am going to take care of everybody. I don't care if it costs me votes or not. Everybody's going to be taken care of much better than they're taken care of now."

So, Donald Trump says he will take care of everybody. It won't cost you votes Donald, it will cost us MONEY. He endorsed this first draft of a healthcare reform presented by Speaker of the House Paul Ryan yesterday, March 7, 2017. It is clear, that by letting Congress take away the mandate, not everyone will be covered. Rather millions will be thrown off the insurance rolls. FACT.

Mr. Know-It-All, healthcare is as complicated as the number of possible ailments and conditions in the medical universe. It seems that most people who have had to deal with doctors, hospitals and insurance companies already know this. You wouldn't construct a building without detailed plans, Mr. President, so why would you build a healthcare system for America without a definitive blueprint? Cost, can we have the cost?

Next, "something great" is what a used car salesman says when you walk onto his lot. Stop hyping things you haven't even read. One should note, even if Trump had read the document, as I did yesterday, he would not even know what it says. It is a construct in legislative form, thus incomprehensible to any mere mortal.

When you say, your new plan will be "very popular" you reveal more of your own personal litmus test for everything instead of defining a good plan, which should be fair, affordable. The cost could be reasonable by inserting enough preventative benefits to keep people out of the hospital and on the job.

The net result of all these layered lies from Trump is that the eventual healthcare act will be nothing like he imagines. And you can write this down, people will end up paying more. There is nothing in there to control costs of doctors, medical professionals or prescriptions. FACT!

No one should fall for this vague notion that the proposed law will increase competition, thus lowering prices. Competition is going away, not because of Obamacare but because hospitals, insurance and pharmaceutical companies are making so much money they are eating up the small companies and creating vast almost-monopolies. There is nothing in the proposed law to stop mergers and impose regional controls. Many states, like Massachusetts and Alabama, have strict rules about which insurance companies can operate in their domains. The states will be more powerful with this reform.

Now let's look at the fat white elephant in the room: Planned Parenthood received 528 million dollars last year from the Federal Government and served and treated, from their 56 independent local affiliates that operate nearly 600 health centers, more than 2.5 million women. We can defund this institution and give the money to other women's centers, but what happens when the patient really needs help and an abortion is their only option? Do those new 'approved by the government' centers send those women back to Planned Parenthood? Women have abortions, and many men in the Congress have probably paid for one somewhere along the line.

So much for the government getting out of telling you what to do. This new flawed document puts the government as much in your face as Obamacare. From making it a law that married people MUST file joint returns, to limiting the monthly amount one gets, this is far from fair. If you are under 30-years of age, you only get 166 dollars to spend on whatever ailment you have. Hope you don't get cancer.

By sending the responsibilities of providing healthcare back to the states, Trump and the feckless legislators can go back to their fans and say, "We promised it, we did it." All the while, those same representatives and senators will enjoy the expensive healthcare paid for by we, the people. Then, the states will have to add more taxes on gas, goods and services, just like the middle class will pay for the damn wall.

Truthfully, this is not a reform of a healthcare act. It's just those people trying to take Obama's name off something to which they didn't contribute. Let's put a name and face on this one, it's TRUMPCARE 1.0 and when it makes you pay more, you'll know who to blame.

18. THE SOURCE OF HATE CRIMES IN AMERICA

If you tell them it's okay to scratch, they will scratch

Posted: 3-10-2017

Lots of people from the #Resistance movement have blamed the President for the rise of hate acts against Muslims and Jews throughout the country. I have always said that in most countries about a quarter of the people see the population through a filtered lens. Quite frankly, some are bigots.

If we were in a court of law, we would find it difficult to link the actions of a few to the most powerful person in our country. What were his exact words? When did he say them? What would be his motivation?

Hatred can begin by painting an entire class of people with a broad brush, for example: all Mexicans are rapists. Trump didn't actually say that all Mexicans are rapists, but it doesn't matter. Some people are so emotionally affected by the first part of the phrase that they mentally apply it to all. Trump links crime and murder to immigrants more than anyone in the world. He would agree with me.

The Donald justifies the bad things he says with, *"I was just being sarcastic,"* or *"I was just having some fun"* to *"It was just locker room talk;"* or as the trophy wife said, *"Boy talk!"* but nonetheless, he said them.

What is his motivation? To elicit a reaction from the crowd and use his power of rhetoric to whip them into a mob. We saw Americans punching other Americans at those rallies. Was that his motivation? He only wants to be right and best, not righteous and fair.

Trump then adds some spice to this by decrying politically correct speech. He launches into a diatribe against the press, going so far as to call them the *"the enemy of the people."* It doesn't take much to link that phrase to many so-called leaders in history.

The Communist leader of China, Mao Zedong, used to call individuals or associations that were critical of his policies "enemies of the people". Soviet leader Joseph Stalin, called people his enemies and had them shot or sent to labor camps. In 1997, Boris Yeltsin made Russian state media call journalist Noyaya Gazeta-Mir Ludei "unpatriotic" and "enemy of the state". And let's not forget President Richard Nixon, along with his criminal Vice President Spiro Agnew, who kept an enemies list.

Trump, along with Stephen K. Bannon, created and disseminated the term "fake news" to give his fans a hook to stab at the "enemies", while Bannon secretly manipulated Breitbart News to craft fake news that he uses to control the President. Joseph Goebbels, a real enemy of the people, would be proud.

We try to heal the wounds of hate and prejudice against people. Then, someone comes along and tacitly gives permission to those on the edge to scratch at the sores. Once the bleeding begins, the loose nuts keep digging. They assume that by desecrating and hating they can get rid of the Jews, or the Blacks, or the Muslims, or the people they disagree with. We all must know that we are mere days away from the "Night of the Long Knives," if we stand by silently. Google it, kids.

If I were called to be an expert witness in the trial against Donald J. Trump for high-crimes and misdemeanor, I would testify that, yes, Mr. Trump created the atmosphere for hate. He gave the masses permission on both sides to be more forward verbally. Trump didn't "drain the swamp," he merely threw millions of people to the alligators. And I might add, as time will tell, he will even throw his most devout followers out with his partially finished taco bowl.

The other day Donald Trump said that if the Republicans don't pass a healthcare bill, he would just let Obamacare fail so he could blame the

Democrats. Here he is exposing himself as nothing but a bloody politician. And in the early morning hours when he says, *"Out damn spots, out,"* and his mother appears to ask him, *"What have you done, Donnie?"* He can look up and say, *"I am the best Mommy, aren't I the best?"*

Haters are just like that Mr. President. They have made you into their father-figure and they are pushing over grave stones, and calling in bomb threats and painting swastikas on walls to please you, or in some cases to show you how much they hate you.

You think you know so much about power, Mr. Trump, when you have never learned the responsibility of power. The misdemeanor you have committed is the promotion of hate. Like screaming fire in a theater full of people, you have given the haters permission to scratch. You must be so proud of yourself.

19. LITTLE MISS CAN'T BE WRONG
Trump's Failure to Lead
Posted: 3-18-2017

In the last fifty plus days we have seen enough from this administration to understand that we have severe on-the-job training on our hands.

There's a great song from the rock band the Spin Doctors, who should be the house band for the Trump team. In their 1991 song, Little Miss Can't Be Wrong, the chorus goes like this:

Little miss, little miss little miss can't be wrong

Ain't no body gonna bow no more when you sound your gong

And so, it goes with Trump insulting the Brits with a comment about spying and refusing to give up the ghost of his Obama conspiracy of a phone "tapp" [sic] in the dark and dastardly Trump Tower. If you are never wrong, you never have to say you are sorry. And never having to admit your flaws is the best path to their nonexistence.

I just finished a 1,600-mile trip down the east coast of America and I talked to a lot of people. The Trump supporters want all the people on the left to back off and give this man a chance. They keep asking why the press is treating Trump so differently than Obama.

They weren't aware of the memes when President Obama was depicted as Hitler? Did they not ask why someone like citizen Trump would keep up the birther conspiracy that filled hours of cable news time?

They also don't understand why the courts are against Trump. They have no knowledge of the dozens of lawsuits that the Obama administration had to deal with from immigration (Deferred Action for Childhood Arrivals order) to environment orders to healthcare. All they did the last five years was defend themselves. This is what our society has become. Look at how many times Donald Trump has been sued in business. There is a reason for that.

People only see what they want to see. Trump tightly wraps a flag around everything to make people believe that his ideas are the best, and if you don't do things his way, we will be in great peril. When he is challenged, he never seems to ask why someone disagrees with him; the mark of a fool in governance.

As much free TV time as he got before the election, he now wastes time with discussions that simply don't matter. His surrogates are silly gang members spouting lies and defensive postures. When your defense of the leader of the free world is that he used air quotes, you know you are in trouble.

Disseminating a lie is called defamation. The original source may be protected by the First Amendment, but the President of the United States is supposed to know. We elected him in the belief he would know. I cannot give this mere mortal a chance without him doing the job correctly. If he thinks coal mines pouring pollution into a stream is okay, then he needs to have his head examined. Let's get rid of all the rules and let the kids in Flint drink the bad water. Really?

And to end this short rant – I must remind the reader that the Spin Doctors song mentioned earlier is on their CD Pocket Full of Kryptonite. As for Donald Trump, his self-absorbed distractions manifest themselves on Twitter, where he lets little boy Donnie out of the box. Tweets are his kryptonite for sure. Sad!

20. THE SIMPLE TRUTH ABOUT DONALD TRUMP

Who Gave Him the Keys to the Car?
Posted: 3-22-2017

According to the National Highway Traffic Safety Administration, the average percentage of DUI repeat offenders is 30%. There is someone killed every 52-minutes in America due to a vehicle accident in which alcohol was involved. NBC's Today provided this stat: The FBI says that every day almost 300,000 people drive drunk, yet only 4,000 are caught by police.

That means thousands of people are behind the wheel at any given moment who can put you and your loved ones in danger. We have Trump at the White House wheel and he is putting America in danger every day. Someone must pull him over.

During the brief time Donald J. Trump has been in office, we have seen some rather bizarre actions, Orwellian use of language and the unfettered use of social media to embarrass himself and our great country.

As we have suggested on these pages before, someone should be controlling both the official POTUS twitter feed and the personal @realDonaldTrump page. Once Trump became President, these sites became official government conduits for establishing administrative policy. Each tweet is a legal US document.

With every fabrication Mr. Know-It-All transmits to the world, the United States of America becomes smaller and pettier in the eyes of the other world leaders. Mr. Trump, to be politically incorrect, the whole world is laughing at you, not with you.

When both the head of the FBI and the head of the NSA testify to Congress that there is no proof the Obama administration wire-tapped your phones, you couldn't let it be. You had to tweet right into the hearing room more untruths.

Like the guy at the bar who has all the confidence in the world that he can drive home after countless doubles, no one on your team has the balls to take the keys away from you. Your power-hungry ego won't allow anyone in your inner circle to at least ask, *"Is this a good idea?"*

You've ended up in the ditch many nights Mr. President, and maybe that is your lame justification for free-base tweeting at all hours of the night. Well, at least I didn't kill anyone. When someone does get killed, you use your account to placate your own self-esteem rather than consider how your words have hurt.

Less than half of the American voters gave you the new car. They are still giving you permission to do things they don't even know will hurt them dearly, soon. What happens when your blind sighted healthcare bill takes medical access away from all those coal miners in West Virginia? What will your "fans" think of you when those premiums and deductibles go up, not down, as you have promised? And your claim that everyone will be covered is a bold-faced lie that is worse than Obama's pronouncement that you can keep your doctor.

Your press secretary is the punchline in a visual joke. No one sees Sean Spicer anymore; when looking at him they see Melissa McCarthy's rage and satire. The fact that you program him to say things, like Mike Flynn was a volunteer in your campaign to lessen the guilt-by-association for his Russian engagement cover-up, is all on you, Mr. President. I even see SNL sketches in my mind rather than a real president. For such a "bad show" they have certainly repositioned you as the fool.

You have failed the Breathalyzer test so many times it's not funny. You have also not been able to walk a straight-line with the American people. Why don't you try to simply tell the truth? Maybe Bernie Sanders is right. You just might be that pathological liar he described.

We would ask for the results of your blood test, but we would rather see your income tax returns for the last four years. Get off the road and get some help, Trump, before someone gets killed. Or you start that war you kept telling us Hillary would've created. You are unfit to hold the office, Sir. Sad!

21. THE DIFFERENCE BETWEEN BUSINESS AND GOVERNMENT

Trump's Assumptions Are Wrong

Posted: 3-24-2017

During the Presidential campaign, we heard the mantra that massaged the maxim into the minds of the under-employed middle class saying what we needed was a great businessman to cure what ails America.

When Trump's loyal followers are questioned about why their man is right for our country, they talk about his business success. That was the same argument they made for Mitt Romney in 2012. And this opens the door for a mature discussion about the difference between the two.

First, let's think about the gap between a privately-owned company and a publicly traded company. In a privately held company, the owners can do whatever they want. They can shout out orders and fire those who don't get the job done. At the end of the year the only person they must face is themselves. Did the company make money or did it lose money?

In a publicly traded company, the top dog answers to investors and their board, or cabinet, as elected by those stockholders. The term fiduciary duty refers in general to the highest standard of care. A fiduciary owes his allegiance to the beneficiary of his or her endeavors. If a person breaches their fiduciary duties, they would need to account for the ill-gotten profit or misdeeds in office.

In a sense, the President of the United States is the head of a large company, but that analogy only goes so far. The president must deal with Congress to get money to run the country. The President does not have the power to unilaterally decide what money goes where. The final budget must be approved by Congress. Since the Supreme Court ruled that the Affordable Care

Act was a tax on citizens, any changes to that Act must be voted on by Congress.

What Trump and many of his voters don't understand is that he must serve more than just those who voted for him. All citizens are the stockholders of this country and Trump's actions must consider the ramifications for all Americans, not just his screaming fans.

Our president's assumption that he can bully his way in and demand that Congress do what he says is wrong. There are factions of fractions within Trump's own party; splinter groups and lobby-controlled partisans, who care only about THEIR money and THEIR re-election.

Trump should think of his hostile takeover of the Republican party and realize that at any time there will be powerful groups, like the House Freedom Caucus that, can stop anything in its tracks; including Mr. Know-It-All President.

Here they are: Mark Meadows of North Carolina, Chair, Justin Amash of Michigan, Brian Babin of Texas, Rod Blum of Iowa, Dave Brat of Virginia, Jim Bridenstine of Oklahoma, Mo Brooks of Alabama, Ken Buck of Colorado, Warren Davidson of Ohio, Ron DeSantis of Florida, Scott DesJarlais of Tennessee, Jeff Duncan of South Carolina, Trent Franks of Arizona, Tom Garrett Jr. of Virginia, Paul Gosar of Arizona, Morgan Griffith of Virginia, Andy Harris of Maryland, Jody Hice of Georgia, Jim Jordan of Ohio, Raúl Labrador of Idaho, Alex Mooney of West Virginia, Gary Palmer of Alabama, Steve Pearce of New Mexico, Scott Perry of Pennsylvania, Ted Poe of Texas, Bill Posey of Florida, Mark Sanford of South Carolina, David Schweikert of Arizona, Randy Weber of Texas, and Ted Yoho of Florida.

These people are the real problem for President Trump because they gave him a standing ovation before the big meeting, then told him they wanted Obamacare gone, period. If you voted for them, how do you feel now?

Nimble companies in business that get things done quickly, even with a few mistakes along the way, can own a market segment and dominate competition. The government in Washington, especially the Hill, shows us the real problem is gridlock, not party affiliation. We had gridlock when Democrats were in power and we have blockage with Republicans in the majority. It's obviously systemic. Trump says vote now and if you say 'NO' he will just move on to something else. Boy, that sounds like avoidance not a fight.

Why did he pick the hardest thing to do first? Why doesn't he stop wasting time, energy and breath on tweets and start figuring out that he should keep his eye on the voters – stockholders – THEY want a return on their investment. So far, he's still in hostile takeover mode. YOU OWN THE COMPANY, run it and stop with this "it's all about me" syndrome. It's not about you at all. Sad!

22. BLINDED BY THE LIGHT
The Mandate Trump Didn't See Coming
Posted: 3-25-2017

By all accounts, Donald J. Trump doesn't seem like a dim bulb, but the light of his own ego blinds him to whatever clever ideas he might have.

The debacle of March 24, 2017 may have been a little late for the Ides of March, but the fact that the Republican majority in the House couldn't pass a Frankenstein healthcare bill might demonstrate they are paying attention. Had they passed that bill, the ill effects would have determined the outcome of the 2018 elections.

Trump seems to be bumping into walls in the dead of night. Wearing his ill-fitting bathrobe, he cannot even comprehend, as he puts it, the strange procedures and rules of the House of Representatives. Did they not teach civics at the Wharton School of Business? Penn graduates are embarrassed everywhere.

And then, the leader of the free (but not free trade) world says this, *"We had no Democrat support. They weren't going to give us a single vote so it's a very difficult thing to do,"* He then added, *"I've been saying for the last year and a half that the best thing we can do politically speaking is to let Obamacare explode."*

Let's review for the folks at home. In the 115th Congress, the House has 237 Republicans and only 193 Democrats. Even with 5 vacancies currently, a fifth grader can see the Republicans have the majority. That is 44 more members and, surely, they could get any bill passed in their chamber. Not so fast. The Republicans stand on states' rights, and anti-mandate is to their detriment.

Trump seems to think his role is to win rather than to lead. There is no responsible governance in what he says when he fails. He first looks to blame someone or something rather than to solve a problem. How did this man do well in business? Oh, that's right, he owned the business. There was no one there to dock his pay or fire him when he did poorly.

Any good business person knows you should never kill a revenue stream. Even if the product people are buying is not the state of the art version, you want to keep them as customers until you can upsell them into the next edition. This means that Trump, if we want to give him some credit, might be thinking that the revenue from the 20 million new insured Americans might be a good thing. Too much credit?

The one thing that Republicans wanted most to scratch in the Affordable Healthcare Act was the mandate. They associated the mandate with the big, bad, evil government being involved in healthcare. Wait, that is simply a tax. If everyone signed up for healthcare and the system took on a more universal approach, there would be more revenue. If all the states would have all gotten on the bandwagon and promoted Obamacare, we would be better off now.

When red states balked at the exchanges for ideological reasons, they were throwing money away. Let's see, where is Bobby Jindal today? He left his state healthcare system in shambles coming in dead last in most categories accept premature death where Louisiana was 47th out of 50 States.

The good idea that Trump kept telling us about at those big loud rallies was creating a marketplace of more competition to lower prices. Increasing costs is one of the debate points people raised saying Obamacare is bad. Trump knows better than anyone that a monopoly in a segment leads to higher prices. That's why he wanted to get Native Americans out of the casino business.

With smart legislation, Trump could cure what ails the AHA right now. All he would have to do is to convince Congress to pass a law saying that states do not control which insurance companies operate in their domains. In a sense, this would be no different than Congress giving Major League Baseball a mandate to operate across state lines without worry about the Interstate Commerce Act of 1887.

Why not write an exception for healthcare providers right now, so that some of the more aggressive players could come into states like Alabama where there is currently only one provider? But that would mean Trump convincing Congress to pass something. I thought he was the deal maker? Turn out the lights Donald, the party is over.

It's right there in front of Trump and he doesn't see it. He wants to win and have everyone kiss his big, fat ass instead of coming up with solutions that would help Americans now. We have said it many times and will keep saying it, the President has the wrong people around him. Sad!

23. SOMEONE STEPPED IN MANURE
Trump and the Nunes Tool
Posted: 3-28-2017

As of March 2017, Devin Nunes is the Chairman of the House Permanent Select Committee on Intelligence. This is the committee that gets to see all the secret stuff from the NSA, CIA and FBI to determine what the legislators should do about these findings. From time to time they are also tasked with investigations and conduct hearings on matters of intelligence that could have major effects on our security.

Nunes graduated from Cal Poly San Luis Obispo with a Bachelor's Degree in agricultural business and a Master's Degree in agriculture. I am sure he has experienced the aroma from one of the great American agricultural by-products: cow manure. And he might have even learned the lesson of not watching where you step when walking around a farm.

The on-going discussion about Russia's involvement in our last election may frustrate and even bore the Trump supporters out there, but perhaps they should ask these questions. Why hasn't the president made a better effort to put all this behind him? Why do we keep hearing that no one talked to the Russians and now it seems lots of people talked to the Russians during the campaign and during the transition? Perhaps they are still talking to them now? If only someone would just fess up and tell us what they are talking about.

Devin Nunes' grandstanding at the White House last week (March 21, 2017) was probably a stunt that he was encouraged to do by the President of the United States. Sorry, but I don't believe that Nunes has the testicles to have done that on his own. He may have thought he was saying something significant, but in the end, he said nothing.

He was so ill prepared to speak that he had to apologize the next day for such an awkward moment and the betrayal of his own committee members. To put it plainly, he was used by Donald Trump as a foil for Mr. Know-It-All's frivolous and unfounded claim that Obama, his imaginary nemesis, was listening to all his phone calls.

Nunes looked weak, silly and ill-informed. From his own admission, he didn't handle things very well. He stepped in it and we can smell it. The press smells it. And every smart Congress person smells it. But they are all being pussies. They should call for an independent investigator. Isn't Ken Starr looking for work?

Here's the good news. The methane gas coming from Mr. Nunes shoes is now protected by Trump's new executive order giving polluters free range to destroy the environment. Clearly, the shit show continues with distraction, devastation and disgrace. Devin Nunes is owned by the Koch Brothers and one might find it interesting that even when he ran unopposed, he was able to raise $1.9 million dollars for his campaign bank. Trump should have known better than to attempt to use someone else's puppet.

Something smells here and someone must stop putting these guys on important committees, or worse, making them the chairperson.

In Washington, the politicians all play by the same rules which help them make their lives better. They do a horrible job of both self-governing and actual governing? They even get to vote on their own pay raises. How can they be unbiased and objective?

If it smells like shit and looks like shit, it's shit, Nunes. And you stepped in it.

24. OUR PING-PONG PRESIDENT
Bouncing Between his Ego and Our Country
Posted: 4-4-2017

Trump opened a recent speech to the trade union's convention by saying how great it is the president knows how much cement can be poured in a day. While he was stroking himself, his press secretary, Sean Spicer, was blaming Obama for the chemical attack on civilians in Syria. (March 4, 2017)

This lethal incident was against women and children and as the President's press liaison expressed, *"The heinous actions by the Bashar al-Assad regime are a consequence of the past administration's weakness and irresolution."*

Okay, we get it. You don't like the last administration. You don't like anything Barack Obama did. You continue to use Obama as your whipping boy because you cannot deal with anything bad without blaming someone else. May I ask a question? Can you let us know when you become President? Your campaign is over and the country is more important than your ego.

You think you can keep hitting the ball back to the other side to isolate yourself from the responsibility of creating policy. If you don't want to draw a red line in the sand, then what is it that you want to do? What are your solutions for babies choking to death? Remember, they will keep hitting the ball back at you and you don't appear to be ready.

Trump fails to realize that Assad is not testing Obama with his latest war crime, he is testing you, President Trump. And you really don't know what to do, do you? You talk a big game, like most bullies, but when some other bully walks onto the playground, you just stand around doing nothing.

You send your son-in-law to Iraq, you prance around with your princess daughter, but you have no knowledge of the way the world really works. Do you realize that your good buddy Putin is on Assad's side? Do you realize that Iran is an ally of Russia? Well, do you? And you do see that you are standing around watching war crimes and you are doing nothing? You are doing exactly what Obama did.

Let it be said, Donald J. Trump, that on March 4, 2017, you embarrassed America with your silence. The world wants to hear from you. You must take a stand. You will have to draw red lines, but can you? Can your ego cope with being wrong on anything? It's not paralysis by too much analysis, it's paralysis by narcissistic mind control.

When will you wake up and get your head in the game? Hillary Clinton and Barack Obama are not here any longer, they are just a part of history. You need to look to the future. What are you going to do to make the world a better place? What are you going to do to make America proud? All I hear on TV is about these friends of yours meeting and talking to Russians, and instead of getting this controversy in your rear-view mirror, you keep tweeting about it, like a 14-year old girl.

Stand up and lead, or get out of the way. We have a country to run.

25. DICTATORS AND DEAD BABIES
Donald Trump's Doctrine of Offensive Remarks
Posted: 4-5-2017

We have a President who defies gravity. He claims he can leap from tall building to tall building in a single bound, which we all know, makes no logical sense. There was this religion he proposed during the campaign. It was simple really: Nationalism vs. Globalism and that any dealings with another nation could be whittled down to a deal.

He keeps telling us and the rest of the world that he and he alone has inherited a mess that he will now fix. Imagine what was going through the mind of Abdullah II of Jordan standing mere feet from Superman. Abdullah, a man who actually wears a military uniform and fights along with his soldiers. Here is a ruler who has been dealing with the Middle East and radical Islam for almost 20 years. Hearing the words, *"I have inherited a mess"* must have sent shockwaves through his royal body.

The drip, drip, drip of dictators and the blood being shed around our earth has finally changed the way our President views certain bad actors on the world stage. Suddenly, he sees that powerful dictators are not deal makers; they are ruthless killers.

Just yesterday he blamed Obama for something that happened yesterday, but today he said, *"It crossed a lot of lines for me,"* and added, *"When you kill innocent children, innocent babies, little babies, with a chemical gas that is so lethal that people were shocked to hear what gas it was, that crosses many, many lines, beyond a red line, many, many lines."* And then, he blames Obama again today, huh?

Was the last time Assad used chemicals on his own people okay, but now it's time to do something? Trump lets us in on his big revelation, *"My attitude toward Syria and Assad has changed very much!"* Oh, really Trump, what was the tipping point for you?

According to the United Nations, since the war began in 2011 an estimated 400,000 Syrians have been killed. And yes, we know that the photo of a lifeless child being washed up on the shore went viral and was seen by millions of people around the world. And we have seen the horrible pictures of children gasping their last breath because of lethal poisons dumped on them. Those realities make a difference, but there is a giant missing piece to this puzzle. And just maybe Trump is about to place that piece into a giant map of the world.

Has the great Donald finally figured out the reason why there are so many refugees, the ones he disdains and fears, running away from this repulsive dictator? Do you think he understands that the ghastly reality of dead babies is the result of no one taking on Russia?

Donald, you can talk about ISIS and brag about how you are going to eradicate them from the face of the earth, which not only makes a great slogan for you, but a dandy recruitment clip for them, but that is only one piece of the enigma.

Dictators who kill people when they get in the way are just as bad as ISIS. If you thought domestic healthcare was complicated, the Middle East is ten times as tough.

Remember, if Assad is as depraved as you think he is and now you believe he should be stopped, you are going to have to face Putin. You will have to tell the Russian leader that you want him to help you STOP ASSAD, not the rebels. The rebels, the Syrian people, are being killed by Russians and Assad's troops and Assad gets aid from Iran, another Russian ally. Who knew it was so complicated?

Obama was tricked by your buddy Putin into believing that all the chemical weapons were taken out of Syria. We know that Putin is now trying to fool you into believing that the rebels gassed their own people. Really? Does that make any sense?

The world is waiting for the President of the United States to develop focus on important issues and stop with the stupid tweets about TV shows and Bill O'Reilly.

America First is a nice chant, but the world is a big place. You say you need 54 billion more dollars for the military, but what you really need is a damn strategy and well-thought-out policy for spending that money. This on-the-job training is fatiguing. Sad!

26. THE SMELL OF TOMAHAWKS IN THE MORNING

Trump Huffs and He Puffs

Posted: 4-7-2017

Finally, the President of the United States has made a statement to the world that he's just like the movie character, John Shaft. Donnie may think he's a bad (shut your mouth), but he should remember one of Shaft's great pieces of advice, *"Next time, you mutha, don't bite off more than you can chew!"*

Yes, we get it, you saw the pictures of the babies, the innocents of war, being poisoned by a chemical that is banned by the Geneva Convention and other treaties and you had to act. You had to bomb the airbase in Syria where the sorties began, but do you have the next step planned? We know that you aren't going to tell US citizens your plans. We get your secret military tactics. But did you tell Congress? You told the Russians you were going to bomb, so much for your big secret plan.

And now that you have decided to teach Assad a lesson, have you considered what happens next with the rebel insurgency and, more importantly, what ISIS is thinking? Mostly likely they consider your actions part of their plan, not yours. Once again, a US President has been drawn into the Middle East.

When you play the screaming pumpkin head at rallies you can talk about how regime change in Libya was bad and blame Obama and Hillary for the situation in the Middle East, but this is real life now and you have inherited a mess.

Stop saying you alone are going to fix it. Ditch that rhetoric and think about who will be there to help you fix it. Remember why we call certain countries allies. You will have to get into bed with some strange dogmatic dudes to keep the peace in the Middle East. Ask your son-in-law.

What a coincidence that King Abdullah II was sitting in the White House while Donald J. Trump was agonizing over an answer to the age-old question created by a blast of human consciousness. At one point, Jordan was accepting 3,000 refugees a day from Syria and it's likely the last person to speak to Trump on the matter of what to do with Syria was the King, a real king. Abdullah got what he wanted, someone else to mess with Assad. And Israel will be happy, too. Sounds like a tribal win-win to moderate Muslims and Zionists everywhere.

Are things looking up for the Donald? He even asked God to bless the whole world. Boy, that sounded like globalism to me. Steve Bannon was probably vomiting out of his limo window on the way home. With so many ex-Goldman people around this president and, of course, the Democrat Trump Kids, are we seeing the turn toward global awareness? Can climate change be next? Baby steps.

A spokesperson for the Kremlin said Putin believes the attack was done under a "trumped-up pretext" and that Vladimir denounced the US strike against a Syrian government airbase as an "aggression against a sovereign state in violation of the norms of international law." Has your buddy has turned against you? Can that tape of whatever happened in St. Petersburg be far behind? And did they actually use the phrase, "trumped-up?" Is that an expression used in Russia?

Now we get to see what you are really made of, Mr. Know-It-All, as we all sing along with the Shaft theme, "Who is the man that would risk his neck for his brother, man? (Trump), Can ya dig it? Who's the cat that won't cop out when there's danger all about? (Trump), Right on!

They claim six people were killed at the base in Syria. Are you counting Mr. President? We know why you did what you did, like George W. going back to Iraq to finish the job his father started. It seems like you are trying to fix all the things you think Obama did incorrectly. Does that make Barack your daddy? Sad!

27. THE RISK OF NOT READING
Donald's Devilish Details
Posted: 4-11-2017

When White House advisors briefed the President of the United States about the events in Syria, they decided to use few words and show pictures to tell the story of the use of chemical weapons.

Everyone learns differently and it has been established that one of the key aspects of our fearless leader is that he doesn't read.

The art of brevity is not a sole providence of this president. Ronald Reagan asked the bureaucrats to reduce all memoranda to one page. Even though we now know that President Reagan toward the end of his command was losing certain memory functions, the memo reduction requirement was a genuine way to get more done. In short, most people over-write.

By showing Trump pictures of the results of the bombing of innocents, including babies, he was moved to not only act, but change his Middle East strategy entirely. Much to the chagrin of the far right and hard line populists, he did what needed to be done. Perhaps this president will eventually move to a moderate position, if only there was a picture we could show him to achieve that result.

By avoiding the "burden" of reading, Donnie does not consume well-thought out research and important intelligence. We would love to have Donald Trump read Richard Haass' book *A World in Disarray: American Foreign Policy and the Crisis of the Old Order*, but it is unlikely that our president would get through the 348 pages.

In one sense, it's good that Trump is not influenced by so-called experts or those who have been in power before him, but that assumes they have absolutely nothing to contribute. The fear we should have is an advisor distorting the truth to achieve their desired result, rather than providing a thoughtful answer to a complex question. We all know that photographs can be doctored and some people have even seen weapons of mass destruction where there were none.

The cause of the Iraq war was equal parts of Saddam Hussein's stonewalling UN inspectors and the trumped-up charges of the intelligence community. Our country wasted one trillion dollars and killed more than 134,000 civilians in the Iraq conflict. This grave mistake was based on some expert's misinterpretation of facts, suspicious miscalculations or sparse information.

There are certain qualifications we apply to most jobs, but for the leader of the free world we take what the electoral college gives us. For the situation in Syria, White House insiders simply placed pictures of the dying children in Trump's hands and he felt compelled to ask his generals, *"What can we do about this?"*

Did Donald not see the other dead baby washing up on the beach? That was the son of a mother and father, you know, refugees of Syria who were trying to escape a land where the leader drops bombs filled with chemicals. Did the president's advisors not show him those pictures? TV covered this sad event, but that image never made it into Donald's flimsy brain to inspire a response.

Now that those around Donald Trump know that all they must do is show him pictures to elicit a Pavlovian reaction, save us from the misdeeds of a few with influence. Judging by how he reads a teleprompter, we can assume that if we asked for more reading from Trump we would bring the country to a stand-still.

Candidate Trump said he knew, even *"more than the generals."* Well he obviously doesn't know. Sorry to crush the feelings of those hardcore Trump fans, but this guy is just a narcissistic builder turned reality TV star who, in his new capacity, is learning on-the-job.

Have patience and keep checking your paystub. Has he reduced your co-pays and deductibles yet? Has he made your roads better? Has he decreased your taxes? Has he made America great yet? What is taking this man so long to get going? Sad!

28. WHY BANNON MUST GO
Chameleon Trump Showing True Colors
Posted: 4-13-2017

We've all had bad bosses in our lives. And there were times that our bosses kept bad employees around much too long. Some big guys like to keep a bad cop around when a dastardly deed must be done, like yelling at the Freedom Caucus. That worked? Others want to be reminded that people are not that important to the success of the enterprise. The deconstruction of the administrative state is an anti-people statement

Some leaders keep negative people around because the person becomes the only buddy a guy has. I have even seen bosses keep someone around because they, too, were a smoker. Strange.

When Donald Trump raged at the rallies, I kept thinking it was an act. He was pro-choice when he was producing offspring, but magically became anti-abortion when he started having grandkids. He appeared to be a real free market man with his actions of having his clothing line made in China and using Japanese steel in his buildings.

He kept screaming about how bad immigrants are, but used immigrants to build his empire. And his immigration ban that separated families, much like what happened during WWII both in Germany and the US, seemed heartless. I guess he thinks it's okay to destroy a family but not okay to kill babies. We get it.

And now we see his liberal, Orthodox Jewish daughter, Ivanka, known as Yael in the Temple, has become the inner conscientiousness of the Donald. According to some reports, she presented the pictures of the babies choking for life in Syria that convinced her father to reverse his policies about Syria completely.

Steve Bannon's ex-wife testified in a legal document in the state of California that Steve didn't want his kids to attend a private school because of the number of Jewish kids at a specific school. Bannon's reason? He didn't like the way 'they' raised their kids to be 'whiny brats' and that he didn't want his girls going to school with Jews.

That remark could be written off if Bannon didn't end up being the money behind and the editorial force in front of Breitbart News. It's the same publication that raised this headline: 'Bill Kristol: Republican spoiler, renegade Jew' and, ironically, the Website that was started by Andrew Breitbart, a person raised in a Jewish family.

Politics is a sticky force and with video everywhere it's easy for researchers to pull up every word one says on any issue. When you so loudly and so strongly claim your position is one thing, then within 100 days you change central platforms, it's more than a midcourse correction. It's a damn flip-flop.

Sooner or later the chameleon finds himself sitting on top of a leaf where he wants to stay for a while; a place he might feel more comfortable. So, he changes to that color and hopes no one notices his transformation.

Imagine how Steve Bannon feels coming to work every day knowing that the person he thought he could control is, quite frankly, uncontainable. And that is also the challenge for son-in-law Jared Kushner and princess daughter Ivanka.

The kids, or as they have been called, the "democrats" must move slowly before they rid the kingdom of the less than worthy. Jared got Chris Christie out of the way, the man who helped convict his father of illegal campaign contributions, tax evasion, and witness tampering and who pushed Charles Kushner into 14 months of federal prison. The kids also drove the big mouth Giuliani out of the picture so Trump wouldn't get distorted by his dogma.

The reason Ivanka couldn't vote for her father in the primaries, was because she was a registered Democrat and didn't understand that in New York primaries you can vote only for candidates in your party. So, the nickname 'democrats' actually works in this case.

Bannon will get in the way and prove to be a distraction that hurts the country and will force the President to be someone he is not.

As the "kids" slowly work their familial magic and massage, Trump's will hopefully move into the middle and Bannon will become an unnecessary third-wheel. The generals certainly don't want him around. The lawyers don't want him around—just look at the messy, poorly written executive orders. And, of course, this is a family affair and the 'renegade Jews' aren't outsiders, they are INSIDERS, and the President listens when they whine.

Within days the Donald declares that NATO is not obsolete and China appears to now be an ally and not a currency manipulator. Are we are starting to see a President who seems to be thinking reasonably?

Okay, he blew off 59 Tomahawks but the attack didn't destroy the runway. The carpet bombs must have been made of real carpet?

Trump now realizes that Russian President Putin is not his friend, but he still won't dress him down as hard as Nikki Halley and Rex Tillerson. We heard how his buddy denies those chemicals were even used in Syria. Putin, using a move out of the Donald's playbook, has pushed back and even called the allegations, 'trumped-up charges."

And the crazy kid in North Korea is ready to test the president. Bannon was against the bombing of the airbase in Syria because his ideology is getting in the way of how the world works. Bannon is an isolationist, while Trump has become a new born globalist. How did that happen?

Even domestically, Bannon sees the world as US and THEM, but in this country, we are a people united, or as some say, citizens united. Who knew being leader of the free world would be so hard. Sad!

29. NO TAXES, NO LOGS, NO TRANSPARENCY

The Trump Illusion of Openness
Posted: 4-18-2017

Donald J Trump likes to put his name on everything. Like a dog urinating to mark his turf, our President thinks that he can just say it, and it is; like his pronouncement the other day that NATO is not obsolete. He continues to play the role of the boy who cried wolf and, when faced with a real wolf, he pets and feeds the animal. Whose side is he on?

Whatever you say about Mr. Know-it-all, you must admit he can lie on a dime. If you believe what he says about his policy, you must also be able to roll with the punches when he tells you that what you believed has changed. Commitments with Trump don't seem to be important. His actions speak louder than his screaming harangues at the rallies.

He says he is open and transparent, but doesn't want you to know who visits him at the White House. Why? That is not his private property; it is an open and free house of the people. Trump's claim that that he's not a guy who telegraphs his moves and maintains an aura of unpredictability in order tho hold power over others, seems rather suspect.

If Trump was really so cloak and dagger, why would he keep using Twitter? He psychological vomits openly, but he doesn't want you to know who enters the White House. Strange.

Trump accused Obama of a lack of transparency, while he wallows in this need to control the narrative. What if a public company in this country decided that the FEC wasn't allowed to see their books? He would call that what, good? Whose side is he on?

Donald, you keep regurgitating that your most recent taxes are under audit. You should be asking the IRS why it is taking them so long to do the audit? You want everyone else in the government to do their jobs and get things done, but not the IRS? If you were to release your tax returns you would cement a precedent that all VPs and Presidents must release them in the future. Wouldn't that be good for America? Whose side are you on?

Many people who support Trump may not really care if he cheated on his taxes, but there are millions, yes Donald, millions of citizens of this great country who truly believe that transparency is a good thing and that you are a servant of the people, not the CEO of a private company. You owe the American people the facts of your financial dealings. What could you possibly be hiding in those forms? Whose side are you on?

Being secretive may have been your method as a builder tycoon, but as your bankruptcy papers reveal, sooner or later people will find out what all this means. You are working for us and we would appreciate you coming clean and explaining what is so problematic about releasing your taxes. Even your nemesis, Hillary Clinton, released decades of tax returns, but as you said the election is over.

And since the election, you have become more isolated and less forthright than what most supporters would have assumed. And your put-down of Obama for playing golf too much really demonstrates your do-as-I-say attitude rather than being an example of your true beliefs and values.

Some reports claim that Trump has played golf 19 times since becoming President, but the sad thing is that the White House won't even comment on that stat. Why? Why would something so mundane as the number of hours Trump spent on the golf course be some government secret? Dwight Eisenhower is turning in his grave.

We don't care how much golf you play Donald Trump, but we truly care about transparency. Be honest, is that possible? Sad!

30. STATES' RIGHTS VS. DONALD TRUMP

Power Delegated Is Power Lost

Posted: 4-21-2017

Most administrations in this great land of the United States have juggled the temptation to take power away from the states with the more conservative viewpoint that states should decide what is right for their people. Attempting to keep both balls in the air has brought tons of lawsuits and taxed the Department of Justice with major decisions and minor peccadillos.

Donald Trump has fallen into the trap quite nicely. His red meat rhetoric that he throws to the hungry masses will reduce his ability to get things done. He obviously doesn't understand that the enumerated powers of Congress, listed in the Tenth Amendment, are not his powers. They are Congressional muscle.

If you read that amendment, you will see that it is very clear: The powers not delegated to the United States by the Constitution, nor prohibited by it to the States, are reserved to the States respectively, or to the people.

Focus on that last phrase, *Powers that are reserved to the people.* When Donald Trump wants to fix healthcare by giving the states more power to determine how it works and what can or cannot be done, he diminishes the power of the president and the federal programs he promised would help people.

In the latest aberration of the Healthcare rewrite, the compromisers have slipped a stick of dynamite into their paragraphs. They are proposing to give a state the right to charge more for those who have pre-existing conditions. Wow, really? If a guy walks in with cancer you can tax him just like a pharmaceutical company? Who the hell are these people?

With April 20, 2017 now just purple haze in the rearview mirror, we find another conflict looming on the horizon, the right of a state to regulate the growing and sales of marijuana. In Colorado, marijuana tax revenue hit 200 million dollars and sales are set to pass one billion dollars this year. What was once a judicial, social and medical over-reach has now turned into a windfall for the mountain state. Even college scholarship programs are being funded out of these taxes and revenues.

When our government was taken over by goodie-two-shoes in the 1920s, the religious right created a constitutional ban on the production, importation, transportation, and sale of alcoholic beverages that remained in place from 1920 to 1933. The ban didn't stop people from making, buying or drinking alcohol. It just made America a dull place for 13 years. Finally, FDR decided that people should have a legal way to let off some steam.

Now some out-of-touch people in power want to take federal legal action against those states that have leveraged medical and recreational marijuana reform into a revenue stream. The new Attorney General knows best about marijuana because he most likely has never smoked it. Really? Donald Trump has said he has never smoked pot or cigarettes and of course, he would be best to judge what smoking cannabis does. Full on irony here, folks.

When you say you want to give more power to the states, but you are selective in how you apply that philosophy, you create confusion. Just like when you ignore scientists' evaluations on climate change, you seem out of touch. When you disregard the medical evidence that marijuana can help people, you are like those people 100 years ago who thought they could defeat alcoholism by controlling everyone. The myths created about marijuana are slowly going up in smoke.

Some polls put the support of national legalization at 61%. That is clearly more people than voted for Trump. Even Canada has taken the move to legalize the herb. What are we waiting for?

Attorney General Jeff Sessions said on a radio interview, *"I am really amazed that a judge sitting on an island in the Pacific can issue an order that stops the President of the United States from what appears to be clearly his statutory and constitutional power."*

Back at you Jeff, I really am amazed that a non-elected cabinet member from a state that doesn't even have a lottery gets to decide how a state handles its medical and recreational use of certain natural plants.

What we really need is for all those who have a vote on marijuana at the federal level to fire up a doobie and relax. It's not 'oxy' or heroin. Keep your eye on the important stuff.

31. THE WAR AGAINST WISDOM
Trump's Anti-People Priorities
Posted: 4-23-2017

We have seen the real Donald Trump and his actions prove that he is against people, their bodies and brains. As the President slashes and murders policies and programs that were designed to protect people, the environment and solid education policy, we all suffer from his war against wisdom.

On Earth Day 2017, we had the usual parades, but this year's celebration included a March for Science to promote science. WHAT? When did we get to the point where SCIENCE needed to fight for respect? The misconceptions, that have been fed into Trump's deformed brain, are obviously the product of other small thinkers who have avoided facts. When you say something is a hoax, you must show the facts in science.

The idea that we can eliminate concepts like the Environmental Protection Agency and curb the destruction that is taking place in rivers, streams and the air we breathe is rash and irresponsible. When we have another water crisis, like Flint, we can all blame Donald for the disaster.

Most military experts agree that job one of the United States State Department is to produce accurate facts and intelligent solutions about simmering spots around the world. Before we send in the Marines, we expect our state department to figure out how to solve the problem before we get into wars and conflicts. Why would Trump cut jobs and decrease the infrastructure of State when the world isn't getting any safer? Even Russia complained about the lack of personnel in the department.

The Center for America Progress reports that the Trump budget would slash 9 billion dollars — 13 percent of the US Department of Education's funding — while investing 1.4 billion dollars of new money in school choice which includes private school vouchers, sending a clear signal that the Trump administration prioritizes ideologically driven voucher schemes over great public schools.

Of course, the middle class may benefit if they have a private school that fits their dogma in their district, but most of the people who voted for Trump will have to suffer with poor public schools. In ten years, we can all blame Betsy DeVos and Donald Trump for poorly prepared graduates who can't get jobs.

On Earth Day, President Tweet wrote: *"I am committed to keeping our air and water clean but always remember that economic growth enhances environmental protection. Jobs matter!"* With this, the President has staked out a position that no money in his budget should be spent on anything that monitors, analyzes or works to solve climate change.

Just because a company makes a lot of money doesn't mean they will protect their workers or the environment. As a Pittsburgher, I remember the 1950s and I can tell you, the air wasn't so clean while U.S. Steel made tons of money.

And what piece of the pie grows in the Trump budget? There will be a 54 billion dollar increase in military spending, but due to Donald's mystical promise to lower the national debt he must cut something else out of the budget.

His minions are going after spending in ways that make it seem they care most about undoing the Obama agenda rather than placing a priority on progress. Trump's departments and commissions are holding up money for projects that have already been approved. Why?

The Federal Transit Administration already approved a 650 million-dollar federal grant for electrification of a San Francisco Bay Area train system but the Trump administration has sent it to purgatory. Any delay will stop California's high-speed rail project, which sounds like the infrastructure upgrade Trump kept touting during the campaign. The train line is more than thirty-years old and needs to be upgraded for environmental and safety reasons. Trump's policies are anti-people that does more harm than good.

According to Fortune magazine, if "parity" reigns, and both sides of the discretionary budget rise 54 billion dollars in fiscal 2017, total debt and deficits over the next decade will balloon by around 1.4 trillion dollars, including interest expense on the extra debt.

So, Donald Trump lied to America when he said he would lower the debt in his first year. The facts are clear. His proposals are no different than Obama's or Bush's with respect to spending money. Let's recall that when Clinton passed a very unpopular tax increase in his first year he was able to lower the deficit. These are facts, not opinions.

Science was used by the Wright Brothers to figure out how to fly. We sure hope President Donald J. Trump understands that every time he climbs the steps to Air Force One, he is benefiting from science. We don't need a March for Science, we need to fund science and education to keep America great. Does the great Orange Leader understand this? Sad!

32. MUSLIMS, MONEY, MEXICANS & MELANIA

Trump's Love-Hate Relationships

Posted: 4-25-2017

If you were to ask me what I thought of Trump buildings, I would say that I neither hate them nor love them. They are plain and, from an architectural eye, appear to be well-built and substantial, but they aren't very innovative. I have never found them inviting and the size of his name on the edifice is gaudy, tacky, kitschy and, well you get it.

When Donald Trump started his egomaniacal trip into politics, most people thought it would be short-lived. Some people hated him and some loved him. When he came down the gold-plated escalator, he stood next to his beautiful immigrant wife and proceeded to tear into immigrants. Hate from day one.

The Mexicans seem to bother Trump the most. Even though he employs Mexicans and Mexican-Americans on his construction jobs, he sounds like he hates them. He used a whole ethnic group to get attention and put himself in the limelight. He wants to build a wall to keep Mexicans out. Why?

Donald Trump would surely hate being psychoanalyzed by a two-bit blogger, but he does expose himself to much of what he gets. Much like the bully on the playground, or the villain in a good movie, we love to hate him. It's not the war against political correctness that he wages that makes him wrong, it's the use of hate to separate us and get what he wants. Gee, what is that?

We know that Donald is a religious man. He worships money and power, which brought in the evangelicals, because they too, are protecting their kingdom on earth with money and power. WWJD? (What Would Jesus Do) And why can't he get that anti-Semitic stink off himself?

He keeps telling us how successful and rich he is. He loves talking about his wins as if anyone else losing makes him them the enemy. He says America first, but then seems to turn on America. He repeats his mantra that we are so screwed up, which is what an abusive father would say to a son who wasn't living up to his expectations. One might say he has a love-hate relationship with the very country he wants to lead.

Hating Muslims is an easy pot to stir. Every time a radical terrorist uses the twisted view of his faith as the justification for taking lives, Trump is there to endorse, encourage and exploit the hate. He can deny that he hates any religious group, like he denies climate change, but the facts are clear. Could you imagine a candidate for the highest office saying they wanted a complete and total shutdown of all Catholics entering the United States?

I am sure Mr. Know-It-All loves his wife Melania, but from this vantage point the relationship doesn't seem so lovey-dovey. Of course, you can spare us the over-the-top public displays of affection we saw with Al Gore and Tipper, and are still trying to unravel the strange sense of codependency that Mike Pence has demonstrated with his wife.

We know that Jack and Jackie Kennedy didn't really have a normal marriage. Maybe being President makes it impossible to have a customary relationship with your spouse, but the jury is still out as to whether Melania staying in New York is really for their son rather than her desire for a life.

In his previous relationships, Donald Trump was not faithful. Maybe he hates being married. Or maybe he is the embodiment of the 70's swinger whose only real vice is sex, without the drugs and rock 'n' roll. Or maybe he finally grew up.

That brings us to this question. Do I hate Donald Trump? Well I don't hate him, I don't like him and I surely don't love him. I feel sorry for him. Some of what he says reminds me of my father, who, if still alive, would be 104 years old. My father's viewpoints were baked in by a generation of people who believed America was a white country, with white bread and white picket fences, and that Italians, Irish, Russians, Jews and all those "other" people should have their own neighborhoods and should stay there except when going out to shop.

Donald Trump probably believes that if he got rid of all the Muslims, Mexicans and minorities who don't "love" America, that magically all the challenges would go away. Hating only gets more hate thrown back at you. Now that he has pulled all the way into his bubble, he will never realize that we are a nation of immigrants who want a better life. Trump's grandfather and mother came to America as immigrants. Does he deny that?

You don't make America great by getting rid of the "others," while catering to the 38% of those people who would look the other way when you shoot someone on Fifth Avenue. It's time for Trump to diminish the hate and increase the love. America is not going to wait for him to catch up with the reality and benefits of love.

33. PRESIDENT OUT OF TOUCH
Has Trump Ever Read the NAFTA Agreement?
Posted: 4-27-2017

Donald Trump fails to see that the world has changed. He may love Twitter and use it as a weapon, but that's only the tip of the technological iceberg floating toward his ship. He has the technology to know every fact, but fails to take the time to use it to his advantage.

His weakest point is the fact that he pushes his misinformed opinion before getting the facts. I truly wonder if he has ever read the NAFTA treaty and fully comprehends how it works for American businesses.

According to Forbes Magazine, Mexico purchased an estimated 2.4 billion dollars of corn from the US in 2015. Now Mexico is threatening to take their corn business to Brazil. Mexico is currently our third largest goods trading partner with 531 billion dollars in two-way goods trade during 2015. Goods exports totaled 236 billion dollars while goods imports totaled 295 billion dollars.

The United States buys 297.7 billion dollars' worth of goods from Canada, which is 76.3% of total Canadian exports. Canada is currently our second largest goods trading partner with 575 billion dollars of two-way goods trade during 2015.

In a nutshell, NAFTA created a "national treatment" of all goods and services from the three countries, the US, Canada and Mexico. The agreement basically means that traders outside the zone must treat all three countries as equals when it comes to the rules and regulations.

It also eliminated any tariffs on goods and services. For example, if Mexico makes a car and sells it in the US, they pay no tax on that good. As well, if Canada produces lumber and sells it in the US, they pay no tariff on the shipment. Why is this good?

Well, if all the US products and services purchased were taxed by Mexico and Canada, the United States would most likely also charge a hefty tariff on the goods coming across our borders. Without NAFTA, there would be an increase on the price of our goods going to those two countries and would stimulate an opportunity for other countries to worm into Mexico and Canada with better prices and might displace US companies as the preferred vendor. The additional taxes we might impose would not offset the loss of profits. After all, taxes don't go directly to companies, they go to the Treasury. The profits our companies are making right now by selling goods to Mexico and Canada might or might not be replaced by tax cuts for businesses. But most experts believe, ending NAFTA would hurt the US economy.

NAFTA helps settle disputes between our three nations and also provides another benefit. With NAFTA, we have Intellectual Property Rights Protections. This prevents a Canadian or Mexican factory from producing knock-offs of our products and ideas and selling them around the world.

Like the fat kid at the table, the Donald wants to take all the cookies from the other kids. And after he has taken all the cookies, he will get all huffy when he realizes that the other kids will get their own cookies from someone else and he will get none. He can't comprehend that his actions will hurt him, even when he gets his unreasonable share.

On April 26, 2017, Trump floated the threat of signing an executive order to withdraw from NAFTA and then received calls from the President of Mexico and the Prime Minister of Canada to discuss the renegotiation of the treaty. President goof-ball smiled because he thought he had won something. Once again, he has been shown to be the bully who doesn't realize that on the long-term, the other leaders are on to him.

As these countries look to their Plan B, which means opening trade with other nations to secure the goods they purchase daily from the US, Trump sits in his little oval office with his big plans that will eventually increase prices on everything we import. He is out-of-touch with the global economy that was created by technology, not ideology. If you are a free-market capitalist, then you will certainly have noticed that our great Orange Leader has just blopped something into the punch bowl.

If he was truly supportive of the common man and on a quest to create new jobs, he wouldn't keep cutting the budgets and destroying our relationships with the customers of our products. He may think he knows how it works, but when Mexico stops buying corn from the U.S. what will he tell that Iowa farmer?

Can we really afford to stop 500 billion dollars in trade with our NAFTA partners? I'm still waiting for all the greatness and winning. Markets want certainty, not gamesmanship and insolent deal making.

34. ANTI-ESTABLISHMENT VS. ESTABLISHMENT

Trump's Outside Agitator Role
Posted: 5-3-2017

I vividly remember when protesters in the late 1960s grew in numbers. President Nixon and his Trump-like bullhorn, Spiro Agnew, claimed that "outside agitators" were behind all the protests against his administration and the Vietnam war. Funny that a President couldn't grasp the concept of regular old Americans against war.

The term 'agitators' goes back to an era of labor disputes when unions would bus thugs to the picket lines at job sites to cause disruption. This would give the local police departments justification to go in and bust some heads. While the owners of the factory accused the unions of bringing in the hooligans, the unions accused the owners of paying the disrupters. The idea was to create fear and thus end the labor dispute. Bricks were thrown, blood was shed.

Like a 1950s politician, Trump uses the expression that *"protesters against him are paid"* leading some to make the joke, "Well, see Trump fulfilled his promise, he has created jobs."

But here's the real question. Is the President anti-establishment, or just modifying truth to build his own establishment? In a world where nepotism is perfectly legal and the only people who have opinions worthy of his attention are those who have as much money as he has or those who are directly related to him, the average Joe is voiceless.

Trump focuses so much on what people are saying about him that he misses the most important part of the job, getting things done.

When he loses a battle in Congress, he wants to change the rules. Sure, it would get more things done if there was a 51% margin on votes but 60% is there for a reason.

Donald Trump fails to understand that by being anti-establishment he is really being anti-constitution and anti-separation of the branches of government.

Article 2 of the Constitution clearly states that: *He shall have Power, by and with the Advice and Consent of the Senate, to make Treaties, provided two thirds of the Senators present concur...* Clearly the founding fathers were establishing an order, especially regarding our treaties with other nations. Jefferson, Washington, Hamilton, et al. didn't want a king, they wanted an executive.

With all the huffing and puffing done by candidate Donnie on the trail, supporters would have believed that their anti-Washington redeemer was going to unleash his wrath on all the terrible things in government as soon as he arrived in office. They joined a cult headed by a charismatic 'leader' who lies. Yes, those are air quotes, Don.

Trump supporters hate the government, until they get dragged off an airplane by police. They hate government, until they discover their drinking water is poisonous. They hate the establishment because Fox News has been feeding their heads with the gospel according to Rupert Murdoch, that everything is wrong, as long as it makes Mr. Murdoch money.

But, the job of heading the executive branch is not as all powerful as it might be in some other countries or in certain companies. If young Donald would have spent more time in civics class, he would have had a fuller understanding of how things worked before he got to the White House.

To say Kim Jong Un is a "smart cookie" is DUMB. Ask Kim Jong Un's uncle how much of a "cookie" he thinks he is. Oh, that's right, you can't, because Kim killed him.

And what does this President think is his top priority? Well, his campaign, which is now taking money for his 2020 reelection pursuit, said they will spend 1.5 million dollars on TV and online to run a commercial that says mainstream media is "fake news." Do your followers know that you are giving their money right back to the mainstream media you decry?

That is what you would call anti-establishment, but what is the next step? Can censorship be too far behind? Why not use the 1.5 million to explain how the budget works, or why your ideas on healthcare are good? Too complicated?

Freedom is part of this establishment we call the United States of America. Protecting people from abuses and schemes is an established goal of government. Keeping citizens safe is a must, but how is tweeting at three-in-the-morning keeping us safe? Get some sleep great Orange one, there's a well-organized establishment out there to get you.

Trump seems to forget established facts, like Andrew Jackson, a Democrat, was not involved in the Civil War. He was dead 16 years when the war started. His only involvement in America's Civil War, and this is a stretch, was his 100 slaves he owned. But then, lots of white people owned dark people back then.

'Old Hickory' might be your hero Mr. Trump, but you ought to learn that Jackson was credited with causing the Panic of 1837, which started an almost ten-year recession. Please don't be like Jackson, Mr. President. Shut up and lead.

35. WHY DO WE NEED A SECOND AMENDMENT?

Trump Needs to Read the First Amendment
Posted: 5-5-2017

Recently, the President's chief of staff said that the administration had considered changing the libel laws in the United States. Donald Trump has constantly used the power of the lawsuit to attack his "enemies" in business. If given the power, he would like to control the press with intimidation and fear. Locking journalists up might not change the way they source or write their stories, but it would spell the end of our democracy as we know it.

Sure, if the libel laws were changed it would help Mr. Thin-Skin soothe his fragile ego, but at what cost? He could haul reporters into court when they wrote something bad about him, but there is a reason the First Amendment was first.

Remember what is says Mr. Trump: *Congress shall make no law respecting an establishment of religion, or prohibiting the free exercise thereof; or abridging the freedom of speech, or of the press; or the right of the people peaceably to assemble, and to petition the Government for a redress of grievances.*

In these 45 words, the framers established the core beliefs of America. I have always said to my gun toting friends, you can have your Second Amendment as long as you protect my First Amendment, which says so much more than giving reporters the right to report freely.

When Trump signed his executive order yesterday (May 4, 2017) thinking he was ending the Johnson Amendment, which bans tax-exempt organizations like churches from political speech and activities, he was dead wrong. The only way the Johnson Amendment can be eliminated is by a vote of Congress. If the Donald took the time to read the First Amendment he would see that he cannot establish a religion or prohibit the free exercise of a religion. So, there is no need for him to sign a worthless piece of paper.

Under the Constitution the President cannot "abridge" freedom of speech. That means he cannot reduce, curtail or cut freedom of speech and this includes the press.

The First Amendment also gives the people the right to assemble in a peaceful way and the right to petition the Government for redress, which can include compensation, reparations, recompense and damages. The founders were smart with their description of the Government as an entity that was not above the people. The Constitution is a valuable piece of paper.

That gets around to why we need a Second Amendment. The founding fathers understood that a tyrant, king, or over-zealous leader might attempt to take away the freedoms of the citizens, thus the reason why we must have the right to bear arms. If someone attempts to take these freedoms away, the framers were more than hinting at a solution. They were giving tacit approval for armed rebellion.

It says: *A well-regulated Militia, being necessary to the security of a free State, the right of the people to keep and bear Arms, shall not be infringed.*

You might be surprised that this blogger would say, YES to the Second Amendment, because we possibly might need that "well-regulated" group of Americans to take our country back one day. It doesn't say anything in those 26 words about mentally challenged people or some ideological driven group of radical terrorists getting guns, does it?

Gun control measures, which most reasonable Americans agree with, are in line with the 2nd amendment's use of the term, a "**well-regulated**" militia. Trump is a puppet of the NRA and always has been. It's rather ironic that the man who rails against lobbyists is controlled by one of the most powerful pro-gun groups. They not only support him, they give him money. In short, the great "swamp drainer" is nothing but a good-for-nothing politician with his hand in the pockets of BIG GUNS. Sad!

36. HEALTHCARE IS COMPLICATED
Trump Unqualified as Insurance Czar
Posted: 5-8-2017

The House of Representatives' poorly written healthcare act is like a guy with a hangover eating a habanero pepper omelet the next day. Crap in, crap out.

They might claim that it's the "hair of the dog," but in reality, it is exactly what they shouldn't have done. When the House passed the American Healthcare Act on May 4, 2017 (by only two votes) 20 Republicans voting against the bill, the Donald played right into Democratic hands.

And here is why:

The GOP accused Democrats of not reading the Obamacare act before they voted on it. Trump forced his party members to do the same thing and thus sabotaged those running in 2018. We must remember the 213 Representatives who voted NO on this one.

The de facto party leader, Donald Trump, said that everyone would get coverage and that pre-existing conditions would be covered, while the same leader let the Freedom Caucus roll him and agree to the deal for a state opt-out for insurance companies.

House members made it seem that they were either expecting their older "brother" the Senate to fix their work or, worse, they were appeasing Trump and displaying the remarkable division within their party. I used the word "brother" because the committee writing the Senate version of the bill consists of 13 men. Why?

We are hearing lots of talk about healthcare and insurance companies. The typical gripe about Obamacare is that there are so few insurance companies in certain states.

Why aren't we discussing the efforts of state insurance commissioners? Some have blocked the expansion of companies into their states. For example, many people don't know that it took GEICO many years to get into the Massachusetts market. WHY? Well, the large insurance companies based in Boston blocked any insurance companies that offered "discounted" insurance. Boy, that is restrictive. That has since been resolved, but it begs a bigger question.

Why would the president keep rotating that hackneyed phrase that he believes in states' rights and wants to give them more control over health insurance? Once you give the states MORE control over healthcare, why even have a national healthcare act? And when all the states raise taxes, the president might think he won't get blamed, but he should think again and stop listening to people like Steve Bannon.

Because of Obamacare, we are no longer debating that there should be a national healthcare plan. We are now debating what it should be and who should pay for it. When the first person with a pre-existing condition dies under Trumpcare, the Donald and the Republican party will have blood on their hands. That Republican lie about death panels will then be rolled out by the Democrats, only this time people will believe it.

With all the companies Donald Trump ran in the past, we are sure that he heard debates about healthcare for his employees. His involvement was probably tertiary with him; either telling someone to do business with someone's company he liked, or just saying get the price down.

Now, we have Tom Price running around repeatedly saying how great the plan is, while never addressing any questions. His presentation, like those of most Trump underlings, is just a mini campaign-like speech fraught with fact-free slogans and fallacies. Is it because he doesn't know what he is talking about, or is it a case of specifics left out so no mistakes are made?

Anyone running a business would ask a few questions before voting on a plan. The first is how much will this cost? The second is what does it do for my workforce? I remember that middle-class rationality of how it would be great to have a true businessman run the government. Well, where can we get one? Or, better yet, can we get a real businesswoman?

Donald Trump has admitted that healthcare is complicated. Obama once opened an explanation with a remark on how complicated the subject was and Jon Stewart called him out. Stewart challenged Obama by forcefully explaining that it's the President's job to help us understand complicated matters.

Let's face it, a simple man who cannot grasp the complexities of things can ever turn them into a well-thought-out plan. Trump does hate, sarcasm and bullying well, but on the mattes of state, he's clumsy, uninformed and foolish. Sad!

37. LAWYERS, GUNS AND MONEY
Trump's Enabler, White House Counsel
Posted: 5-9-2017

We learned two things on May 8, 2017. The private education Donald Trump was awarded did not teach him how to spell and when confronted with any legal warning, he will stonewall. He learned all his lessons from the late lawyer and mentor Roy Cohn. Some, who know both personalities, would say that Trump is channeling Roy.

The Donald is correct that during the Senate hearings, Sally Yates did not disclose any new facts about what happened. This is because she knows a lot more about the investigation and as a good law enforcement person, she didn't want spill any beans to those being investigated. What she did reveal was a solid timeline that exposes the president's decision-making process when it comes to potential legal threats to his legitimacy.

The acting Attorney General asked for a meeting with White House Counsel Don McGahn. At two face-to-face meetings, she warned the administration of problems with Michael Flynn. McGahn posed several interesting questions during those encounters.

He wanted to know whether the acting AG had thought Flynn had broken any laws. He also wondered why it was a Department of Justice matter if two administration officials lied to each other. WHAT? Even more damaging, he asked if any action the DOJ might take would interfere with an on-going investigation. Yates said, *"No, because Flynn had already been interviewed by the FBI."*

Clearly McGahn, coincidentally another "Donald", was fishing for whether there was a probe into Flynn. Of course, McGahn is no stranger to the dirty underbelly of Washington politics. Trump may have said he was going to drain the swamp, but he kept one of the alligators as legal counsel.

McGahn was Chief Counsel for the RNC for nine years, before George W. Bush appointed him to the Federal Election Committee (FEC), where he had his fingers on governing the election process. Don McGahn, as counsel for the RNC, defended Tom DeLay, who was indicted and convicted of illegally transferring funds from his campaign to a super PAC in Texas. Rather than get into the lengthy details here, which include information about Russian money as well, simply just google: DeLay-Abramoff Money Trail.

McGahn shouldn't be judged by the clients he's kept, but he did work for the Koch Brothers' Freedom Partners. In short, Don McGahn is apparently more swamp than Trump and thought to be able to navigate around the alligators at the Justice Department.

In Warren Zevon's classic song, *Lawyers, Guns and Money*, one line stands out, *"Send lawyers, guns, and money, the shit has hit the fan!"* As for Trump, "it" seems to keep hitting the twirling reality of Washington, and in some cases, the President seems to be picking the stuff up and throwing it back into the fan himself, like an orange orangutan.

It's too late for Donald Trump to defend his pal Michael Flynn to the press or the people of this great nation. Even the press secretary keeps saying *"the President had made the right decision and we've moved on,"* but have we? We have lawyers, we have more guns in Afghanistan and we have MONEY involved in everything Trump and his relatives touch.

The two Donald's waited 18 days to pull the plug on what they knew was a problem. That doesn't sound like the fantasy character Donald Trump created on the campaign trail. The whole Flynn-gate affair prompts a question. If there was no Washington Post article, would Flynn still have his job? If the answer is yes, then the President is guilty of putting personal loyalties above national security. His actions demonstrated a lack of political and business judgement. In business, you cut your losses and move on.

There was a great article written by the National Review's Tom Rogan that was posted on November 20, 2016. It quoted someone who knows Flynn well, *"Flynn had a tendency to bully anyone who disagreed with his assessments on operational strategy."* That sounds a lot like the man who wanted him by his side for all the big decisions on security. The whole premise of Rogan's article was that Michael Flynn was the wrong pick for National Security Adviser.

I always look for strange connections that don't mean anything, like the fact that Don McGahn's mother is Noreen Rogan and the article was written by a man name Rogan, no relation.

Now, I know our President might brew that into a conspiracy theory saying that someone born in the UK like Rogan, shouldn't be allowed to write about American politics. However, if Trump took the time to read this article when he was deciding who to appoint for National Security, he would have seen what everyone else saw in Flynn, a right-wing whack job who has no business being on the people's payroll. If only our President could read.

38. DONALD TRUMP IS NO AXEL FOLEY

The President Is Always on Defense

Posted: 5-10-2017

What if you started a new job and the first thing your boss said to you was, *"I'm right about everything and you must never disagree with me about anything."* Anyone worth their salt and without a large mortgage payment would flee the building.

We don't get to vote for our bosses but we do vote for our president. Hillary Clinton got 65,844,610 votes, which was 48.2% of the popular vote, while the man who is President got 62,979,636 votes, only 46.1%. Also, there were 7,804,213, or 5.7% of the voters who cast their ballot for someone other than the two headliners.

According to a May 9, 2017 Rasmussen Reports Daily Presidential Tracking Poll, 46% of Likely US voters approve of President Trump's job performance, while 54% disapprove. This means that more than half the people in the USA don't think Trump is doing a very good job. And in my unscientific poll, there is a large percentage of people in the country who truly hate him.

Most Presidents start out by presenting their case and through their actions slowly warm up the citizens who might not have voted for them. People aren't as dumb as Bill Maher claims they are, but there still are massive numbers of people in the country who follow Trump like a cult leader. One of the meanings of cult is a misplaced or excessive admiration for a particular person or thing.

Trump thinks he's the master of the redirect, which was aptly demonstrated in the movie Beverly Hills Cops II. Gilbert Gottfried played a guy named Bernstein at City Hall in charge of all city records. Eddie Murphy and his cop sidekicks used intimidation to trick the timid clerk. The fun begins when Murphy's character holds a stack of parking tickets he claims belong to Bernstein's wife:

Sidney Bernstein setting up a bribe says, *"Wait, I have an idea. Is there something that I have in this office that I could hand to you and that would make you kind of forget that you're holding those little pink tickets there?"* Gottfried proceeds to propose a $200 bribe to have the tickets go away. The metaphor and sleight of hand helps the police get into the city computer.

And the innocent question, *"You'd go, what did I have there? I don't remember."* Of course, *"forgetting"* was code for just disremembering that he just gave a large bribe to the cops. What is in one hand, made what was in the other hand go away.

On the one hand, Sally Yates testified about warning the Trump about Michael Flynn and the president and all his men did nothing for 18 days. On the other, Trump fired James Comey, Director of the FBI, on May 9, 2017.

On another hand, Jared Kushner's sister used the image of the president and her brother's position at the White House to sell EB-5 visas to Chinese investors.

So, for 500,000 dollars anyone, without clearance, without vetting can purchase a Green Card and move to the United States. While other workers, future immigrants and refugees seeking asylum must wait in line. Trump approved this measure a few days before Jared's sister did her pitch, but on the campaign trail he was so worried about how people get into the country.

How is the "Golden Visa" EB-5 program even legal? I guess Trump knows best. I mean, how could a terrorist afford that much money? They can't just take it out of the ISIS bank, or can they?

As the cable news channels regurgitate diatribes assigned to their political formats, the American public is, once again, fooled by the master liar in the White House. Even Fox News wasn't quite sure how to handle the firing of James Comey.

It was delightful to watch them try to vocalize whether this was good or bad. You can't keep switching your position on major issues and expect the American people to understand your true values.

The real journalists need to step up right now. They should keep on the Russian story. Why is Donald J. Trump so defensive about this? It sure does feel like Nixon. Remember what really got to the bottom of the whole Watergate mess was a special prosecutor. We've already seen the movie, now let's read the script.

And the administration should be taking the press secretary to the wood shed on the EB-5 visa program and how it makes America less secure.

Why not find the answers, or is the Donald afraid that what he has in his one small hand might show that the other small hand has been signing things at the urging of some dark force from a faraway land?

Someone should follow the money. A thorough analysis of everything Trump does would be in order. How will every decision affect his kids and their wealth? The signing of the budget with the extension of the EB-5 just happened. What else has he done? Maybe it's nothing, but why not clear the air? What are you afraid of, Mr. President?

I for one, will not be silent, #NotOnMyWatch.

39. THE ATROCITIES OF AMERICAN POLITICS

Trump Will Destroy the Republican Party

Posted: 5-11-2017

When the White House had Sarah Huckabee Sanders field questions the day after Donald Trump fired the FBI Director (May 9, 2017), we saw a combative B team player who really isn't ready for prime time. Sorry, but even though she is the DNA offspring of deep southern conservatives, Mike Huckabee and Janet McCain (no relation), we blame the President for not having the guts to come out to the press and take questions himself. He is mostly chicken-shit when confronted.

Sarah, the word, "atrocity" means an extremely wicked or cruel act, typically involving physical violence or injury. When you claim James Comey was guilty of atrocities you moved him into the same level as Bashar al-Assad, Saddam Husain or, wait for it, Vladimir Putin. You owe the guy an apology for your horrible word choice and lack of comprehension.

As the Republican opportunists and sordid politicians line up to get behind the President on his obvious move to thwart investigations, there is a flaw here beyond repair for the Republican party. Poor Sarah could not have expected that the day she was to fill in for her co-worker who was busy with Naval Reserve duty she would make things worse. If she is the future of the party, then you might as well bring her father back.

The thinking Republicans, not Paul Ryan, who are asking good questions will be able to say they stood up and challenged the Liar-in-Chief when he tried to shut down investigations into Michael Flynn. The Democrats are not without sin on this one. After all you can't call for Comey's head and then, when our great Orange Leader delivers said head, pull out the word, "Watergate."

The debate will go on for a few days as to whether this is worse than Watergate, or perhaps Watergate Lite, or maybe nothing at all; but from this vantage point we make our case that Donald J. Trump has always been the wrong person to lead America. If this leads to impeachment, historians can say this was just like Watergate.

This is only the tip of the iceberg, which Donald Trump is trying to melt with his executive orders and lack of judgement. The most astonishing aspect is the administrations' lack of awareness about how this would be interpreted. If you just worked this through a logic process you would say, boy that is how they got Nixon.

Trump hijacked the Republican Party, and they let him. He hijacked the Presidency and millions of people helped him. BUT, he cannot hijack the structure of America. He cannot stop the truth from coming out, much to his frustration. He wants Mommy and Daddy to back up every one of his lies. And when someone keeps saying that he lies, they are added to his enemies list.

Richard Nixon was an ideologue, with an enemies list, who was the last person to see that the country was changing. He was a scotch-drinking Quaker who was so out of touch with reality, he listened only to those around him. Donald Trump may not drink alcohol but he is clearly addicted to fame. He needs to have his ego massaged everyday by those around him. This makes him dangerously manipulatable.

The RNC may be all happy that they control the Senate, the House and the White House, but are they truly in control of anything? In 2018, when healthcare is costing more and hurting people, those seats will go away and the cycle will continue. Sadly, when the Democrats regain a majority, the atrocities of American politics will kick in. That's when nothing gets done.

What Donald Trump has brought to the surface are the many cracks in the Republican party and those who claim the country is better off with an elephant in the room. With hearings on TV so often, we get to see those ridiculous GOP ideologues like Ted Cruz who wastes hearing time with questions designed to put down Democrats rather than discovering what is really going on. Cruz might think he is smart and impressive, but he comes off like the guy at the party who only wants to talk about what he thinks is important. Save us.

The exposure of public hearings puts on trial the lack of depth within many of those serving on important committees. It also showcases that the Dems are not all tree-hugging, left-winged whackos as Fox News paints them. They are generally well prepared and ask good questions. Whether you like Al Franken or not, he does have a way of getting people to talk.

My advice to everyone in America is to keep your eyes open. Remember what you said about Obama? Well double that with Trump. Are you better off yet? Are you winning? Did you get a raise? How much did they charge for that medicine today? The Republican party owns healthcare and they own Trump. Poor babies.

40. BAD WEATHER IN WASHINGTON
Prognosis: No Hope in Trumpville
Posted: 5-12-2017

As the weather in America rips a path of destruction across this great nation, we do not hear the President talk about climate change. The personal tragedies and demoralizing death from ever-increasing weather fronts are never mentioned by the Donald. It's as if domestic agenda is being written by his inability to quell the ongoing controversies about himself while not delivering hope to the people. Why can't he solve that problem?

It's clear by the tweet storms that the president's White House has no control over his message because, quite frankly, he's making it up as he goes along. His people run out to the podium to unsuccessfully sandbag the negative flow affecting the President.

There are some people who have said. "I have heard this," that Donald Trump is suffering from Dissociative Identity Disorder (Multiple Personality Disorder), a complex psychological condition that can be caused by many factors, including severe trauma during early childhood.

Along with pathological lying (also called pseudologia fantastica and mythomania), a behavior of habitual or compulsive lying, Trump has few sunny days. He feels compelled to repeat certain phrases incessantly because of an insecure need to be understood. Or perhaps, the repetition solidifies lies as a truth in his own mind.

We see what a poor reader he is when using a teleprompter. This could be the result of attention deficit disorder and would explain why he dislikes reading.

Trump lashes out when the clouds roll in and he feels the world is against him. He lusts after praise, and when he doesn't get any he inserts compliments into his speech. This might be caused by an inferiority complex, a lack of self-worth and uncertainty about himself. He constantly has feelings of not measuring up to standards. His extremely asocial behavior manifests itself by putting down people, especially Barack Obama, who he considers to be mentally superior.

But let's get back to the weather. When destruction hit parts of America, previous Presidents commented about the people's hardship and gave them some hope. Sometimes the leader of the free world would go to see the damage and experience the pain first hand. This president ignores the very people who voted for him. He goes out only to do his shtick at restricted, ticket-only political rallies.

After the airing of the interview with NBC's Lester Holt, our great Orange Leader proved once again that his version of the truth should be our focus. He finally admitted a "slight mistake" that his surrogates cannot be "perfectly accurate" because there is so much going on? What? I thought being President would be easy.

As the weather gets worse in Washington and the Trumpettes attempt to bail out Mr. Know-It-All, we need hip boots to splash through the excrement shoveled out these days.

Trump is now threatening to end press briefings. Rather than just passing out fact sheets with your points, Mr. President, why don't you take your significantly fat ass over to the press room and take the questions yourself?

In a recent interview Trump attacked Stephen Colbert claiming he isn't funny, while the more Donald belittles him the bigger Colbert's ratings grow.

Why is the President of the United States wasting his time talking about comedians? It's ironic that Stephen Colbert coined the term "Truthiness," which is now in the dictionary. Donald Trump is the glowing example of living on the thin edge of truthiness and that's no joke.

Everyone knows Comey didn't bow to the King and that is why he is gone. Who elected this orange guy? Time will tell if James Comey will become the John Dean of this administration. Younger readers, please Google.

The morning of May 12, 2017 brought Trump's latest tweet, *"James Comey better hope that there are no 'tapes' of our conversations before he starts leaking to the press!"* When have we ever seen a person fire someone, personally put them down, and then publicly threaten them? Our "leader" is truly a very small man.

Obviously, the President lives in the eye of the storm, but someone needs to tell him the other side of the hurricane will get him. The winds are blowing and the currents are not in his favor.

41. TRUMP'S CABINET EXPOSED PT. 1.
Judge a Man by the Companies He Keeps
Posted: 5-15-2017

When the time comes to write the history of the Trump reign in Washington, we will look to the people he picked to sit at the big table. The President's Cabinet are the most important members of his team. These members are so powerful in the government that they must be confirmed by Congress.

Many articles are written as the season begins in any specific sport. The armchair coaches and managers at the newspapers, magazines, web sites and TV networks tell us why one team is better than the other. It's only been a little over 100 days since this administration started and some of these characters weren't confirmed right away. However, they all are now official, so let's look at each player on the Trump team.

One of the most important people influencing how our country deals with the many hotspots and countries in the world is the Secretary of State. Traded from the EXXON MOBIL team and playing this position is Rex Tillerson. Rex carries himself well and has the gravitas and voice that can impress you, but don't expect to have him ever say anything that matters. You can't see the strings coming from his arms, but Trump speak is in his speak. I loved it when he said what Trump wanted him to say, then a minute later, retorted that Russian hacking was a bad thing. He's no Hillary Clinton, but you knew that.

The person in charge of the Treasury, Steven Mnuchin, was brought in from Goldman Sachs and has a nasty curve ball. While at ESL Investments he helped Trump secure dough for his building projects. He gave Trump cash and the Donald paid him back with a job taking care of our money. This guy was involved in the OneWest housing crisis and foreclosed on many Americans while his company reaped rewards. Of course, this is too easy. It's putting the wolf in charge of the hen house. We just hope that our nest eggs aren't cracked by this inarticulate banker.

On defense, and we mean Secretary of Defense, we have James N. Mattis. He is a lifelong military man with excellent credentials, but, sadly, many critics of President Trump believe that the driving force on this decision was Mattis' nickname, "Mad Dog Mattis," which Trump loved saying at his rallies. Mattis carries a big bat and understands global conflicts and the nuisances of specific cultures. If Mattis stays, we will have some sanity in the ranks.

The Attorney General's job went to longtime supporter and campaigner Jefferson Beauregard Sessions III, whose law and order message was blended with Trump's exaggerated views on crime and who commits them. Sessions is not only a team player, he is the umpire who wants a certain crowd to like him.

Under Sessions, we will fill up the prisons due to his mandated sentencing decree, which will help some of Trump's contributors, GEO Group, the largest for-profit prison firm and the other large prison company, CoreCivic, who both gave as much as a quarter of a million dollars to support Trump's inauguration. Sessions also had to recuse himself from any Russian election investigation because of his failing to admit under oath that he, too, met with the Russians. Rule of Law? He claims his recusal was driven only by his involvement in the campaign.

Ryan Zinke, appointed and confirmed as the Secretary of the Interior, may have a degree in geology and a military record but what stands out here is his service on the board of the oil pipeline company QS Energy. During the primary, Zinke said that Hillary Clinton was "the real enemy" and the "anti-Christ" due to her position on freedom of choice for women. While Zinke wants to decide what a woman does with her interior, this guy wants to destroy our land. He wants to burn more coal for electricity and has zero care about Native Lands. To the Native people of America, he is indeed an evil spirit.

Sonny Perdue may be the Agriculture Secretary, but he is NOT related to the Perdue Chicken Company. As governor of Georgia, he once asked his state to pray to ask God to end a drought. This is a guy who wanted to return to the stars and bars flag for the state of Georgia (the one that looked confederate). Ironically, he was sworn in as Secretary of Agriculture by Clarence Thomas. It's too soon to see if this guy has any real understanding of farms, but he is a "Bull Dog" and has a degree from University of Georgia College of Veterinary Medicine. So, he knows animals.

Finally, let's take a quick look at the Secretary of Commerce, Wilbur Ross. He is a son of a New Jersey judge. When Ross was the Senior Managing Director of Rothschild Inc., a firm that specialized in bankruptcies, good old Wilbur figured out a way for Donald Trump to keep control of his failing casinos. In settlements that came after a Securities and Exchange Commission probe into overcharging of fees by WL Ross & Co, his most recent firm, he paid more than 100 million dollars in fines and shareholder reimbursements. He only deals with trade, so his background won't keep him from pissing off Canada, Mexico and eventually all our trade partners.

42. WHERE DID TRUMP FIND THESE PEOPLE? PT. 2

Rotten Cabinet, Shaky Legs

Posted: 6-25-2017

Let's start with the Department of Health and Human Services. It has a budget of one trillion dollars and is the primary source of funding for medical research. Tom Price heads up this department. Although he is a doctor in real life, most recently he was the six-term congressman from the sixth district of Georgia.

To prove Tom Price is the typical wheeler-dealer politician, CNN, the New York Times, and the Wall Street Journal all reported that Price bought more than $300,000 worth of stocks in companies that stood to benefit from legislation he supported or drafted. The Democrats tried to postpone his nomination, but Trump was whining about how long things were taking. A full investigation into his stock dealings was never completed before he was confirmed.

According to Wired magazine: *Price recently drafted a budget that would have cut spending on Medicare by $449 billion over the next ten years. When Senator Elizabeth Warren asked him how that squared with Trump's pledge to not to touch Medicare or Medicaid, Price said money was the wrong metric. "I believe the metric ought to be the care to the patients."* Price is so full of it, it's amazing his kidneys can clean that much political excrement. Loser.

Ben Carson is the United States Secretary of Housing and Urban Development, probably because he owns a house and grew up in Detroit. There are no other logical reasons for him to have the position. He says stupid things much of the time.

Rick Perry is our Secretary of Energy, a department whose name he once forgot when it was on his list of departments to abolish when he was running for President. Sadly, the nuclear codes are in his domain now. God save us.

The guy that Trump put in charge of the EPA is Scott Pruitt, who will be more specifically skewered in this book, just keep reading

Dan Coats, as Senator from the State of Indiana, served on the United States Senate Select Committee on Intelligence and was tapped by President Trump to become the Director of National Intelligence. Aside from being a soccer player at Wheaton, there is some question whether his age, or too many headers, made him think he didn't have to testify during recent Senate hearings. Dan Coats is supposed to be heading up the investigation of the Russian tampering of our 2016 elections, but he must be under some loyalty pledge that prevents him from doing that job.

We will give David Shilkin (Veterans), John F. Kelly (Homeland Security), Mike Pompeo (CIA) and Nikki Haley (U.N.) a pass here because, as of this posting, they appear to be doing their jobs.

Let's now turn to the future of our children and the Department of Education, which is run by a person who has never been in a public school or had any of her children attend a public school, Betsy DeVos. Ms. DeVos' father was a billionaire and her husband is Dick DeVos Jr., the multi-billionaire heir to the Amway fortune. Not that being rich prevents insight about how education can work for the kids, but this pick is the number one doozy for the Donald. Betsy was awarded her post because she and her husband are big donors not only to conservative causes, but also to Trump himself.

In the New York Times reader poll, Betsy won Worst Trump Cabinet Member. Her mission is to destroy public schools and create a voucher program in which families can pay for private or parochial education. Under the myth that people really want a choice about what and where their kids are taught, DeVos' war on public education will only set back communities and make them dip into their own pockets to bail out local communities and schools.

People have complained about her lack of experience, knowledge and education, but the truth is she would have never been considered if it wasn't for the pay-to-play reality of money. She literally bought the position. She has no vision, no real plan and whatever she comes up with will be victim of the draconian budget cuts from Mick Mulvaney the Director of the Office of Management and Budget.

To wrap up this post on the dysfunctional Trump cabinet, let's focus on the guy who also says stupid things most of the time, Mike Mulvaney. He was a member of the House of Representatives from South Carolina before he got the job figuring out how to make the budget work. He attended Georgetown and has a law degree from the University of North Carolina. He has no practical experience or education in finance or business.

In 2015, Mulvaney was part of the 'Shutdown Caucus,' willing to close the government down instead of extending the debt limit. He achieved notoriety through his tea party roots and has now become the guy who will decide how OUR money will be spent.

Rather than discredit Mick with my opinions, let's just walk through some of his quotes:

Mulvaney has said that Meals on Wheels is one of those programs *"not showing any results."*

Mulvaney argued for the elimination of children's food programs because they do not lead to *"demonstrable"* improvement in school performance.

Mulvaney reported that Trump considers climate research *"a waste of money."*

Mulvaney, when asked about cuts to humanitarian programs, said, *"That should come as a surprise to no one who watched the campaign"*

Where did Trump find these people? Someday we will all wake up and realize that not only did the nation elect the wrong person for President, but that same person picked unqualified and dangerous people for almost every position in the cabinet. The faster these people leave; the better off America will be.

43. TRUMP'S "ABSOLUTE RIGHTS"
Mother F**king Laptops on These Mother F**king Planes
Posted: 5-16-2017

There are two things happening at the same time and if you open your eyes wide enough you will see that America has a problem. Let me simplify this into grains of truth.

First, we have a President in Trump who is being told by lawyers and over-zealous advisors about how to leap over his latest lie. Is this democracy or is it something a kingdom must do when a teenager becomes King after his old man died? The people who voted for Trump's big mouth made a huge mistake. Donald Trump has some abnormal affection and bizarre loyalty to Russia. We must find out what that's all about.

He may have the right and power to declassify at will, but once he does the intelligence is no longer a secret and then can be circulated to anyone – ISIS and newspapers for example. That's dumb on his part.

Trump made a threat, now unveiled, to his fired FBI Director and tweeted a cryptic statement about 'tapes' in the White House. He then proceeded to claim he didn't leak anything to the Russians about a threat of ISIS laptop bombs. Next, he used the phrase *"humanitarian reasons"* as a justification for leaking information about the plot to the Russians in the Oval Office. Does he realize that if there are any 'tapes' they can be subpoenaed by Congress?

Our great Orange Leader has painted himself into a legal corner which he cannot escape without laying down some heavy footprints, but that is not the biggest part of this intrigue. The story within the story is the insane idea of making people check their computers on all flights. There are very good reasons that this would put more people in danger.

Laptops generally run on nickel cadmium (NiCad), nickel metal hydride (NiMH), or lithium ion (Li-ion) batteries, with Li-ion being the most common in newer laptops. There's a reason why the airlines currently ask you to take any device that has a lithium battery out of luggage you plan to check.

In February of 2016 The Department of Transportation, which oversees the FAA, banned the use of lithium batteries on planes. Due to the risk of fire, lithium-ion batteries cannot be shipped as cargo on passenger planes.

Now we are hearing this call to make people check their laptops in baggage. Is Homeland Security this stupid? Someone will close their laptop and forget to turn it off. They will then place it in the middle of their clothes to protect it and create an overheating situation that could create a luggage hold fire. Who's your terrorist now?

Let's get back to those 'absolute rights' the Donald claims. It's about time for the Congress to read Article 1, Section 1 of the Constitution: *All legislative Powers herein granted shall be vested in a Congress of the United States, which shall consist of a Senate and House of Representatives.* The President cannot make law.

And the Donald should read the last paragraph in Article 1, Section 3: *Judgment in Cases of Impeachment shall not extend further than to removal from Office, and disqualification to hold and enjoy any Office of honor, Trust or Profit under the United States: but the Party convicted shall nevertheless be liable and subject to Indictment, Trial, Judgment and Punishment, according to Law.*

The President is not above the law, be it in the office or out of the office. What he told the Russians may or may not destroy a relationship we have with another government's security services, or it might get someone killed, but Trump doesn't care. He's focused only on how he looks to whomever is in the room, friend or foe.

With each justification and lack of communication with Congress, the greater the number of Republican skeptics he will create. Meanwhile, we hope that a laptop in a suitcase doesn't start a plane fire. Trump may be a baboon, but someone should stand up to bad security policies. We cannot trust Trump to keep a secret or make a good decision. Sad, really, really Sad!

44. WHOLLY APPROPRIATE – HOLY CRAP!

Trump Recorded in the Oval by the Russians?

Posted: 5-17-2017

Wake up America, Trump and Putin are having a love affair. We must ask the question, when do Republicans step up and do something about it? Let's just walk through seven days of presidential disgrace.

The Donald decided to fire the Director of the FBI on May 9, 2017 because of the investigation into Russia's tampering with the US election. Then, he had the Russians in the White House the next day, where he gave them intel that was provided by Israel.

Let's rewind a bit now. On Valentine's Day 2017 the New York Times told us that Trump asked the FBI's to "let go" the investigation into Michael Flynn. Incredibly, this happened just one day after Trump fired Flynn. Now we have half-baked experts discussing if this was obstruction of justice.

Obstruction consists of any attempt to hinder the discovery, apprehension, conviction or punishment of anyone who has committed a crime. The acts by which justice is obstructed may include bribery, murder, intimidation, and the use of physical force against witnesses, law enforcement officers or court officials.

When I heard Congressman Adam Schiff say we must look at "intent" I almost laughed. Trump, in his own style, asked Comey to end the investigation into Flynn and then later he fired him. That should be a giant period at the end of the sentence and as much intent as any logical person would need.

Just when we thought that all the shoes have dropped, Putin announced that he can provided a transcript of the discussion that took place with the President on May 10, 2017 in the Oval Office. Trump not only got played by the Russians with photographs of them yucking it up, but Putin says he knows every word that was said there. This begs the question, what is secure?

If this seems to have gone too far, then you are being a logical and loyal American. If you see all this as some conspiracy to get Donald Trump, then you obviously are a member of the cult of unawareness; God bless you.

What are we going to do? We have already gone through this before. It was called Watergate. There is a moment in time when we realize that absolute power corrupts absolutely. It's time for people like McMaster, Tillerson and Mattis to stop their attempts to bail out the loser. Whatever credibility they have is hanging in the balance.

Yes, we aren't winning because we have a loser in the White House and it's time for him to go. President Pence will be inadequate at best, but we must stabilize the Republic and get this government back on solid American Sovereignty. There are times when people want change. Wanting something different is okay, but we also need to be open to that comprehension that our choice might not have been what is best.

Why wait four years to fix this mistake? It's time for thinking Americans to decide what they want their country to be. We are either going to permit this perverse vision of our country or go back to a standard operating procedure that has worked for more than 240 years.

Donald J. Trump has just proved that he is unfit to be President of the United States. Is that clear enough?

45. WITCH HUNTS AND SMOKING GUNS

Trump Leaves America in Denial
Posted: 5-18-2017

Donald J. Trump, ready to embark on his long trip to meet with leaders of the world, sends his first tweet in 24-hours (5-18-2017). And he posted, *"This is the single greatest witch hunt of a politician in American history!"*

He lives in total denial. We can only hope that he could endure the extreme vetting that an immigrant would suffer coming through customs on his back into the country.

We are seeing things melt away fast. Between the Comey memos, creating the possibility that Trump asked the FBI Director to let go the investigation of Michael Flynn and his ties to Russia, we also get the news that Trump was warned about Flynn by Susan Rice, Sally Yates and President Obama. Nonetheless Trump, named him National Security Advisor. So much for extreme vetting.

Trump uses short little phrases, he probably writes on his little hands, to deflect truth and promote his agenda of lies. He claims this is the biggest "witch hunt" in American history. Did he did use the word "politician." I didn't think Donald Trump was a politician, I thought he was different; a real swamp drainer.

As for witch hunts, the Salem witch trials between February 1692 and May 1693 resulted in the executions of twenty people, fourteen of them women, and all but one by hanging. I'm not sure you want to dredge up that piece of history with your rhetoric, Mr. Know-It-All. Witch hunts don't usually end well for the witches.

There are many smoking guns here, but most of the people who voted for the Orange Wonder cannot see the smoke from the witches. They think the media are lying and they are the witches and bitches; when, in fact, the press is being played by the leakers who have this righteous viewpoint that democracy is better when people know what is going on. The operative word here is "righteous."

The Department of Justice has appointed a special counsel to review what happened and possibly bring charges against those who abused their power, Donald Trump is on the defense with a large smear of denial. Perhaps someday, Trump will wake up to the reality that the United States of America is bigger than him and his fragile ego. His self-esteem is so delicate that when the slightest breeze of truth hits it spins him round and round uncontrollably.

Robert Swan Mueller III, may have a beautiful middle name, but he will be Donald Trump's biggest problem in his life. Male swans of all species will ferociously guard their nests and, in this case, the nest is our country. While the President runs around the world trying to impress other leaders, Mueller will be hard at work finding the facts.

We deserve to know the facts and get to the bottom of this ridiculous charade this administration has perpetrated on America. If Trump did nothing wrong, then he can be managed better when both parties know the extent to which his incompetence and unethical actions have damaged the presidency and our country.

If he did something wrong, he needs to be removed from office. He cannot make money on his short stay in the White House, which means he will have to divest many properties to pay for lawsuits that will fall from the sky.

It is sad that, as great as our country is, it could have been hijacked by a con man. Is there really any difference between Bernie Madoff and Donald Trump? Maybe that's going too far, but hey, you never know.

46. POOR DONALD TRUMP

"Believe me, there was no collusion!"

Posted: 5-19-2017

We should feel sorry for Donald Trump because he has been treated so unfairly by the media, the press, Democrats, zoning boards, Congress, the legal system, interest groups, lobbyists, women, Billy Bush, the intelligence community, the Justice Department and now the Special Counsel. The whole world is against him.

When Richard Nixon uttered the words, *"I am not a crook"* most of America knew that this was one of the great examples of what I call the 'implication of the opposite.'

When people use defensive terminologies and then repeat them too often, the listener slowly flips the meaning. The more Nixon said that he was **not a crook,** the more we believed he was. Nixon also called Watergate a *"witch hunt,"* and when he obstructed justice he was forced out of the office by Congress.

When Trump says the appointment of Special Counsel is *"respectable"* but in the same sentence calls the whole investigation a *"witch hunt"* he combines opposite propositions.

Trump uses words *"believe me"* a lot when he speaks. Some would say that is the mark of a very insecure speaker, but it just might be a tell. The tell being, I am lying so I must ask for belief before my words are spoken, like a hypnotic suggestion.

Another behavior occurred after one of his unbelievable tweets. We heard Trump and his surrogates say, *"the tweet speaks for itself"* which is almost like blaming the tweet for what was said.

Then there was the question from Fox News' Jeanine Pirro about whether conversations are being recorded in the White House. Trump answered, *"That I can't talk about. I won't talk about that."* Why not explain yourself and the tweet?

This is what Trump does when he cannot back up his opinions with facts or truth. It is quite clear that our president is not a student of history. If he had studied what happened to Richard Nixon, he would have known what not to do. But he is more interested in being known for someone who did it his way. Where is Frank Sinatra when we need him?

I would like to remind all those evangelical power brokers about the ninth of the Ten Commandments, bearing false witness against thy neighbor. Scholars make a distinction between lying in general and bearing false witness (perjury). Funny how there wasn't a specific commandment regarding everyday lying. I guess if Trump perjures himself in future cases, the Bible crowd will have to leave him.

This pattern of lying is disturbing. The quick darting from one story to the next hurts America. The stock market, allies and the citizens need to have a consistent and well- thought-out plan. We are not getting that from this administration.

Trump will learn that having only 39% of the public behind him and constantly playing to his base will earn no value abroad. They don't care how popular you are or think you are.

But what should concern us most is a sign that our President is losing his grasp of putting words together in a meaningful way. When asked about the investigation, he said these words:

"...there certainly is no collusion between myself and my campaign, but I can always speak for myself and the Russians, zero."

You can brush off this as more hamburger helper or you can take this sentence for the way it was constructed. Is this a soundbite for a courtroom drama? The man said there was no collusion between him and his campaign. Was that a way to plant the seed that he didn't control what his campaign and transition team did? Is he that smart?

Perhaps you could also say there was a Freudian slip there, that he was confessing that he can speak for the Russians. Really? Who made him the Russian ambassador?

Adding the word *"zero"* at the end doesn't change the meaning of the sentence. When the leader of the free word has a major problem with syntax, this is a real problem. When people translate these words into other languages, he might be very surprised how misunderstood he is.

When Trump peppers his speech with *"everybody thinks so,"* or bragging about the *"fantastic job"* he is doing, he doesn't cloud the negative moments that can appear in the same paragraph, even in the same sentence. He's elevated George W. Bush to valedictorian status.

The pressure is getting to poor Donald. Everybody is treating him so unfairly. Why? He should be analyzing why so many people are against him.

47. TRUMP SIDES WITH THE SUNNIS
Presidential Gunrunner Changes Tune
Posted: 5-22-2017

Mohammed united the tribes of Arabia through religious doctrine and force, while Donald Trump, no Mohammed indeed, drove a firmer wedge between the Sunni and Shia believers with a single trip to the Middle East.

His vitriol against Iran deployed the old philosophy, the enemy of my enemy is my friend. To the tune of billions of dollars in armaments and technology, the Royal Saud family secured Donald Trump's loyalty.

To be fair, this is no different than what the former CIA Director and President George H.W. Bush did to have 'normal' relations with most of the Arabs in the area. The US President has to deal with kings and dictators to keep the wheels of diplomacy and industry rolling. Stated more directly, Saudi Arabia has oil and we have weapons and great software.

In Donald Trump's speech to the gathered tribes and countries of the Muslim faith, he failed to comprehend the nature of Islamic banking. For someone who has spread his footprint around the world, Trump's naïveté on the way money flows from legitimate sources to the terror groups is astounding. His state department experts could have told him that the men listening to his speech in Riyadh have no idea what the Islamic banks do with their money because those banks are under no government's reach. This is how Mohammed wanted it.

Hats off, no pun intended, to the First Lady and Daughter Ivanka for not covering their heads while in a Muslim country. However, First Lady Obama already blazed that trail. It was interesting how Trump's daughter made a statement in Saudi Arabia, but then covered her head in Israel. So, noted.

Donald J. Trump, who called for the ban of all people coming from Muslim nations, was much more tempered when facing the force of dozens of

Islamic nations sitting before him. He didn't use the term "radical Islamic terrorism" out of respect for the religion. Wow, how he adjusts his act to his audience. When he gets to Israel he will don a yarmulke so not to offend. When did he become so politically and socially correct? What will his base think?

The trip to Saudi Arabia will no doubt improve Trump's ratings, but while he is away, the plot against him continues in the States. Watching him look so presidential, with no damaging tweets this week, will he learn from this trip? Like someone on vacation without a care and with loads of procedural respect dished out and obviously patronizing anointment from the hosting countries, he shouldn't let it go to his head. Trump will find the trip less positive toward the end.

He will face the holy pontiff in the Vatican. The Pope will not kiss Trump's ring or give him a gold necklace. He will ask hard questions about South Americans, climate change, walls and what have you done for the poor?

With the big NATO meeting and the G7 Economic Summit in Italy, Trump will find less adoration and more hard questions. For now, he leaves Saudi Arabia with the feeling of success, but with a hard road ahead.

People in America don't care about whether the Sunnis and Shia hate each other; that has been going on for 1,400 years. What America sees on TV this week will probably fool some into believing that this man of orange has a plan for America.

Peace in the Middle East and deals for bombs won't give the US a better healthcare system. Trump having lavish banquets abroad will not produce a fairer tax plan for the citizens of this country. But he did say we would get tired of winning. The hype is painful.

48. THE DEFENSIVE FOOL IS BACK
"I never said the word Israel."
Posted: 5-23-2017

There is a great term that many have used to describe people who either act or speak inappropriately. They say the person is being 'tone-deaf' to demonstrate the feelings of those who are affected by the statement.

When the President's travel ban was rolled out and confusion reigned at major airports, instant protests popped up all over the country, Trump was in the movie room at the White House watching Finding Dory. Albert Brooks, one of the voiceover actors in that drama summed it up best, *"Odd that Trump is watching Finding Dory today, a movie about reuniting with family when he's preventing it in real life."*

Another tone-deaf moment came that same weekend when Ivanka Trump tweeted out 'Date Night' picture of herself and Jared dressed to the nines. Many critics of the royal family were quick to point out the insensitive nature of the tweet. What was the big deal? She has always been rich and will always be rich. That's what rich folks do while others suffer.

After an optically enticing visit to Saudi Arabia, Trump traveled to Israel and was greeted warmly by that country's Prime Minister Benjamin Netanyahu. Everything was going great, until the Donald couldn't resist the screaming press after the hand-shake photo opportunity. He had to talk. He had to defend himself. He has no discipline.

The look on Netanyahu's face said it all. While Bebe smiled and repeated his stock answer to the controversy, Trump hushed the reporters so they could all hear his words, *"I never mentioned the word or the name Israel during that conversation!"* This was about his conversation in the Oval Office with two Russian diplomats the day after he fired James Comey.

Once again, Mr. Know-It-All opened his mouth and put his foot in it. It was beyond 'tone-deaf.' It was disrespectful to the leader of our ally and a totally uncouth remark. While Trump denied that a conversation about Israeli intelligence took place with the Russians, he confirmed there was a conversation about the ISIS plot. I'll bet his lawyers were groaning out loud.

While our president may think that declassifying intelligence at will is his prerogative, he should remember that what he claims he doesn't know is in direct conflict with all his previous statements about knowing everything about ISIS.

And low and behold, just as he makes a short trip to meet with Mahmoud Abbas, the President of the State of Palestine, he is greeted with another terrorist attack. This time in Manchester, UK on April 22, 2017.

As he stood there and declared the terrorists *"Evil Losers"* he demonstrated his knack for being 'tone-deaf' on the global stage. That word *"loser"* might connote that those suffering through the attack are the winners. What?

Knowing that President Trump is not manageable, by the large entourage he brought with him, doesn't lessen the calamity of poor communication. Just as he is pointing out how the perpetrators of such a horrific act are such losers, he throws in, *"It will happen again."* Maybe when the teenage girls in Manchester hear his warning of the terrorists returning he achieves his goal of spreading fear with no empathy.

He may think he is the King of deals, but still gets low grades for seeming uncaring and wanting to be more 'right' than compassionate. He declares what people think. He pronounces what people should feel. But what he will find out painfully is that his words matter. Laws are based on words.

Donald J. Trump's great presidential scam continues, but in this show, he doesn't control the final scene. He can't fire public opinion. He cannot declare winners and losers as he did on his reality TV show. Twenty-two people lost their lives. That is the reality for their families.

Real reality is so much more difficult than he ever imagined.

133

49. CRISIS MANAGEMENT TEAM
Trump Meets Pope Behind Closed Doors
Posted: 5-24-2017

It was great to see the first lady Melania Trump wearing a veil when meeting the Pope with the President. It was said that she did this out of respect for the Pontiff, while being uncovered in Saudi Arabia. I guess respect is a subjective matter with them.

While the Trump team was making its way across the Middle East and Europe, the President was, as they say, 'lawyering up' by hiring a New York law firm to defend himself in the matter of Russia interfering with the election.

This comes within the same week as Michael Flynn, the fired National Security Advisor of the United States, sent letters to both the House and Senate committees investigating him saying he would plead the Fifth Amendment and not turn over evidence or testify. One of the reasons given was the appointment of Special Counsel to get to the bottom of the matter.

For those of my readers who need a quick refresher course on the Fifth, here is what it says:

No person shall be held to answer for a capital, or otherwise infamous crime, unless on a presentment or indictment of a Grand Jury, except in cases arising in the land or naval forces, or in the Militia, when in actual service in time of War or public danger; nor shall any person be subject for the same offence to be twice put in jeopardy of life or limb; nor **shall be compelled in any criminal case to be a witness against himself,** *nor be deprived of life, liberty, or property, without due process of law; nor shall private property be taken for public use, without just compensation.*

I added the bolding of the words pertinent to this case. Michael Flynn has the right not to answer any question that could incriminate him. However, because Flynn is a military officer and the matter of possible collusion with another nation to knowing interfere with our National election, some might want to play the treason card.

The Constitution defines treason as specific acts, namely *"levying War against [the United States], or in adhering to their Enemies, giving them Aid and Comfort."* The key word here is *"adhering"* which in this case could mean *"obeying"* orders from a foreign government. That would be much worse for General Flynn.

Trump is not dumb in matters of lawyers and courts and suits of all kinds. He has lived most of his life defending his business practices and conduct. He knows that once James Comey, Michael Rogers, Director of the NSA, and Dan Coats, Director of National Intelligence, are under oath and testifying to Special Counsel Mueller, Trump will be exposed as an over-zealous politician attempting to obstruct the investigation into Michael Flynn.

What possible reason would Donald J. Trump have to put his entire presidency at risk to defend Michael Flynn? If he would just let it go, turn over all the information he and his staff might have and let the facts speak for themselves, we could get beyond this. If Michael Flynn was simply an embarrassingly bad choice, fine. Flynn would be collateral damage in the quest to restore trust in our election and the President himself.

The news of Trump putting together a crisis management team to deal with this issue is truly sad, and might be more proof that we have a real crisis on our hands.

It's like the Tylenol people trying to find the answer to sabotage and working the PR angle as fast as possible. Tylenol survived as a product, but this Russian matter will give the leader of the free world headaches throughout the summer.

And it does get hot in DC in the summer, especially when there is a crisis in the house.

50. BODY-SLAMMING IN MONTANA
Trump Bad Mouths Media
Posted: 5-25-2017

The state slogan of Montana is Oro y Plata, which means Gold and Silver. Perhaps, their recent political headline will set the gold standard on how a Republican should handle the press. Tomorrow we will learn whether the alleged man-handling of a reporter, who just asked a question, had any effect on the special election for their sole member for the House of Representatives. Greg Gianforte wants to fill that vacant seat.

From Fox News web site (5-25-2017): *"Ben Jacobs of The Guardian — walked into the room with a voice recorder, put it up to Gianforte's face and began asking if he had a response to the newly released Congressional Budget Office report on the American Health Care Act. Gianforte told him he would get to him later. Jacobs persisted with his question. Gianforte told him to talk to his press guy, Shane Scanlon."*

At that point, Gianforte grabbed Jacobs by the neck with both hands and slammed him into the ground behind him, the Fox News reporter continued, *"I watched in disbelief as Gianforte then began punching the reporter. As Gianforte moved on top of Jacobs, he began yelling something to the effect of, 'I'm sick and tired of this!'"*

Nixon, the first president to regularly refer to reporters as "the media" stayed away from the more Constitutionally acceptable term, "the press" lives on in the Trump Administration.

From the First Amendment: *"Congress shall make no law respecting an establishment of religion, or prohibiting the free exercise thereof; or abridging the freedom of speech, or of the press."*

I believe that Gianforte's actions were based on a whisper or permission slip from someone else higher up in power. Perhaps Gianforte was just having a bad multi-millionaire day, or was he acting out what Trump suggested at his rallies?

The "press" says that Gianforte and his wife founded the customer relationship management software company called RightNow Technologies. They certainly must have a grasp of helping customers be successful, or in this case, the voter, for positive gains and results. What positives can come from a body slam?

Trump is the source of the negative energy toward the press and the "mainstream media." A very dear friend of mine just said, *"I don't know what to believe anymore."* Deep inside that sentence is the dogmatic doubt and disingenuous evaluation of our press as all evil, all wrong, all uninformed. How can one TV news network keep belittling all the other media outlets, when they themselves are a media outlet? No brotherhood, no defense when you do wrong. Read: Fox News' sexual harassment crisis.

When the President focuses on the leaks rather than the truth, he drives a wedge between the purpose of the press in a democracy and the responsibility of any administration to manage its information.

Trump's team is horrible at messaging and their boss is worse. With all the golf Donald plays, he certainly should understand what a wedge does. Certainly, he knows the difference between a pitching wedge and a sand wedge.

Instead of thoughtfully using a wedge to get himself out of the sand trap of anti-press philosophy, he generally pulls a driver and whacks the press with it. Instead of making the press wither, it makes them stronger. His harangues motivate the media to work harder. The greater the number of shots the press takes from the administration, the more significant things they will uncover. They will know right from wrong.

There is no physical contact in golf and shouldn't be any in politics. During the campaign, Donald Trump said it's very appropriate for his supporters to beat protesters at his rallies. Candidate Trump added as a protester was being escorted away, *"The guards are being very gentle with him… I'd like to punch him in the face, I'll tell you that."*

Now that Donald J. Trump is President of the United States many seem to disregard what the 'candidate' said compared to what the President utters. But, really folks, the damage is already done. Trump said it was okay, he won the election, therefore those activities are permissible. He has already declared war on the press. The media armies are not going away. They are marching toward him. Even Fox News at times are forced to tell the truth.

Any fool can launch a web site and blast out their true feelings and thoughts. We are all THE PRESS. We are all THE MEDIA.

51. DYSFUNCTIONAL DISTRUST
Trump's Family Flaw
Posted: 5-28-2017

Did it ever dawn on anyone that the reason Donald Trump ran for President was because he doesn't trust anyone? He distrusts government and holds a penchant for conspiracy theories, such as the government cooking up the case against the Trump Organization about housing discrimination in 1973. He lives in a world where everyone is out to get him.

His thin skin and quick to the defense behavior is linked to a disorder driving him to be the bully so that he can feel good. Without a fight, without controversy, without tons of press, he is a frightened little boy making sure there is nothing under the bed.

Perhaps this was how his father viewed the world, but most likely the silver spoon that has been in Trump's mouth since birth has leached just enough metal into his brain to deliver permanent damage.

With this premise of distrust, I will advance some of my own theories of how things work in our government and Washington. Let's start with a basic truth: the structure of our nation is powered by tons of lawyers. Being an attorney is a valid and important profession, but when things get tough attorneys are quick to tell their clients to shut up and stay away from cavalier statements.

Next, we have the history of Nixon, who kept saying he was not a crook and then ended up being the kingpin in a cover-up and conspiracy to obstruct justice. We had Bill Clinton saying on TV, *"I did not have sexual relations with that woman,"* when indeed he did. So, who can we trust? I'm sure the reason Bill Clinton told Hillary to have a private server was because he worried that the NSA would see all of his and Hillary's emails.

George W. Bush told us Iraq had *"weapons of mass destruction,"* and then we found out that was a trumped-up charge which cost America thousands of lives, wounded one million soldiers and wasted a trillion dollars; much more damaging than sex with an intern.

When America welcomes back President Donald Trump from his nine-day trip to the Middle East and Europe, he will be greeted with the weight of the Russian controversy and the ego trip of being on the world stage will melt away quickly.

Trump focuses on leaks, while the free American press is focused on Russian intervention in our election. Would it surprise anyone that the source of the leaks might be the White House itself?

One conspiracy theory is that Steve Bannon is the leaker, using his back-channel press connections. Leaks keep Trump angry and pliable by a world-class manipulator like Bannon. If Bannon's main goal is disruption, he would be able to do more disruption and keep the base angry, as well but making it seem like the world is against Trump.

Clearly Bannon is smarter than Trump. His many allies in the administration have surrounded the President with more enablers than thinkers. The latest leak about son-in-law Jared Kushner makes him radioactive and this is just what Bannon wants. Jared has been forcing Bannon into a lesser level in the Trump circle. This leak might be the payback.

Okay, those are just theories but do they make sense? That is what you are supposed to say right after you utter such outrageous claims. It starts the elevation of a rumor on the journey to plausibility, and the most gullible don't have to chew too much before they swallow it.

Maybe the attack on Kushner is coming from the Russians in retaliation for the floated comment that sanctions against Russia might get worse. That is how they have been playing Trump through this whole election cycle. Again, that is just a theory.

You shouldn't have your family work for you when you are president. You shouldn't own things that would suggest you are in violation of the Emoluments Clause, which states you may not take money from foreign governments for your personal benefit.

When people in power don't admit that something happened until the press discloses it, how are we possibly going to trust these liars and deceivers? They are all part of a debilitating, dysfunctional family we elected. Well, we didn't elect the rest of the family, we just got them for free. And as they say, there is always a good reason why something is free. They will take their profit on the back end and we will be no better off. You cannot trust someone who Donald Trump can't fire. Think about it.

52. TRUMP INVADES GERMANY
Attacks Fake News on Twitter
Posted: 5-31-2017

Donald Trump once again has shown the world exactly who he is and it's embarrassing. On the morning of May 30, 2017, he proclaimed that Germany is somehow hurting the U.S. economy. This is a funny tweet coming just days after the man was face to face with the Chancellor of Germany. Angela Merkel is surely thinking, "What just happened?"

I'm sure many of Trump's rich friends drive Mercedes Benz and BMW cars, so why the post G-7 attack on the country that makes these quality automobiles? Mr. Know-It-All President says his trip was such a success, while the leaders in Europe are wondering what drugs this guy is on.

Let's just look at the concept of cars. Sales people at Mercedes dealerships are some of the highest paid people in automotive sales. The technicians at their dealerships are also highly paid specialists. They are American workers who benefit from the products that Germany makes.

Mercedes claims that more than 350,000 Mercedes cars are sold in the US every year, while Media Monitors, a research company, says there are 360 Mercedes dealerships in this country. Lots of jobs there.

We also build Mercedes Benz vehicles here. The Mercedes-Benz GLE-Class Sport Utility and the full-sized GL-Class Luxury Sport Utility Vehicles are built at the Mercedes-Benz U.S. International production facility near Tuscaloosa, Alabama.

It's simple. When a news story is negative, it is fake news. When Trump tweets, we are asked to assume the position of, *this tweet speaks for itself.* Really? What does it mean to say that we have a *Massive Trade Deficit* with Germany?

According to the CNN Money web site: in 2016, the US trade gap with Germany was 67.8 billion dollars, the second largest in the world. America's trade deficit with China, at 310 billion, was the only one larger.

Germany bought 80.4 billion dollars' worth of American goods and services last year, more than was purchased by any other European country except the United Kingdom.

Does Donald Trump really understand how trade works? We are starting to see that his priorities on policy are based on how things make him look, rather than what are the most important aspects for America. Rather than putting America First, it appears that putting Donald Trump first is far more important.

His rants and tweet storms may be fun for him and his 30% devout followers called his "base," but what about the 70% of Americans who just want him to do a good job? Every decision he makes is driven by the penchant to disrupt rather than lead.

You can't keep attacking friends like Germany and expect every news story to be bright and positive. Sean Spicer can pronounce that the nine-day trip was a success, but, the damage that Trump left behind will hurt us for years to come.

Who is the real enemy here? Russia seems to be winning. Why is that?

53. SCREW THE PLANET
Trump Pulls Out Early
Posted: 6-1-2017

On June 1, 2017, Donald J. Trump showed he really doesn't care about human beings. He relies on people who cherish money and business over the life of this very planet on which we live. Trump said *"No"* to survival and to science today. I must ask who is cheering him? Who is on his side on this matter? This is just one more indication that he is not fit to be president.

Nixon established the Environmental Protection Agency (EPA) and Ronald Reagan signed legislation to help eliminate acid rain, but our great Orange Leader in the White House went against the good judgement of hundreds of major U.S. businesses, 147 other countries and, more importantly, some of the smartest scientists of the world.

This was not a little deal to build a casino in New Jersey. This was the agreement with every major nation to change the way we treat the earth. Once again, Trump is marching toward a slippery precipice which will surely take this country over the edge. This new decree from King Trump might be wrapped in an unrecyclable foil package marked America First, but it really should have a large sign that says, **"Earth Last!"**

The world is not flat, Donald. It's a round sphere with a circumference of more than 25,000 miles moving at the speed of one thousand miles per hour. 7.34 billion people live on this blue planet. Why are you strangling her? I am sure you think you can hold it in your tiny, grimy hand, but it's not your world to hold.

One of the biggest mistakes the Trump administration made was placing Scott Pruitt as the head of the Environmental Protection Agency. Scott is a brain-dead politician from Oklahoma who, through his legal and legislative actions in that state, created more earthquakes than God. I mean real earthquakes that have measurably increased due to the relaxation of laws against fracking, thus causing the conditions for tectonic shifts under the earth.

Earthquakes are now common in Oklahoma thanks to Scott Pruitt. He is the most dangerous person to the environment in our country and he now heads the agency. It's Trump's fault. He picks bad people. Now Pruitt can help screw the whole planet. Why does this man have power?

Not only has Pruitt filled positions at the EPA with people having clear conflicts of interests, he scuttled the Clean Power Plan, diluted the Mercury and Air Toxin Rules, shut out scientific advisors, took down valuable data from the public EPA website, called for a 31% decrease in the EPA budget and has been the loudest voice against the Paris accord. They have even censored the words "Climate Change" from important government reports. He has been shouting in Trump's ear and polluting his mind with non-facts, hearsay and denial. Pruitt will destroy America and the world. A truly aimless, soulless human being. And remember, Donald Trump brags about this appointment.

The only way people can understand the impact of these actions is to talk to some of the people most recently affected by the lack of rules and thoughtless politicians. Ask the mother's in Flint, Michigan about how their children will never recover from a bad decision about the water for that city.

Ask the people who are downstream from polluting plants and rule breakers who have bribed politicians with contributions. Commissions and departments look the other way while these industrial whores slowly kill our babies.

Donald Trump's concept of half-tweets in the middle of the night and his inability to comprehend how things work in Washington cannot compare to his pure destruction of good things and the addition of bad things. Sad!

While we were sleeping, Trump signed a law that says Internet companies can sell your personal data without your permission. The Donald has taken away more of your civil rights in 100 days than any president, and we slept. This president embarrassed our country on the world stage and was rude to our allies, and we slept. Now, Donald Trump is moving to destroy the environment and we must ask, "WHEN WILL WE ALL WAKE UP?"

54. "IT'S A TRAVEL BAN!"
Trump's War with Words
Posted: 6-6-2017

This morning, before 7 a.m., Donald Trump tripled down on his desire for the first executive order travel ban to be the law of the land. His tweet on June 5th, 2017 has legally connected both orders and once again reinforced his real intent. His fiery surrogates got it wrong, the commander has decreed, it's a *"TRAVEL BAN"* dummies.

Any judicial mind can clearly see that the order has its roots in keeping people of a certain religion out of the U.S. It's not a temporary pause for us to figure out how people are vetted elsewhere, it's simply a goal on a list that was created by Team Trump. A list of campaign promises that have been given a free pass outside of a constitutional clearance or citizen mandate.

We have knowledge that the original order was to keep Muslims out of American; the man said it. And in his tweets today he said what he really wants and we must take him at his word. The first ban is his real intent. The president legally married the two orders this morning. His tweets are legal documents because he is the President of the U.S. He cannot have two personalities, one on paper and one on social media.

The other problem with the order is the clear proof that it will do nothing to stop terror. One could say that if the order was necessary to prevent terror, we would already have had a terror attack. There has been no logical evaluation of a situation with new facts. We are doomed as a nation if mistakes occur by involuntary actions by this neophyte, bumbling president.

It's clear that all of Trump's words and actions are a reward for those who voted for him, not for the entire country. It's so repulsive that the majority of those who didn't vote for him must put up with his self-serving narcissism. The more he caters to his base the less he's America's president.

Donald, you are right, the other counties are laughing. They are laughing at you.

The travel ban is a bad idea. The true test of any immigration system is how it's administered. If 700,000 people over stay their visas, what are you doing about that? Are we monitoring people who have been radicalized here and then travel to countries of risk? That seems to be a connection to terrorism. Do we know when they come back in? Who are you trying to catch with this travel ban, poor refugees or real terrorists?

Why not add more state department people so we can study *"what the hell is really going on?"* Are you at all interested in what.is going on? Using your faulty logic in the last three weeks, surely the U.K. would be put on your list. Your whole administration seems to be talking around the truth and trying to figure out what you mean. Why don't you figure out how to properly communicate so that everyone understands you?

STOP TWEETING and start communicating. Your language is poor and unclear. And you obviously have a very low reading comprehension. The Mayor of London was talking to his people and being very clear. Londoners are not used to seeing people walking around with guns like we are. He was saying, no need to be alarmed by seeing lots of people with guns. Observational awareness is not your strong suit.

You misread Sadiq Khan's statement and you decided that when an ally is attacked you insult them. Now we know why you didn't reinforce our commitment to NATO's Article 5, you really don't believe it. And by the way Donald, Sadiq is not a terrorist.

Rather than making things worse, please figure out why Russia has increased trade to North Korea by 40%. Wouldn't that be something you should care about? Before you tweet about your stupid travel ban and how everyone gets it wrong except you, why not slow down and THINK.

Surely you have the intelligence to understand that our country was attacked during the election. Why aren't YOU leading the charge to get to the bottom of this mess? Or, is that just how you roll? Is making nice with Russia your priority above all else?

Trump is off the tracks and must be stopped. We may find out that he broke the law, but it's totally clear that he's a bad administrator, a poor communicator and a malicious president.

55. TWITTER, TERRORISM & TIMING
Trump Shows His Trigger Finger
Posted: 6-7-2017

Imagine if the President of the United States was addicted to crack cocaine. All the responsible parties would be meeting to work on an intervention before he would either hurt himself, or hurt other people.

In this case, the social media platform Twitter has given Donald Trump the love that he maybe hasn't been able to get in real life. The instantaneous high from his tweet 'fans' is the drug he needs every day. The first thing those who care would attempt is separating the addicted from their drug.

To date, Donald Trump has tweeted more than 35,000 messages to his 31.8 million followers. To put that in perspective, if we assume they are all those following are truly "fans," that is only 10.2% of the population of the country. And we now know that besides the thousands of bots that have electronically attached themselves to the Donald wagon, **people who hate him also follow him** to see what the great one will tweet next. In fact, I follow both the POTUS and RealDonaldTrump twitter feeds. Just numbers.

Social media platforms are designed for a generation of people who are seeking instant gratification and the reward of believing that people like them. These narcissistic platforms reinforce viewpoints by showing a member only those things the service's algorithm thinks are compatible with their likes, dislikes and responses. So, Trump sees only what he wants to see, just like a twelve-year-old middle schooler.

If the President used Twitter strategically to dispense his views on issues and to help explain the why behind some of his policies, one could argue that it wasn't an addiction, but rather a tool in his multi-media box. At 35,000 tweets, however, we have a problem.

We saw what happened when his reading comprehension didn't sync up with the power of the presidential tweet when he attacked the Mayor of London. And we saw him declare an incident as a terror attack, even before the smoke had cleared. His irresponsible actions move our country closer to the brink of a possible disaster.

His addiction, as he rightly says, doesn't have the mainstream media filter and, in fact, has no filter whatsoever. The account @RealDonaldTrump has no official connection to the government and is a direct link to the brain of the president. And his tweeting late at night and early in the morning just might be the downfall of this "great" man.

We saw the #Covfefe moment and Trump's quick action to take credit for the Arab states declaration of Qatar blockade, when some believe the whole affair was motivated by a Russian hack of their news service. There's a fact Mr. Know-It-All could have learned from his own intelligence services had he bothered to ask. By the way, the United States of America has a very important Air Force base in Qatar, a good reason our president should research before broadcasting his thoughts on the matter.

Then there is the matter of Trump's TRAVEL BAN which the Supreme Court is considering. Why would the central figure in the case be on social media putting down his Justice Department and the ban itself? This lack of maturity is something we would reference to a person sixty-years younger.

The only way to deal with this kind of addiction is to take the phone away and send the boy to his room. If there was a legal way to take Trump's Twitter account away, I would surely sign on to that campaign. As I have stated on these pages previously, a tweet is a legal document, a legal document with all the weight of something the President has signed or decreed.

Someone must act on this issue, or we should remove the man from office.

56. COMEY'S STATEMENT

Statement for the Record Senate Select Committee on Intelligence

Posted: 6-8-2017

James B. Comey

June 8, 2017

Chairman Burr, Ranking Member Warner, Members of the Committee. Thank you for inviting me to appear before you today. I was asked to testify today to describe for you my interactions with President-Elect and President Trump on subjects that I understand are of interest to you. I have not included every detail from my conversations with the President, but, to the best of my recollection, I have tried to include information that may be relevant to the Committee.

January 6 Briefing

I first met then-President-Elect Trump on Friday, January 6 in a conference room at Trump Tower in New York. I was there with other Intelligence Community (IC) leaders to brief him and his new national security team on the findings of an IC assessment concerning Russian efforts to interfere in the election. At the conclusion of that briefing, I remained alone with the President Elect to brief him on some personally sensitive aspects of the information assembled during the assessment.

The IC leadership thought it important, for a variety of reasons, to alert the incoming President to the existence of this material, even though it was salacious and unverified. Among those reasons were: (1) we knew the media was about to publicly report the material and we believed the IC should not keep knowledge of the material and its imminent release from the President-Elect; and (2) to the extent there was some effort to compromise an incoming President, we could blunt any such effort with a defensive briefing.

The Director of National Intelligence asked that I personally do this portion of the briefing because I was staying in my position and because the material implicated the FBI's counter-intelligence responsibilities. We also agreed I would do it alone to minimize potential embarrassment to the President-Elect. Although we agreed it made sense for me to do the briefing, the FBI's leadership and I were concerned that the briefing might create a situation where a new President came into office uncertain about whether the FBI was conducting a counter-intelligence investigation of his personal conduct.

It is important to understand that FBI counter-intelligence investigations are different than the more-commonly known criminal investigative work. The Bureau's goal in a counter-intelligence investigation is to understand the technical and human methods that hostile foreign powers are using to influence the United States or to steal our secrets. The FBI uses that understanding to disrupt those efforts. Sometimes disruption takes the form of alerting a person who is targeted for recruitment or influence by the foreign power. Sometimes it involves hardening a computer system that is being attacked. Sometimes it involves "turning" the recruited person into a double-agent, or publicly calling out the behavior with sanctions or expulsions of embassy-based intelligence officers. On occasion, criminal prosecution is used to disrupt intelligence activities.

Because the nature of the hostile foreign nation is well known, counterintelligence investigations tend to be centered on individuals the FBI suspects to be witting or unwitting agents of that foreign power. When the FBI develops reason to believe an American has been targeted for recruitment by a foreign power or is covertly acting as an agent of the foreign power, the FBI will "open an investigation" on that American and use legal authorities to try to learn more about the nature of any relationship with the foreign power so it can be disrupted.

In that context, prior to the January 6 meeting, I discussed with the FBI's leadership team whether I should be prepared to assure President-Elect Trump that we were not investigating him personally. That was true; we did not have an open counter-intelligence case on him. We agreed I should do so if circumstances warranted. During our one-on-one meeting at Trump Tower, based on President Elect Trump's reaction to the briefing and without him directly asking the question, I offered that assurance.

I felt compelled to document my first conversation with the President-Elect in a memo. To ensure accuracy, I began to type it on a laptop in an FBI vehicle outside Trump Tower the moment I walked out of the meeting. Creating written records immediately after one-on-one conversations with Mr. Trump was my practice from that point forward. This had not been my practice in the past. I spoke alone with President Obama twice in person (and never on the phone) – once in 2015 to discuss law enforcement policy issues and a second time, briefly, for him to say goodbye in late 2016. In neither of those circumstances did I memorialize the discussions. I can recall nine one-on-one conversations with President Trump in four months – three in person and six on the phone.

January 27 Dinner

The President and I had dinner on Friday, January 27 at 6:30 pm in the Green Room at the White House. He had called me at lunchtime that day and invited me to dinner that night, saying he was going to invite my whole family, but decided to have just me this time, with the whole family coming the next time. It was unclear from the conversation who else would be at the dinner, although I assumed there would be others.

It turned out to be just the two of us, seated at a small oval table in the center of the Green Room. Two Navy stewards waited on us, only entering the room to serve food and drinks.

The President began by asking me whether I wanted to stay on as FBI Director, which I found strange because he had already told me twice in earlier conversations that he hoped I would stay, and I had assured him that I intended to. He said that lots of people wanted my job and, given the abuse I had taken during the previous year, he would understand if I wanted to walk away.

My instincts told me that the one-on-one setting, and the pretense that this was our first discussion about my position, meant the dinner was, at least in part, an effort to have me ask for my job and create some sort of patronage relationship. That concerned me greatly, given the FBI's traditionally independent status in the executive branch.

I replied that I loved my work and intended to stay and serve out my ten-year term as Director. And then, because the set-up made me uneasy, I added that I was not "reliable" in the way politicians use that word, but he could always count on me to tell him the truth. I added that I was not on anybody's side politically and could not be counted on in the traditional political sense, a stance I said was in his best interest as the President.

A few moments later, the President said, "I need loyalty, I expect loyalty." I didn't move, speak, or change my facial expression in any way during the awkward silence that followed. We simply looked at each other in silence. The conversation then moved on, but he returned to the subject near the end of our dinner.

At one point, I explained why it was so important that the FBI and the Department of Justice be independent of the White House. I said it was a paradox: Throughout history, some Presidents have decided that because "problems" come from Justice, they should try to hold the Department close. But blurring those boundaries ultimately makes the problems worse by undermining public trust in the institutions and their work.

Near the end of our dinner, the President returned to the subject of my job, saying he was very glad I wanted to stay, adding that he had heard great things about me from Jim Mattis, Jeff Sessions, and many others. He then said, "I need loyalty." I replied, "You will always get honesty from me." He paused and then said, "That's what I want, honest loyalty." I paused, and then said, "You will get that from me." As I wrote in the memo I created immediately after the dinner, it is possible we understood the phrase "honest loyalty" differently, but I decided it wouldn't be productive to push it further. The term – honest loyalty – had helped end a very awkward conversation and my explanations had made clear what he should expect.

During the dinner, the President returned to the salacious material I had briefed him about on January 6, and, as he had done previously, expressed his disgust for the allegations and strongly denied them. He said he was considering ordering me to investigate the alleged incident to prove it didn't happen. I replied that he should give that careful thought because it might create a narrative that we were investigating him personally, which we weren't, and because it was very difficult to prove a negative. He said he would think about it and asked me to think about it. As was my practice for conversations with President Trump, I wrote a detailed memo about the dinner immediately afterwards and shared it with the senior leadership team of the FBI.

February 14 Oval Office Meeting

On February 14, I went to the Oval Office for a scheduled counterterrorism briefing of the President. He sat behind the desk and a group of us sat in a semi-circle of about six chairs facing him on the other side of the desk. The Vice President, Deputy Director of the CIA, Director of the National Counter Terrorism Center, Secretary of Homeland Security, the Attorney General, and I were in the semi-circle of chairs. I was directly facing the President, sitting between the Deputy CIA Director and the Director of

NCTC. There were quite a few others in the room, sitting behind us on couches and chairs.

The President signaled the end of the briefing by thanking the group and telling them all that he wanted to speak to me alone. I stayed in my chair. As the participants started to leave the Oval Office, the Attorney General lingered by my chair, but the President thanked him and said he wanted to speak only with me. The last person to leave was Jared Kushner, who also stood by my chair and exchanged pleasantries with me. The President then excused him, saying he wanted to speak with me.

When the door by the grandfather clock closed, and we were alone, the President began by saying, "I want to talk about Mike Flynn." Flynn had resigned the previous day. The President began by saying Flynn hadn't done anything wrong in speaking with the Russians, but he had to let him go because he had misled the Vice President. He added that he had other concerns about Flynn, which he did not then specify.

The President then made a long series of comments about the problem with leaks of classified information – a concern I shared and still share. After he had spoken for a few minutes about leaks, Reince Priebus leaned in through the door by the grandfather clock and I could see a group of people waiting behind him. The President waved at him to close the door, saying he would be done shortly. The door closed.

The President then returned to the topic of Mike Flynn, saying, "He is a good guy and has been through a lot." He repeated that Flynn hadn't done anything wrong on his calls with the Russians, but had misled the Vice President. He then said, "I hope you can see your way clear to letting this go, to letting Flynn go. He is a good guy. I hope you can let this go." I replied only that "he is a good guy." (In fact, I had a positive experience dealing with

Mike Flynn when he was a colleague as Director of the Defense Intelligence Agency at the beginning of my term at FBI.) I did not say I would "let this go."

The President returned briefly to the problem of leaks. I then got up and left out the door by the grandfather clock, making my way through the large group of people waiting there, including Mr. Priebus and the Vice President.

I immediately prepared an unclassified memo of the conversation about Flynn and discussed the matter with FBI senior leadership. I had understood the President to be requesting that we drop any investigation of Flynn in connection with false statements about his conversations with the Russian ambassador in December. I did not understand the President to be talking about the broader investigation into Russia or possible links to his campaign. I could be wrong, but I took him to be focusing on what had just happened with Flynn's departure and the controversy around his account of his phone calls. Regardless, it was very concerning, given the FBI's role as an independent investigative agency.

The FBI leadership team agreed with me that it was important not to infect the investigative team with the President's request, which we did not intend to abide. We also concluded that, given that it was a one-on-one conversation, there was nothing available to corroborate my account. We concluded it made little sense to report it to Attorney General Sessions, who we expected would likely recuse himself from involvement in Russia-related investigations. (He did so two weeks later.) The Deputy Attorney General's role was then filled in an acting capacity by a United States Attorney, who would also not be in the role very long.

After discussing the matter, we decided to keep it very closely held, resolving to figure out what to do with it down the road as our investigation progressed. The investigation moved ahead at full speed, with none of the investigative team members – or the Department of Justice lawyers supporting them – aware of the President's request.

Shortly afterwards, I spoke with Attorney General Sessions in person to pass along the President's concerns about leaks. I took the opportunity to implore the Attorney General to prevent any future direct communication between the President and me. I told the AG that what had just happened – him being asked to leave while the FBI Director, who reports to the AG, remained behind – was inappropriate and should never happen. He did not reply. For the reasons discussed above, I did not mention that the President broached the FBI's potential investigation of General Flynn.

March 30 Phone Call

On the morning of March 30, the President called me at the FBI. He described the Russia investigation as "a cloud" that was impairing his ability to act on behalf of the country. He said he had nothing to do with Russia, had not been involved with hookers in Russia, and had always assumed he was being recorded when in Russia. He asked what we could do to "lift the cloud." I responded that we were investigating the matter as quickly as we could, and that there would be great benefit, if we didn't find anything, to our having done the work well. He agreed, but then re-emphasized the problems this was causing him.

Then the President asked why there had been a congressional hearing about Russia the previous week – at which I had, as the Department of Justice directed, confirmed the investigation into possible coordination between Russia and the Trump campaign. I explained the demands from the leadership of both parties in Congress for more information, and that Senator Grassley had even held up the confirmation of the Deputy Attorney General until we briefed him in detail on the investigation. I explained that we had briefed the leadership of Congress on exactly which individuals we were investigating and that we had told those Congressional leaders that we were not personally investigating President Trump. I reminded him I had previously told him that. He repeatedly told me, "We need to get that fact out." (I did not tell the President that the FBI and the Department of Justice had been reluctant to make public statements that we did not have an open case on President Trump for a number of reasons, most importantly because it would create a duty to correct, should that change.)

The President went on to say that if there were some "satellite" associates of his who did something wrong, it would be good to find that out, but that he hadn't done anything wrong and hoped I would find a way to get it out that we weren't investigating him.

In an abrupt shift, he turned the conversation to FBI Deputy Director Andrew McCabe, saying he hadn't brought up "the McCabe thing" because I had said McCabe was honorable, although McAuliffe was close to the Clintons and had given him (I think he meant Deputy Director McCabe's wife) campaign money. Although I didn't understand why the President was bringing this up, I repeated that Mr. McCabe was an honorable person.

He finished by stressing "the cloud" that was interfering with his ability to make deals for the country and said he hoped I could find a way to get out that he wasn't being investigated. I told him I would see what we could do, and that we would do our investigative work well and as quickly as we could.

Immediately after that conversation, I called Acting Deputy Attorney General Dana Boente (AG Sessions had by then recused himself on all Russia related matters), to report the substance of the call from the President, and said I would await his guidance. I did not hear back from him before the President called me again two weeks later.

April 11 Phone Call

On the morning of April 11, the President called me and asked what I had done about his request that I "get out" that he is not personally under investigation. I replied that I had passed his request to the Acting Deputy Attorney General, but I had not heard back. He replied that "the cloud" was getting in the way of his ability to do his job. He said that perhaps he would have his people reach out to the Acting Deputy Attorney General. I said that was the way his request should be handled. I said the White House Counsel should contact the leadership of DOJ to make the request, which was the traditional channel.

He said he would do that and added, "Because I have been very loyal to you, very loyal; we had that thing you know." I did not reply or ask him what he meant by "that thing." I said only that the way to handle it was to have the White House Counsel call the Acting Deputy Attorney General. He said that was what he would do and the call ended.

That was the last time I spoke with President Trump.

57. THE SWEET SMELL OF VINDICATION
Trump Lives in Denial
Posted: 6-8-2017

Today is the big day for James Comey, former FBI Director, to testify in front of the Senate hearing. And in keeping with Comey's style, he released his opening statement the day before the big hearing, as seen above. There is much to learn from this document he plans to put on the record.

On May 18, 2017, President Trump was asked at his joint press conference with Colombian President Juan Manuel Santos if he had ever asked James Comey to close or back down the investigation into Michael Flynn. Trump flatly said, *"No, no, next question."* Later in the conference he added, *"There has been no collusion between certainly myself and the campaign -- but I can always speak for myself -- and the Russians: zero,"* Once again Mr. Know-It-All was only interested in protecting himself.

The irony of a man who asks for loyalty, but seems to have no loyalty to anyone else is representative of, at least, a major character flaw. Trump takes no blame for anything his campaign or administration does.

His lawyer issued a statement after the opening remarks were released that said, *"The President is pleased that Mr. Comey has finally publicly confirmed his private reports that the President was not under investigation in any Russian probe. The President feels completely and totally vindicated."*

The use of the word "vindicated" is quite interesting. The meaning, "to clear (someone) of blame or suspicion." Now this may be wishful thinking on the part of the Trump camp, but the head of the FBI is not a court of law. And to be fair, if you judged Comey's actions with regard to the Hillary Clinton server situation, you might think he was more judge than investigator.

If Trump set up a quid pro quo by asking Comey if he wants to stay, then requesting him to back off the investigation into Flynn, that feels like obstruction. Then Trump fired Comey when he didn't back off the investigation, thus linking the request to his employment.

If justice has been harmed in firing Comey, then Trump's words and actions were a clear indication of obstruction of justice. The President of the United States is not above the law.

We shall see what is unveiled during the hearings and investigations but, for any thinking American, we have seen the man behind the curtain, and he is a wicked con artist who may believe he is above the law. Or, maybe Donald Trump is so naïve he has no business being in the Oval Office. This drama should be canceled, not for lack of ratings and audience, but because our whole country is being put at risk.

Let it be said that June 8, 2017 was the day we learned what kind of man Donald J. Trump really is.

58. LEAKER vs LIAR
Trump Plays Defense
Posted: 6-9-2017

It's time to take a stand: Do you believe Jim Comey or Donald Trump? And the biggest question remaining is whether Donald Trump is fit to be the President of the United States.

People will cherry pick the things they liked and didn't like from the Comey testimony, but the damage has been done. Reasonable doubt has been established here and we must look beyond the pundits to find the truth.

One of the fallout items of what the internet called "Comey Day" (June 8, 2017) was some people saying that Trump has no experience as a politician or the knowledge of the legal boundaries required for the presidency.

Paul Ryan, Speaker of the House, said, *"The president wasn't trying to obstruct justice, but just doesn't know enough about political protocol."* Oh, I guess Trump missed the orientation class for being President, Sad!

If you thought 24-hours of no tweeting set a new tone, that evaporated with new tweets today and the post hearing statement from Donald Trump's personal lawyer. In that statement, Marc Kasowitz made the following points:

1. The President was not under investigation as part of any probe into Russian interference and there is no evidence that a single vote changed as a result of any Russian interference.

2. The President never sought to impede the investigation into attempted Russian interference in the 2016 election.

3. The President never, in form or substance, directed or suggested that Mr. Comey stop investigating anyone, including suggesting that that Mr. Comey "let Flynn go."

4. The President also never told Mr. Comey, "I need loyalty, I expect loyalty" in form or substance.

So, I guess there are no recordings of the meetings. The use of the word "cloud" in Mr. Kasowitz's statement is quite interesting. This was the word James Comey used in describing the conversation he had with Donald Trump. We do have imprinting here, and a key to Donald Trump being the author of his own defense.

The question one might ask is why, in almost every conversation, does Trump seem to be obsessed with clearing his name from some investigation that no one ever said he was under? Is he is doing a pre-emptive denial?

If in fact Michael Flynn talked to the Russians and took money from a Russian news service and his company was highly compensated by the Turkish government, then Michael Flynn is part of the investigation into Russian tampering. Therefore, any defense of Flynn after his firing would seem to say that, at least, Trump was offering a character testimony for his "good guy" Michael Flynn. Using the presidential podium to argue Flynn's innocence is an attempt to affect the outcome of charges and a form of obstruction.

The idea of vindication seems premature. Assuming things are moving forward with Robert Mueller, the Special Counsel, there is now an additional element to his investigation of obstruction.

Jim Comey admitted, under oath, that he leaked the facts of the memos he had written after each meeting with Trump to the New York Times through a professor "friend" at Columbia University. He said that the reason he leaked the information was based on a tweet from Donald J. Trump, typed on May 12, 2017, *"James Comey better hope that there are no 'tapes' of our conversations before he starts leaking to the press!"*

Kasowitz claimed in his statement that Comey leaked the memos before that tweet. This is a major mistake in the timeline. The New York Times never quoted the Comey memos prior to Trump's May 12, 2017 tweet and the first time the story ran was May 16, 2017. This fact came from Julie Hirschfeld Davis of the New York Times.

Acting out of a sense of loyalty to his country, the FBI and, I am sure, his own reputation, Comey wanted to get the word out so that the Department of Justice would appoint a special prosecutor, or counsel. And like a great chess player, he got exactly what he wanted.

The Trump machine has started to accuse Comey of being part of the deep state and they will try to sue their way out of this mess. One would think that after being in office for four and a half months they would have found the deep state already. This legal action will only make it worse. I don't think Trump is naïve about the job, I think he is just plain dumb.

The UK has now rejected some of the politics of Theresa May. The French rejected the dark politics of Marine LePen. And now it's time for America to figure out how to get rid of the liars and start to listen to the leakers.

Donald Trump may be a leaker and a liar. There are web sites dedicated to his lies, but now we know that his twitter account leaks his personal inner thoughts. And if you look through 35,000 tweets, you can find all the leaks in his logic.

59. A CORRUPT INTENT
Trump Paints Himself into a Corner
Posted: 6-12-2017

There is a kind of arrogance that some people carry and which can be spotted a mile away. This trait gets passed to the next generation and sticks out like a sore thumb on a small hand. Donald J. Trump has the audacity to think that hoping something will happen will make it so, even when it's good only for him.

The lead on a story from the web site The Hill on June 9, 2017 ran: *"Former US Attorney Nick Akerman, who prosecuted the Watergate case, says fired FBI Director James Comey's testimony about his conversations with President Trump establishes 'corrupt intent up the wazoo.'"*

Now I don't know Nick, but I do know Trump's pattern of telling people they could stay in a job only to toy with them in a dance of loyalty. Ask former U.S. Attorney for the Southern District of New York, Preet Bharara. Preet was just another victim of this first glad handing, then back stabbing, routine. Bharara, one of the great investigator and prosecutors in America, was brusquely fired by Trump after Donald promised Preet could stay on the job.

With his everyday words and actions, President Trump dismisses the millions of citizens who didn't cast their vote for him. If he cannot fire you, he ignores you. The episodes of him playing to his "base" are getting old and bothersome.

There have been three presidents in American history who have faced impeachment, or the imminent threat of it. They were; Richard Nixon, who resigned in 1974 before the House could consider four articles of impeachment related to Watergate; Bill Clinton, who came within 17 votes in the Senate of being removed from office on obstruction of justice in the Monica Lewinsky scandal of 1999 and the biggest "almost" loser, Andrew Johnson, came within a single Senate vote of removal due to his handling of the country during Reconstruction.

Nixon was so ambitious that his ego was manipulated by corrupted cohorts who were working to keep him in office at any cost. Clinton is a lot like Trump, only where Bill has immense intelligence, Donald has money. Johnson, poor old Andrew, like Lyndon Johnson, really "inherited a mess" after the leader of America was gunned down by sinister forces. Andrew Johnson was a trial balloon for how we can right our ship when the wrong person gets into office

Donald Trump is far from being impeached at this date, June 12, 2017, but he has done nothing for his ratings outside of his 'base' and he might have weakened his favorability with some of the moderate Republicans. **If confronted, he will lie.** Trump keeps playing the role of president, rather than actually being the President.

What Comey's testimony, and Trump's terrible interview with NBC's Lester Holt created, was a picture of a man who focuses on the wrong things. If he wanted people to think he was firing Comey because of "a thing" then he should have said that "thing" from the beginning. What he did was push smart people into asking for further investigation, not into Michael Flynn but into the President himself.

Why would the President of the United States make a threat of recordings on Twitter to a director of the FBI after he fired him? And then why would he play with the press about whether those tapes exist?

The possibility that the President has been recording conversations in the White House, sets up the Donald and paints him into a corner. If tapes are available, then THOSE TAPES CAN BE REQUESTED for investigation. If no tapes were made, then it points to a pathological lying spree perpetrated on the American people.

Trump seems like Nixon with his hell-bent desire to stay in office at any cost. Democracy and Law and Order be damned, this guy will do anything to keep his job. That is what he wants out of all the president's men and women. They must do what he asks to keep their jobs.

Trump is a public relations nightmare. For a businessman, these kinds of diversions would be unnecessary wastes of a bunch of money to lawyers. These are colossal presidential mistakes that get in the way of making America great or, as I see it, keeping America as great as it was before Trump.

When Trump's surrogates and lawyers call James Comey a coward, they are using playground language to belittle the tall man of honor. When they call him a leaker, they suppose that all conversations with the king are the property of the king. This "I own my words" is something that Donald Trump has sued people over in the past. In any other circumstance, calling James Comey a liar would be layers of libelous slander and pillory stacked up on a giant bullshit sandwich.

Trump may think he can wait for the paint to dry and walk out of the corner Scott-free, but there are other footsteps a-coming. This was the bulletin from the Washington Post on June 11, 2017: "*Attorneys general for the District of Columbia and the state of Maryland say they will sue President Trump on Monday, alleging that he has violated anti-corruption clauses in the Constitution by accepting millions in payments and benefits from foreign governments since moving into the White House.*"

It may take time, but the Orange Leader will certainly not get renewed for another season and the network executives are debating whether to pull his reality show sooner rather than later. We all hope that President Pence will at least bring closure to this ugly chapter in American history. Like Andrew Johnson, Pence will certainly inherit a mess. Sad!

60. THE SERIOUSNESS OF IT ALL
The Day I Finally Figured Out Trump
Posted: 6-15-2017

Today, Flag Day 2017, gun shots rang out on a baseball field in Virginia. The GOP baseball team was practicing for their annual charity game with the Democrats. Both parties take this event extraordinarily seriously; to the point of practicing early mornings in the weeks leading up to the event.

I've often said that I am not very smart. I don't mean that in a self-deprecating way. I truly don't understand people. How I have been able to understand things at times is by converting the abstracts of life into pictures. My emotions are tied to visuals of every kind. My father was born on Flag Day, so when I see the flags on the streets of our great nation I think of my father. He used to joke, *"Hey, look, everyone is celebrating my birthday. They've put their flags out."*

When I learned of a man shooting members of the GOP baseball team during their practice today I had a sick feeling. Not just because it was an act of violence but that, as we later learned, there probably was a political motive to the shooting.

For me to understand how politics work I draw a circle. At the top of the circle, say 12 o'clock, exists a place I call the middle, or the moderate position. Then I move to the right or the left on that circle. When I get so far down, say around 6 o'clock, it's hard to distinguish the far right from the far left. They galvanize into this raw, exposed nerve ending. The far right, Alt-Right or white supremacists, are like the far left, Patriot fighters, anarchists and Marxist revolutionaries.

On Fox News, Newt Gingrich, a political financial exploitation artist, talked about the meaning of the shootings. He said, *"It's part of a pattern. You've had an increasing intensity of hostility on the left."* Maybe you see only the intense increase of the left, Mr. Gingrich, but there has been an increase intensity on both sides, and the catalyst is Donald Trump. You either own that and take your rewards from dirty dark political money, or stop your intellectual charade.

Trump opened a can of worms, and no one wants to eat worms. No matter how you serve it up, someone, somewhere, should stand up and say, TRUMP put the worms in the can, and here is how he started it.

It began with his message against political correctness. People got the message. It was banged in the media for weeks and weeks. It's okay to say what you want. So, when we had violent rallies the emotional band aids were ripped off and people screamed. They screamed at the Bernie rallies, they screamed at the Donald rallies.

The moderate people, like Hillary Clinton, bounced between 11 o'clock, to lure some Bernie voters, and 1 o'clock, to attract some of the normal Republicans. But Hilary's moves didn't matter. The distrust that was sown over the years by critics and the bombardment of hateful fake news and mistruths on social media created a myth far too big for Clinton to overcome in the Electoral College.

Trump was louder than Bernie and the Democrat machine didn't want to turn over the reins to a part-time Democrat, full-time Independent socialist. On the other hand, the avarice of the Republican party permitted Trump to hijack their club. Winning mattered more than principals, which is page one in the Trump and Gingrich playbook. Trump needs to cut the silly game show crap and start to become serious about America and ALL THE AMERICAN PEOPLE. Become the President you dick-wad.

The fact that the Capitol Hill Police killed the gunman who targeted Republicans on that field means we won't get to hear his side of the story, but his electronic footprint is the same as those angry "let's take some action" radicals on the right. You see, when you go so far to the right, you meet up with the crazies who have taken the message of hate too far to the left. They see themselves as freedom fighters, like the minute men, oppressed white people with guns, far right, or far left?

Trump needs to lead or leave. If he had a brain and better people around him, he would see that he has stirred the pot and added hate toward immigrants, putting just enough salt into the wounds of people who have been economically displaced by years of globalization. He has "called for things" rather than really getting anything done. He is as fake as the real news he dislikes and bashes.

Wait until the people figure out that his "great movement" has achieved higher drug prices without oversight, fake job creation without training, mediocre education without a budget, environmental mistakes and healthcare that doesn't work for the very people who voted for him. They will be screaming, *"Lock him up!"*

I loved the irony of Congress members quickly cancelling their hearing on gun control because of the shootings. What, too soon? The language they used in the halls of democracy: *"An attack on one of us, is an attack on us all!"* Finally, they understand why NATO exists. Doh!

The Trump administration should realize the harder they push the more push back they will get. Where are all the "best people" Trump said he would get to help him? All the President's men, and a few women, sat around the cabinet table the other day kissing his fat ass and wasting taxpayers' money. Embarrassing.

The more Donald Trump governs exclusively for his base, the angrier the rest of America becomes. What gets in the way of any good idea Trump has is his inability to float above his emotional level and sell why the idea is good. It's not a bad piece of advice to be a moderate in America, especially with so many guns in the hands of lunatics.

61. PREPARING FOR PRESIDENT PENCE
The Vice Tightens on Trump
Posted: 6-16-2017

A very well-written book by Allan J. Lichtman called *The Case for Impeachment*, was recently released. In it, the author outlines facts about impeachment, our country's history with impeachable offenses and some of the lesser known aspects of impeachment, which our founding fathers put into the Constitution to protect the democracy from power-hungry tyrants.

With Donald Trump, we have someone who probably has no idea that his presidential groundbreaking or, as the mainstream media calls them, unprecedented actions, will eventually cause him to be seared in broad daylight by the magnification glass of facts.

The impeachable activities are slowly being revealed by a zealous press corps, which has been unfairly belittled by the administration, and a special counsel whom the Department of Justice has appointed.

Logically, unless a person with as much flowing wealth and international properties can clearly isolate his family and himself from those profits, he can be easily impeached because of the Constitution's Emolument Clause: ARTICLE I, SECTION 9, CLAUSE 8"

"No Title of Nobility shall be granted by the United States: And no Person holding any Office of Profit or Trust under them, shall, without the Consent of the Congress, accept of any present, Emolument, Office, or Title, of any kind whatever, from any King, Prince, or foreign State."

It would have been far better for our country if Donald Trump had off loaded his businesses to a blind trust instead of his family. Trump is conning America once again and no one has been seriously questioning, until now.

The Attorney General's in the District of Columbia and Maryland have sued the President using the Emolument's clause, saying that he is enriching himself and his family through the commerce that takes place at properties in those states and district.

200 Congress people are going to sue under the same banner, and the Special Counsel is moving quickly having a clear mandate to investigate the President for obstruction of justice in the wake of the firing of James Comey. Not to pour gasoline on an open fire, but let it be said here and now (June 16, 2017) judging by Trump's tweets and previous behavior, he will fire Robert S. Mueller III because of the impeachment time bomb that he himself has armed.

Let's move forward here. After we rid ourselves of a hateful, lame, unaware, megalomaniacal narcissist, we will have to rebuild reality around someone who must take the mantle of the executive branch and keep the trains running under the present laws. Hopefully, with the assumption that Mike Pence is clean, he will be our next president.

Many of my friends have asked me what I think of Mike Pence, a highly religious ideolog, who up to this point, has been a B-actor in the role of VP. Pence is not a substantive thinker and his organizational skills can be judged by his handling of the state of Indiana and Trump's transition. He obviously has no vetting skills and he sounds like a bad radio announcer when he talks.

We can rule out any judgement on the transition, knowing that most of the people who Trump involved were amateurs at government and loyal dogs to the dogma of Bannon. In Indiana, Pence showed the LGBTQ community that he is being guided by what the bible tells him to do, without any regard to the ramifications flowing to all the people in his state. In short, he was like a replacement baseball player during a strike, not that good, but we all know we will just have to wait until 2020 to get a real President again.

There are times when I wake up and think that all Trump needs to do to end all this Russia stuff is to stop stonewalling and release his tax returns. Step up to the microphone and really talk to the American people and explain why he seems more positive to Russia than to the UK, France, Germany and our other allies. Donald, stop tweeting and start working on getting needed changes accomplished.

Then I have my first cup of coffee and remember that, by the President's actions, those great achievements he talked about will never be as important to him as how he is perceived. What people think about him is more important than respecting justice and law. Trump is incapable of being an authentic leader of the greatest nation in the world. More importantly, he is not personally worthy of the office.

And in the end, playing the role of Gerald Ford, our new white-haired leader, President Pence, will pardon Donald Trump so he can go back to making money and being the source of deep-state conspiracy theories about how the White House was stolen from him. Only this time, he will be right.

62. CUBAN MISSIVE CRISIS
Trump Turns the Clock Back to 1960
Posted: 6-16-2017

Donald Trump wants a better deal with Cuba. What he doesn't understand is that Cuba will get a better deal from someone named Vladimir Putin, the same Mr. Putin who used similar language saying he would protect Russians in the Ukraine without any respect for their sovereign state. Now with Donald Trump slapping the sanctions back on Cuba, he has opened the door for Russia to return to Cuba with gifts and money.

Trump's denunciation of Cuban policies yesterday in Florida might have incited the large community of anti-Castro Cuban-Americans in Miami, but didn't match his actions. It's a selective sucker punch against the current regime in Havana, but after sixty-years of blockades, sanctions and containment by America, you can bet Raúl Castro is already on the phone to Moscow.

Trump used terms like maintaining blockades and sanctions and canceling the policy, but he simply modified Obama's executive order. The new order from Trump might block US citizens and companies from doing business with establishments that are controlled by the Cuban military, but it doesn't stop Americans from going to Cuba. It merely adds red tape and more bureaucracy. His rhetoric of making it easier to do things and ending unnecessary regulations has been thrown out the window.

The speech in South Florida's Little Havana was full of stories about the struggles Cubans and Cuban-Americans have endured since Fidel Castro converted the island to communism. The real changes that Trump claimed his new approach will deliver sound more like an attempt to dictate the terms of how Cuba will be governed, a la 'nation building.'

Sure, asking them to have elections sounds like a good idea. Elections in Cuba involve nomination of municipal candidates by voters in nomination assemblies, nomination of provincial and national candidates by candidacy commissions, voting by secret ballot, and recall elections. But then, Trump speech writers probably don't know that Cuba already has some elections.

Donald Trump's declarations of the human rights violations in Cuba might sound righteous on the surface, but not once did Trump cover the human rights and cruel and unusual punishments of his hosts in Saudi Arabia. And lost in this whole reality is that our government is still holding people without charges or due process at Guantanamo Bay Naval Base, on Cuban soil. As they say, this man speaks with forked-tongue.

Is this his way of thanking Cuban Americans for their votes and keeping a campaign promise, while creating another opportunity to say something bad about Obama? Why do his actions feel like a way to fulfill, rather than introducing a well-developed way to change the way we deal with challenges?

Trump may have sent a strong missive to other nations who abuse their people, but if America could help the Cuban people better with tourism and more American influences. They might just take things into their own hands. We don't need another Bay of Pigs invasion and tourism is certainly better than isolation.

Due to the lack of free speech in Cuba, Trump's harangue will not be heard by its people, but the stifling of the tourism industry will surely hurt Cuban workers. Were Trump's actions only a way to get back at the Marriott corporation, his business competitor already doing business in Cuba?

The question that one might ask now, if you didn't cut off diplomatic relations with Cuba, why not appoint an ambassador and start talking about a better deal? Or does Trump feel like he's finished with it?

63. NOT ALL TWEETS ARE EQUAL
Trump's Newspeak Man: Jay Sekulow
Posted: 6-19-2017

In the classic book *"1984"*, by George Orwell, the term *"newspeak"* was introduced. This noun is defined as ambiguous euphemistic language used chiefly in political propaganda. The Wikipedia page on it says: *"Newspeak is a controlled language, of restricted grammar and limited vocabulary, a linguistic design meant to limit the freedom of thought—personal identity, self-expression, free will—that ideologically threatens the régime of Big Brother."*

While there are those in the Trump administration who hold a belief in some "deep state" is controlling everything, there are those Americans who believe that if our President was given more power he would become Big Brother.

Steve Bannon, Trump's right brain, declared his desire to destroy the "Administrative State", whatever that is. Now we have a new dance partner in this affair. His name is Jay Sekulow and his job is that of personal lawyer for Donald Trump. Good luck, Jay.

While the multiple personalities in Trump's head float in and out of existence, it will be Sekulow's responsibility to explain and defend the Donald. His role is already off to a rocky start with the tweet that was heard around the world.

Jay Sekulow went on all the Sunday morning talk shows to say to make it *"crystal clear that the President is not, and has never been, under investigation."* And the attorney attempted to dismiss the tweet in which the President said that he **is** under investigation. Jay also expressed that the tweet was simply acknowledging the Washington Post article. Huh?

Trump did not use a question mark in his tweet. He used an exclamation mark, which meant he wasn't questioning the Washington Post story. He wanted any interpretation to be based on exactly what he wrote. The lame claim by Sekulow that his client was limited by 140 characters is complete bullshit. Anyone familiar with Twitter and how it works, including Trump, can create a short string of tweets to add more meaning. In fact, the Trump as candidate and President has many times done precisely that with his use of ellipses.

Trump goes out of his way to say that he is not under investigation. And he says, he doesn't know anything that was going on with the Russians. How can he say, he's not under investigation? They wouldn't tell him if he was under investigation. And they probably didn't tell him he wasn't under investigation. They never talked to him. I could say Donald Trump is a woman, but I have no proof he's a man or a woman. I just know that he says he's a man.

The best question on the issue came from Chris Cuomo on a June 19, 2017 CNN report when he confronted Sekulow with this: *"You are his attorney of record, why not just pick up the phone and ask Robert Mueller if your client is under investigation?"* Chris, who has a law degree from Fordham University, asked the right question, one that the media never knew to ask.

Trump and his legal team have a responsibility to ask that question. A prosecutor does not have to tell a citizen if they are under investigation, but it would be proper for an attorney to, at least, ask the question.

Over the weekend one of my friends claimed I was being *"hysterical"* about this political stuff. "Hysterical" seems to be the new go-to word when trying to explain why a person adamantly disagrees with something. I told my friend that I just want to make sure we really understand all this when the smoke clears. I want to be counted with those who spoke out against a president who is wasting time, tax dollars, acting guilty and becoming untrusted in the world. Surely our country suffers.

Newspeak, with its linguistic design meant to limit the freedom of thought. This is precisely the intention of Donald Trump. His lawyers may try to bend the meaning of his words by saying things like, *"Oh, he is not very good at using social media."* Perhaps, but he's an abysmal writer and cannot communicate effectively with his grade school sentence structure. If someone else needs to explain what his tweets mean, then he didn't write them very well.

When a surrogate says, *"The tweets stand on their own,"* we must take that statement at face value. The worst thing about Trump is he uses his tweets as a psychological vomiting tool. He should invest in a therapist who can come by at 3:30 a.m. to help him over these emotional mole hills.

If I was Donald's shrink, my first question would be, *"Why do you obsess about whether you are under investigation?"* Now you know, Mr. Trump, how Obama felt when every action he made was questioned with a lawsuit or an investigation of congressional blockade. You wanted the job and you go it. Now, get to work and stop bitching!

64. THE INSANE BLAME GAME
Trump Must Look Forward
Posted: 6-21-2017

Donald Trump more than insinuated that the death of Otto Warmbier right after he was released from a North Korean jail was caused by the slow diplomacy of the Obama administration. One could ask why it took the Trump administration five months to free Mr. Warmbier. A better question might be, how soon can you get the other American's Kim Dong Chul, Kim Sang-duk and Kim Hak-Song freed from this horrible regime in North Korea?

Sometime soon, Donald J. Trump needs to look forward and stop blaming the last administration for everything that goes wrong. He's got just as big a problem in Syria right now with the confusion being created by Russia. Within the last 24-hours we have shot down one Syrian jet and two Iranian made drones that the Syrian army was using to scope out their enemies. The imaginary red line in Syria was matched by team Trump with 59 tomahawks, but what did that do? Nothing.

When the Chinese pulled back on trade with North Korea, Russia stepped up and moved their coal and supplies to Kim Jong Un. Let's be clear, Russia is on the side of Assad, Iran and North Korea; and Trump wants to be open to a productive Russian relationship. Why?

Trump needs a dose of reality. Putin will do anything to bring him down. Time will show that if he cannot control Trump, he will certainly attempt to destroy him.

There are serious problems in the world and the Trump administration can hardly handle an investigation into their stupid mistakes with Russia and election meddling. How can they be effective with crazy demonic leaders like Un or the crafty and soulless Putin? Trump is outclassed by Putin and misunderstands North Korea.

The President's legal document, called a tweet, sent a message to China today (June 20, 2017) *"While I greatly appreciate the efforts of President Xi & China to help with North Korea, it has not worked out. At least I know China tried!"* Why does he broadcast this rather than just sending a communique to the President of China? Trump has let everyone in the world know that he thinks what China did was not good enough for him. Is he really blaming China for the actions of Kim Jong Un?

If Trump can get the other three Americans out of North Korea, we can all salute him and believe that he has some leverage with Un, but that seems unlikely. Trump could end up being played by Un and Putin, while never knowing they have the upper hand. Could he be that naïve?

It would be great if Trump would help with the investigation and get rid of these distractions. There are too many important things in the world to deal with right now. With the Treasury Department sending documents to those on the Congressional oversight committees, it's getting more and more critical for the president to admit if there are tapes, show his full tax returns and help rid himself of this cancer on his Presidency.

We don't need more dead Americans shipped home from North Korea. We don't need to hear the President's concerns laced with blame and exploitation. We need the President to be a leader and help America. So far, we have someone who is floundering while acting on such basic levels.

65. SECRETS, RIDDLES AND LIES
Trump's Russian Roulette
Posted: 6-22-2017

There is a great word that helps us understand the current president. The word is publicity, the notice or attention given to someone or something by the media. It also has a second meaning, the spreading of information about a product, person, or company for advertising or promotional purposes.

With all the complaints about leaks from somewhere inside the White House, Donald Trump could be the leaker. He loves to talk and brag and, when no one else is in the room, how do we know what he is saying on the phone to the hundreds of people he talks with in any given week?

The Russia story is a saga because Trump and his surrogates have never been able to say the right things. Their push-back only exacerbates the matter. Donald Trump did business with Russians, that is a fact. Just look up the company Bayrock, which Trump was involved in SoHo and Florida.

According to USA Today: *"Trump addressed potential investors in Moscow and bragged to Real Estate Weekly about his access to Russia's rich and powerful, 'I have a great relationship with many Russians.'"*

To make matters worse, Donald Trump, Jr. went on the record in September of 2008 by saying, *"In terms of high-end product influx into the United States, Russians make up a pretty disproportionate cross-section of a lot of our assets; say in Dubai, and certainly with our project in SoHo and anywhere in New York. We see a lot of money pouring in from Russia."* Could Donald Trump, Jr. be a thorn in his father's side?

According to Bloomberg News: *"One of Bayrock's principals was a career criminal named Felix Sater who had ties to Russian and American organized crime groups. Before linking up with the company and with Trump, he had worked as a mob informant for the US government, fled to Moscow to avoid criminal charges while boasting of his KGB and*

Kremlin contacts there, and had gone to prison for slashing apart another man's face with a broken cocktail glass."

The first secret isn't so much a riddle but an out-and-out lie on Donald Trump's part about involvement with Russians. Why Congress hasn't demanded total disclosure of the President's financial entanglements is an enigma which can possibly be understood using the old maxim, "Winning is all that matters."

The President of the United States is playing Russian roulette, the practice of loading a bullet into one chamber of a revolver, spinning the cylinder, and then pulling the trigger while pointing the gun at one's own head. He can say that this story is a "hoax" and part of "fake news" and deep inside Trump may feel some guilt about his involvement with the Russians. What is the source of that guilt?

John Harris, the Co-Founder and Editor-In-Chief of Politico, was on Comedy Central's *The Daily Show* (June 21, 2017). He made an extremely cogent point about the Trump era by saying this is one of the most transparent White Houses he's covered.

Harris added, *"It's the most secretive and transparent administrations."* He saw that the President is so obsessed with press coverage, many of the staffers, immersed by infighting, can get their message to their boss only by leaking to the press.

They are aware of his lack of openness and cannot find any other way to deal with his isolation as a leader. He's inaccessible and a poor listener.

One of the sad things about this administration is its need to hold political rallies to keep a fist-grip on the base and to extract funds from the middle-class to pay for his ego massages. Donald Trump has created nothing short of a cult that believes his lies and listens to his harsh rhetoric as something pure and patriotic. He insults them with, *"I'd rather have a rich person than a poor person running the economy."* (June 21, 2017) I assume he means that poor people aren't smart enough to make economic decisions because they are poor. Sad!

With each bold-orange-faced lie we learn more and more about the American populace and how far one man can abuse power and obstruct justice. The insults are free. Trump has business dealings with Russians and he has been lying about this all along. The bullet in the chamber is Michael Flynn. Will Flynn bring the President to his knees?

66. NO TAPES, NO PROOF
Trump Incessantly Playing Games
Posted: 6-23-2017

Donald Trump was pushed off cable TV for a few hours when the Senate released its healthcare bill, but he returned to the headlines again after his latest tweet: *"With all of the recently reported electronic surveillance, intercepts, unmasking and illegal leaking of information, I have no idea whether there are "tapes" or recordings of my conversations with James Comey, but I did not make, and do not have, any such recordings."*

And with this, he called a TV blackout on the daily press conference, which was run by Sarah Huckabee Saunders (June 22, 2017), to keep his daily "Shit Show" off the airwaves, but after the briefing they allowed the audio to be released. So, there were tapes of the press conference and after the press briefing CNN and others ran the audio.

Donald J. Trump doesn't have a mental filter when it comes to Twitter. With the admission that there are no tapes of his conversations with fired FBI Director James Comey, his original tweet was more of a threat than a question. He knew there were no tapes of the conversation, but moved forward despite that fact. His action is tantamount to **witness intimidation**.

The statute is: *"Witness tampering is the act of attempting to alter or prevent the testimony of witnesses within criminal or civil proceedings."* Laws regarding witness tampering also apply to proceedings before the U.S. Congress, executive departments, and administrative agencies.

The Legal Information Institute embellishes: "Whoever knowingly uses intimidation, threatens, or corruptly persuades another person, or attempts to do so, or engages in misleading conduct toward another person, with intent to:

(1) influence, delay, or prevent the testimony of any person in an official proceeding;

(2) cause or induce any person to:

(A) withhold testimony, or withhold a record, document, or other object, from an official proceeding;

(B) alter, destroy, mutilate, or conceal an object with intent to impair the object's integrity or availability for use in an official proceeding;

(C) evade legal process summoning that person to appear as a witness, or to produce a record, document, or other object, in an official proceeding; or

(D) be absent from an official proceeding to which such person has been summoned by legal process."

As Robert Mueller begins his quest to find the answers behind Russian interference in the election, President Trump said today (June 23, 2017) that Mueller is good friends with James Comey and the friendship is *"bothersome."* Our great Orange Leader is planting doubt and staging the next firing, for sure.

Trump is spanking the press with his news briefing blackout, but his passive aggressiveness makes no sense. The White House released the audio right after the event. Does he want to be able to stop the release of the audio if the briefing doesn't go well?

The press is not amused. World leaders are not entertained by this childish deception. The credibility of the highest office in our country has been lost with Donald Trump. It will never be restored until Donald Trump is gone.

You cannot be impeached for being stupid or obsessed with issues that have little to do with being a great President. Some of his actions have moved from inappropriate to incompetence to obstruction.

Keep your eyes on Trump as the investigation gets closer to his front door. He has taken the heat off the Senate and their secret healthcare bill but, in the end, we will still have a country when the Donald is back in New York as an irrelevant ex-president.

67. THE GRAND CON
Trump's Fake Promises
Posted: 6-24-2017

Imagine during a contract negotiation your boss promised you that he would never lower your wage. So, you accepted the new deal and at some point, he reduced your wage. What would you think of your boss?

On the campaign trail Donald Trump was forceful with his promise that he would not lower Medicare, Medicaid or Social Security. And with this grand con, many low income and older Americans connected with that promise. It may have determined their votes in the election. But now the President is silent while the Republican Senate and House of Representatives create large cuts to those programs without his squeaky high voice saying, *"No."* What kind of leader is he?

AARP Executive Vice President Nancy LeaMond said, *"The Senate bill which imposes an 'Age Tax' on older adults—increasing health insurance premiums and reducing tax credits, makes cuts to both Medicare and Medicaid funding, and yet gives billions of dollars in tax breaks to drug and insurance companies. AARP calls on every Senator to vote 'NO' on this harmful bill."*

It's obvious that Donald J. Trump is just a typical politician who promises things to get elected and then does what he wants, or what the party tells him to do. This spineless bundle of white fat with his oversized neckties has little empathy with the poor, the middle-class or the millions of retired Americans who depend on these services and programs. He just wants to be loved by his slowly dissolving base and get reelected; cringe the thought.

The National Coalition for Cancer Survivorship posted this on their Website today: *"The Senate GOP recently released their version of the ACA repeal bill that they crafted in secret. Under this bill, millions of Americans, including cancer survivors, will lose health insurance. Cancer survivors are at risk of losing vital protections for people*

According to a recent Gallup poll, Congress has only a 20% approval rating, while Donald Trump in the RealClearpolitics.com average gets around 40% approval with 54% disapproval of the job he is doing. Yes, he can blame Congress for the slash and burn healthcare bill, but remember that the President must sign it. If he does, he owns it. Recall when people talked about "Death Panels" and Obamacare? Well, with Trumpcare, we are going to get them.

There are many liars and lies in politics and the average Joe doesn't have the wherewithal or time to discern the numbers, language and deceits from the truth. Free market healthcare, like trickle-down economics, is a diabolical myth perpetrated on the American public. Math doesn't lie. Rich people, the upper 1%, are getting richer while the middle class is getting poorer.

You might not want to trust someone like Donald Trump, or Treasury Secretary Steve Mnuchin, who on the side just made a boatload of money producing the Wonder Woman movie. They have no credibility when it comes to what they do with your money. Mnuchin, for example, just sold his interest in Dune Entertainment and then named his fiancée Louise Linton CEO to protect his wealth while he toils at his job in government. I assume Steve and Louise have a swell healthcare plan at Dune. She sure dresses well.

This healthcare bill is going to give the upper 1% more money! Trump and his great disrupters are running a scam, a con, a scheme on the American public. In the next three years, they want to justify tax cuts for the rich by taking services away from the poor, the disenfranchised and the elderly.

They aren't good people and conservative Republicans truly believe that giving rich people more money will help them get elected. After all, rich people give money to super PACs and campaigns, the middle class will never finance their greed.

Trump has already abolished the death tax with the stroke of his pen. His kids will greatly benefit by what he has already done. But we should realize how much a burden the rich people must endure by moving their money around so the IRS doesn't see where it actually is going. Trump is no better than the steel and train magnates of the late 1800s. Winning may be everything to the Donald, but the middle and lower classes of America will not tolerate much more of his poisonous political pain.

If you thought the voters were angry during the election, wait until they find out you screwed them with a horrendously false promise, Mr. Trump.

68. TRUMP'S TRUE COLORS
Inherently Racist Messaging
Posted: 6-26-2017

I don't profess to know what is in another man's heart, but after many years of observations I do believe I have found some answers to many of my questions about Trump.

One of the things that an expert might tell you about pathological liars is that they hate when someone proves they are lying. Also, they usually embody the following characteristics: narcissism, selfishness, abusive attitude, obsessive, compulsive behaviors, impulsivity, aggressiveness, jealous behaviors, manipulative behaviors, deceptiveness, socially awkwardness, discomfort, low self-esteem, temperamental outbursts and anger. Why do these words feel like they were written about Donald Trump? Indeed, those are straight-off-the-shelf descriptions of most pathological liars.

There is a toxic combination of jealous behavior, low self-esteem and anger that can also deliver another dark disorder called racism, which is prejudice, discrimination, or antagonism directed against someone of a different race based on the belief that one's own race is superior.

If we dip into the Donald's past, we know that one of the most embarrassing things that happened to the Trumps in New York City was the lawsuit accusing them of discrimination in the housing market. According to the Business Insider Website, a civil-rights lawsuit brought by the Justice Department against Donald Trump and his father Fred Trump in 1973 claimed that African-Americans and Puerto Ricans were prevented from renting apartments from Trump. In 1975, Trump agreed to a consent decree, whereby no admission of wrongdoing would be given, however, his management company was ordered to take out ads telling ethnic minorities that they were welcome to seek housing at Trump properties.

Trump's well-established modus operandi is to blame those who disagree with him or who stand in the way of him either getting away with a lie or making money. Blame the accuser and hit back hard. Could the President be harboring deep-seated feelings that African-Americans are out to get him in some way? That is a strange form of racism.

Trump brags constantly about his wealth and success and attributes it to his genetic makeup. He told Playboy in 1990 that he is, *"a strong believer in genes"* and *"my kids can be brought up without adversity and respond well if they have the genes."* Forget about whispers to the Alt-Right, this is a scream.

According to the Independent website: *"The [Trump] family subscribes to a racehorse theory of human development. "They believe that there are superior people and that if you put together the genes of a superior woman and a superior man, you get a superior offspring."* Doesn't that sound a bit like what the Germans were talking about in 1939? And, just to throw a little whisper in here, the use of plastic surgery to repair those gene flaws.

Let's look at his weird responses to white supremacist groups. In The Guardian: *"Activists who recently gave Nazi salutes and shouted, "hail Trump!" at a gathering in Washington will revolt if the new US president fails to meet their expectations, the leaders told the Guardian."* Haven't we heard the President declare his contempt for these groups?

Steve Bannon stokes the gene fire and white supremacist messaging. Trump is being played like a limp puppet by Stephen Miller, Sebastian Gorka and Bannon who believe that nationalism trumps pluralism. They want to divide the nation and give the "power" back to white people. Trump, at least, is an accomplice in this terrible affront to American citizen equality.

Now that brings us to another argument on the racist in the White House. Let's assume that some of the material that was in the now famous dossier that was prepared by a British spy was less than accurate. However, one point stood out to me. The fact that Donald Trump did not like Michelle

Obama and, if Trump's backward blaming is to be believed, he dislikes the former President even more. That's a fact and a sad example of racism.

For years, Donald Trump claimed Barack Obama wasn't born in America, only to later half-heartedly admit that he was wrong. Trump believes that he can attribute everything that is wrong in his America to Obama.

This week Donald Trump blamed Obama for not doing more about the Russian attempts to get him elected. Does he really think the people are that stupid? Yes, he does and, sadly, some are.

Deep down inside, this constant use of Obama as whipping boy speaks to Donald's real true color, prejudice. Some will say I'm being unfair, but it's all there in front of you. Think about it:

- ✓ Trump knows that Obama is a better speaker and smarter man (jealous behavior).
- ✓ Trump knows that no matter what happens in the world, Obama's legacy will be lower unemployment, saving the US auto industry and moving the economy back into the black (low self-esteem).
- ✓ Trump's real job seems to be doing everything he can to justify his presidency by creating a narrative that Obama is inferior to his perfectly planned genome (manipulative behaviors, deceptiveness).

Trump will find himself all alone in a country whose diversity will never be stopped by racism or tied down by stereotypes. It appears from this vantage point that Donald Trump, our President, is at best, a part-time racist.

69. MUSLIMS BAD, RUSSIANS GOOD
Trump's Travel Ban Begins
Posted: 6-29-2017

The Supreme Court wanted to show some respect for the office of the President, so they gave him the benefit of the doubt with a baby-ruling on the travel ban. While pushing the bigger decision about how America's image will be morphed by arguments this October, the court gave the president the power to manage who enters this country.

Taking Trump's ban on face value, it allows our government to research the credibility of the vetting of visas, and to create a system that would provide better security of our country. One of the things that happened in the last year, which most experts and representatives agree on, America was the victim of a cyber-attack by Russia.

The administration has done nothing to protect America from that threat. Every President says these words with his hand on a Bible: *"I do solemnly swear that I will faithfully execute the Office of President of the United States, and will to the best of my ability, preserve, protect and defend the Constitution of the United States."*

The protection of our democracy and the defense of our Constitution are paramount. Donald Trump has done nothing about the issue of electronic invasion by Russia, and some people around him say he considers most questions about Russia to be alarmist over-reaction. Others, who have taken a more psychological approach, believe Trump has combined the Russian hacking scandal and any possible collusion into one large bucket of dissent against him and disdain for him personally. Someone has programmed his tiny brain to believe that if the Russian probe goes forward, America will find out that his whole presidency is a fraud.

Trump is so used to hearing critics calling him a phony or a con that he assumes he must have done something wrong. However, this time he really is doing something wrong by ignoring a threat to cyber-security. Our Orange Leader has a Mister Magoo vision of protecting and defending this nation.

The Senate approved a bill to lock in sanctions against Russia by a 98-2 vote. Interestingly, Republican Rand Paul of Kentucky and Independent Bernie Sanders of Vermont voted against the measure. The bill, which includes both Russian and Iranian sanctions, heads to the House for approval before President Donald Trump gets to sign it. Should Trump veto the bill, it will disclose his reticence to ruffle Russian feathers. Trump seems to be able to intimidate the House, where the Senate sees him as a necessary evil.

As the summer tornadoes, hurricanes, droughts and fires rage across America; our representatives will get an earful at their town meetings, if they are brave enough to have them. We can sit here and take this bad management on the part of Donald Trump's White House, or we can start to scream.

The House of Representatives has an interesting balancing act right now. Their members don't want to have Trump in their faces. However, if they stand by and let Trump screw up the country, they will surely be losing their jobs in 2018 and beyond. The leadership on both sides are so full- of ideologues nothing will get done. As much as the President claims the Democrats are keeping him from being successful, he has never invited them to his house to sit down and talk. He's the problem.

Trump is doing nothing about Russia and has pushed it aside. Why? Trump moved very quickly on his Muslim ban, which was blocked by the courts. He modified it, even going so far to say he liked the first one better, but at least he compromised. If he would have applied logical verbiage to his order, and not flame out online, he could have gotten what he wanted in the first place.

We don't hear Trump screaming about Russia, so we can only assume he really doesn't care about its interference with our election. Someday he will have to explain. From this vantage point, he's clearly declared, *"Muslims bad, Russians good."* The real question is why?

70. THE CYBER BULLY-IN-CHIEF
Trump: Unhappy in His Own Skin
Posted: 6-29-2017

Donald Trump has once again demonstrated his thin skin and relentless, mean streak. In a morning tweet, the President of the United States put forth a silly immature, cruel and misogynistic post deriding MSNBC morning host Mika Brzezinski.

The tweet read as follows, *"I heard poorly rated @Morning Joe speaks badly of me (don't watch anymore). Then how come low I.Q. Crazy Mika, along with Psycho Joe, came to Mar-a-Lago 3 nights in a row around New Year's Eve, and insisted on joining me. She was bleeding badly from a face-lift. I said no!"*

Now I could have simply chalked it up to his modus operandi and how Trump shows us his true colors through Twitter, but there is a problem here that is not going to go away. It's impossible to have respect for the office of the President of the United States with Trump and all his men and women.

Melania Trump, the first lady of this country, said through a spokesperson, *"When her husband gets attacked, he will punch back ten times harder."* I know that English is not Melania's first language and I hope we didn't miss anything in translation, but I must say, there goes that whole bullshit concept of her being the titular head of some anti-cyber bullying campaign. Now, zero credibility.

The protectors of our drunk uncle president were out in full force today. Sarah Huckabee Sanders commented, *"I don't think that the president's ever been someone who gets attack and doesn't push back. There have been an outrageous number of personal attacks, not just to him, but to frankly everyone around him. This is a president who fights fire with fire. And certainly, will not be allowed to be bullied by a liberal media and the liberal elites within the media or Hollywood or anywhere else."*

I'm not sure that the president of a country with a First Amendment can allow or disallow what others say about him. We have now seen the real enemy of the state and they are, indeed, those who are working for the White House. We are all getting burned by Trump's fire and disregard for human beings.

The people around our president are soulless. They lie and disregard common decency to show their love for this power-hungry tyrant, Donald J. Trump. How do they sleep at night?

Whether you like Joe Scarborough or Mika or not, you should consider that the imaginary battles between the free press and the oppressive regime of Trump are now, in fact, real. The media, be it liberal, conservative, or far right, has a duty to find facts, write stories, conduct broadcasts and inform the American people.

This president doesn't care about anyone but himself. Those who support his abuse of power will be tried not only in the court of public opinion, but perhaps even called to testify in a real court about whether they were instructed to lie to the American people. If lying to the citizens is not an impeachable offense, then what is?

71. FAKE NEWS OR FAKE PRESIDENT?
Trump's War on the Constitution
Posted: 7-7-2017

Occasionally I see, hear or read a journalist saying that Donald Trump has some grand strategy. When pressed, the author says that this latest move was pure genius, or the tweet did exactly what he designed it to do, as if the Donald is an intelligent media designer.

There's not much difference between Trump's tweets and a nine-year-old boy grapping the microphone at Walmart and yelling stupid kid-things into the store's PA system. The kid's grand plan is to get attention, same as the "leader" of the free world.

In the President's latest tweet (July 2, 2017), he proclaimed, *"The FAKE AND FRAUDULENT NEWS MEDIA is working hard to convince Republicans and others I should not use social media - but remember, I won the 2016 election with interviews, speeches and social media. I had to beat #FakeNews, and did. We will continue to WIN! My use of social media is not Presidential - it's MODERN DAY PRESIDENTIAL. Make America Great Again!"*

When I read this, my mind heard that same spoiled nine-year-old brat saying, *"Mommy made me president. I'm the president. I get to be president and do whatever I want!"*

This over complaining and endless whining about news coverage in the media isn't new to presidents. Trump has decided, however, that anyone who disagrees with him, critiques him or attempts to cover his misadventures, is the enemy. One could change the term "Fake News" to "People who hate me" and it would fit perfectly in all contexts. If I don't make it on the enemies list, I am going to be pissed.

Steve Bannon, the administration's dark, evil, twin of Spiro Agnew, has said openly that the media is the "opposition party." He, along with Trump surrogates, Miller, Conway and that overtly obnoxious, fake intellectual

Sebastian Gorka, have crafted a White House position that is obstinate and cantankerous. Any thinking America hearing them speak can clearly see through the pretentious, defensive droning of their propaganda.

Richard M. Nixon did the same thing when he was president, even using the same terms about the media. However, Trump is no Nixon. The 37th President had to resign in disgrace. This president, when the time comes, will have to be removed from his current residence by the Secret Service, Capitol Hill Police or maybe the Army.

Even Trump's slogan is not new. It is a total rip-off of Ronald Reagan's campaign motto, demonstrating that Trump is an even better actor than Ronald Reagan. An actor takes the stage and plays a part, while not being the real thing. We now have a fake President and everything he does is directed to making his character likeable, rather than forging policy and decisions that are righteous and good for the country. #FakePresident

Trump bellyaches that his achievements are not covered in the "fake news" but he broadcasts his tirades on the very same "fake" mainstream media he continually slams. His complaints about not being covered are total lies. The media covers every speech, every signing, every tweet. His "key promises," such as reforming healthcare, getting a better, fairer, tax code and creating jobs, have become fake, rally fodder rather than reality.

Months ago, President Trump and VP Mike Pence rode their white horses into the Carrier furnace plant in Indianapolis to announce they had convinced the company to abandon a plan to move to Mexico. They stated publicly that this would save hundreds of jobs. Update: many employees will soon be losing their jobs at that very plant. On June 22, 2017, CNBC reported that: *"Carrier's plant in Indianapolis is scheduled to lay off about 600 workers by the end of the year. The jobs are going to Mexico."* Nice work, little boys.

Donald J. Trump will probably write that off as "FAKE NEWS," but the road to success for this president must go through the media. You cannot be a great president in a vacuum. You cannot dearly guard the Second

Amendment while spitting in the face of those who employ the First Amendment to keep democracy strong. Without the First Amendment, we don't need the Second Amendment.

Fake means fraudulent, and the usage of that term by our president in the context of media coverage is troublesome on many levels. When something is fraudulent, it is obtained, done by, or has involved, deception, especially criminal deception. The American public, the Congress and the courts must be on-guard with this president. There's a very small step from complaining to outlawing and, in this case, the outlawing would be executed by an elected outlaw.

At this date, the fake president may not like the fake media, but if all media outlets stopped talking about Trump, he would probably melt into a damp, mushy pool of man tan and makeup. Sad.

72. AN OPEN LETTER TO THE BASE
Dear Donald Trump Fans
Posted: 7-2-2017

It is unlikely that you are reading this but, if you are, I just want to say a few things to you before you slap on your silly red baseball cap or put on that "Lock Her Up" T-shirt and jump in your car and drive to the next rally. I know that you are as American as I am and you really do want this country to be successful, but we must talk. This isn't funny anymore.

You probably haven't gotten a raise in years. I get that, it's horrible. In some cases, your raise was eaten up by the banking crisis that was created by greedy bankers with an immoral disregard for the common man and their mortgages. I get that, too. In other cases, your employer may have used some buzz line about how we live in an age of financial insecurity to justify keeping your wages at a level where profit for the owners takes precedence over your long-term benefits.

Donald Trump was hyper critical of Obama and Bush and government in general, maybe that is why you like him. Do his anti-government, anti-immigrant, anti-free trade, anti-anyone else's methods make him the great law respecting leader you voted for? Provided that law lines up with what Trump wants to do, he will apply it. If it doesn't, he will attempt to break it. That's who he is.

Trump is for state's rights, until they interfere with his grand plan to remake America in his image. Go ahead, admit it, you are just as radical as those people who marched against the Vietnam war. Oh, you're not? You sure fooled me, the way you are so anti-government.

Trump says he is going to change things, but do you listen to what he says and then match that up with what he does? He says he is out for the blue-collar worker and he preaches he wants to bring back manufacturing to those places that once boomed with industry, BUT HE IS AGAINST

INCREASING THE MINIMUM WAGE. Gee, why wouldn't he fight for you on such a simple thing as a few more bucks an hour?

Donald Trump has yet to explain why being nice to Russia is a good idea. He has yet to demonstrate why a country which doesn't give a rat's ass for the American worker would be something we shouldn't fear. Trump seems to be afraid of most things that are NOT AMERICAN, except PUTIN, WHO IS NOT AMERICAN.

Our great Orange Leader has confused you with his mantra that he didn't collude with Russia in the attempt to disrupt our election process. Then he eventually admitted that Russians did launch a cyber-attack against our beloved country. You did hear him say that, right? RUSSIA IS NOT OUR FRIEND AND YOU SHOULD BE ASKING TRUMP WHY HE HASN'T DECLARED CYBER WAR AGAINST THEM. If Trump is so strong, why are Russia, Syria, Iran and North Korea not changing their disruptive ways?

Many of you believe that Donald Trump is a great Commander-in-Chief, but when he launched 59 tomahawks into Syria for their use of chemical weapons, the airport was up and running only a few days later. WHY DIDN'T WE DESTROY THE AIR BASE IN SYRIA? Some strike, huh?

Now I know, you think Congress is a useless institution and if you believe your leader, the court system is just as rigged. Aside from God, however, who do you believe in? Now I have been quite critical of your addiction to the cult-like Trump dogma, but I want to have a man to man with you, or, man to woman with you.

Let me ask you a question. Why do rich white guys always think they can fix things? Well, it's because no one confronts them when they are wrong. Let's zero-base this, Trump's Base people. You claim the Donald is smart because he got rich being a great business person, right? You say he makes a good president because the country is benefitting from a strong businessman running the country like a business. Well, okay, let's work this premise.

YOU DO REALIZE THAT DONALD TRUMP IS $315 MILLION IN DEBT, RIGHT? Why? If he is so rich, why does he carry debt? Now let's see how he stacks up with other great American born success stories. Donald Trump is worth 1.4 billion dollars, while Warren Buffet, the head of Berkshire Hathaway is worth 76.1 billion. Mr. Buffet disagrees with Donald Trump on many issues. Last time I checked, Warren Buffet pays his taxes and carries no debt at all, so, why aren't you listening to Buffet instead of Trump? Speaking of wealth, Amazon's Jeff Bezos is worth 84.3 billion dollars, Bill Gates is worth 88.7 billion and Facebook's Mark Zuckerberg comes in at 63 billion. You should be listening to them. Beating the IRS is more important to the Donald than paying his taxes on time like you do.

Now let's address the big fat orange elephant in the room. When Donald Trump screamed it was okay to smack protestors at his rallies, you were on his side. Of course, when he said, *"It's time for us to take our country back!"* you liked that message. You also enabled him with his war against the press which you no longer trust. ***In Donald, You Trust.*** Where did God go?

You like the idea of America First because deep-down inside you believe that immigrants and African-Americans and gay couples and people with a liberal progressive agenda have taken advantage of you personally. In many cases, you have been enabled by your evangelical leaders. When did church folk decide that white Christians are more important than the poor? WWJD? For the atheists in the crowd, that means What Would Jesus Do?

When you say you want to take back your country, you are ignorant of the history of North America. Our land was stolen from its native peoples by European colonists. Those people with guns and horses took land from unarmed peoples. Is this why you want to keep your hands on your guns and the Second Amendment? I get that, too.

What really made America great were waves of immigrants from all over the world who came here to have a better life. DONALD TRUMP'S GRANDFATHER CAME FROM GERMANY FOR A BETTER LIFE. The

Donald is more immigrant that those who want to take back their country. Trump's mother was not born in America; she was born in Scotland. That makes the Donald only second or third generation American, depending on how you'd like to split hairs.

Here's the most important issue for the Trump loyalists. What is it that you really want? Are you in this for "endless winning" or are you interested in more jobs, better healthcare, a better, safer life and an opportunity for your kids to do better than you did? DOES THIS RING TRUE?

Donald Trump has spent most of his time with rich people and famous people and the urban elite. I am sure he paid for more than one abortion in his life. His political and moral positions change when they get in the way of what he wants. We know that he gave money to the Washington elite, he admits it. Donald Trump will bounce between helping rich people and his kids first, then, if there is anything left, maybe he'll throw you a bone. You don't have to believe me, you just need to ask a simple question. IF TRUMP IS SO GREAT, WHY ARE YOU STILL PAYING MORE FOR MEDICINES AND INSURANCE?

The debacle in Congress over the healthcare bill is but one example that shows we didn't send someone to the White House to drain the swamp. In Washington, the swamp must be navigated by someone with a map. Our government was designed so that one person could never dominate it. WHAT DO YOU WANT, A RAISE AND LOWER TAXES OR DO YOU WANT DONALD TRUMP TO SPEND ALL YOUR MONEY ON A WALL?

As strong as you think Trump is, open your eyes and see that he's just a rich, silver-spoon-in-his-mouth golfer who fooled you once, twice, and again, and again. Ask yourself this. Are things better? And if they are not better now, when will they get better? You can say he's not a miracle worker and, "please give him a chance." But remember, HE TOLD YOU HE IS A MIRACLE WORKER.

73. IMPATIENT AND "UN" AWARE
Trump's Challenge: North Korea
Posted: 7-4-2017

That great term, "sword rattling" takes us back to simpler times, which were actually just as complicated as they are today. We don't get to pick the leaders of the nations of the world. Some leaders move to the top of a government because of birthright, while others kill their way to the top. In democratic countries, candidates run campaigns and get elected. Their viewpoints will either light the way or cast a shadow over the land they rule.

Donald Trump ran his campaign on hardened opinions based on his consumption of extremely skewed media outlets and conspiracy theories. He railed against China at almost every rally by mentioning their currency manipulation and trade advantage over the US. He said few negative things about Russia. Trump also claimed he knew more than his generals about terrorist groups such as ISIS. Now that he is President, however, it's important that he listens carefully to his generals.

On the day before the 4th of July 2017, this nation's 241st birthday, Kim Jong Un ordered the launch of what his press described as an ICBM that could reach the United States. Trump is now becoming aware that Little Kim is taunting him. In fact, the missile traveled 578 miles and made it two-thirds of the way to Japan.

In the Rose Garden (June 30, 2017) Trump made an announcement about the Asian country when he said, *"The era of strategic patience with the North Korean regime has failed. And, frankly, that patience is over."* Okay, not quite a red line, but, in a communist country, red is not such a bad color.

Once again, our federally paid tweeting teenager took to the internet even before he knew the nature of the missile to weigh in on this crisis, *"North Korea has just launched another missile. Does this guy have anything better to do with his life? Hard to believe that South Korea and Japan will put up with this much longer. Perhaps China will put a heavy move on North Korea and end this nonsense once and for all!"*

I laughed when I read that tweet. The line that stuck out was, *"Does this guy have anything better to do with his life?"* I thought, yeah, that little monster, lucky-sperm leader is launching missiles and our great Orange Wonder is launching tweets. Why isn't he talking with Japan and South Korea? It sounds like he is pitching a movie idea to China. What does he mean by *"heavy move."* Isn't that what Trump said he did with women he thought attractive?

According to the New York Times (June 26, 2017): *"South Korea's foreign minister indicated strongly on Monday that her government would honor an agreement to deploy an American missile-defense system despite protests and economic retaliation from China."* That seems a bit far from what you want China to do, Mr. Trump.

The Donald is impatient with North Korea because he doesn't understand that country's complexities. If General MacArthur in the 1950s would have been allowed to continue his march beyond the 38th parallel, who knows what Korea would be as a unified country, today. China wanted a buffer between a working democracy, albeit corruptible, in South Korea and what they want to believe is modern communism in China. Remember, it was China that convinced Truman to "stand down" and then Truman fired MacArthur to avoid another world war.

Trump showed his feelings about China's lack of involvement in his tweet (June 20, 2017), *"While I greatly appreciate the efforts of President Xi & China to help with North Korea, it has not worked out. At least I know China tried!"* Why is our President attempting to shame leaders of major countries into action? It's almost more important for him to have a running commentary on his feelings. Our president is like a teenage girl writing in her diary every night: Dear Diary…

While China and South Korea would like more discourse between countries, Trump is doing his best to make this about the cult of personality rather than political diplomacy. Trump is simply not a diplomatic person. Why is he President again?

Our boy president toys with people on Twitter and screams about his big bad enemy, the press, at his politically motivated rallies, while Kim Jong Un taunts nations with missiles. The frightening reality is that Un would sacrifice his country's 25 million people just to prove that he is the boss. What are Trump's priorities?

Trump may say he is impatient, but what is next? If the President of the United States cannot rally nations and the strong characters who care about the world, he is wasting his time with those 140 characters on Twitter. World leaders want to know the plan, and that includes what happens after Kim Jong Un is gone. Unfortunately, most of those same leaders are also looking forward to the time Trump is gone.

74. PLAYING THE TRUMP CARD
The Jester at the World Leader Table
Posted: 7-5-2017

If you play a trump card during a game of Spades, you take the whole trick or, in non-card terms, you get to pick up every card on the table. That makes you the winner. The trump card sounds like the strong member of the deck, but the roots of the name might surprise you. From old English (1500s), *trump,* and then from Middle English *trumpen,* meant to "*deceive* to *cheat.*" The old French *tromper* also meant "*to deceive.*"

We should remind our readers that Trump's last name is not the original version of his name. His family name in Germany was Drumpf, which they later changed to Trump. Regardless, the word Trump doesn't always have positive connotations.

The leaders of Argentina, Australia, Brazil, Canada, China, France, Germany, India, Indonesia, Italy, Japan, Republic of Korea, Mexico, Russia, Saudi Arabia, South Africa, Turkey, the United Kingdom, the United States and the European Union will gather at the 2017 G20 summit in Hamburg, Germany. The meetings will begin on Friday, July 7, 2017.

In an interview in the German weekly, Die Zeit, Angela Merkel said, "*While we are looking at the possibilities of cooperation to benefit everyone, globalization is seen by the American administration more as a process that is not about a win-win situation but about winners and losers.*" It was clear that she was taking the first shot across the bow of the USS Donald Trump.

Here is a great lesson in the destructive power of over-statement. In the hours and hours of titillating campaign tirades and over-modulated microphones, the Donald made it very clear that his way was going to be "America First!" In his bombast, he belittled the whole notion of globalization.

His raspy bleating convinced many voters that the rest of the world was ripping off America and this was the reason for the torment of our middle class. Guiltless, in Trump's accusations, were the rich Wall Street oligarchy, who Trump relates to more than the common man.

The President's conundrum was produced by his own reckless mouth. He talked about how it would be good to befriend Russia so that they can help us beat ISIS, without any apparent regard that Russia is an ally of Iran and will only go so far in the Middle East quagmire. Can Donald Trump not comprehend that Putin likes Assad and wants him to stay on top of Syria? You know, the guy who gassed the kids?

Trump probably forgot that Russia, as the former USSR, spent ten years of direct involvement with and occupation in Afghanistan. They may fly some sorties and drop some bombs where Assad tells them, but they certainly aren't going to bomb Damascus. They don't even believe that chemical weapons have been used in Syria. Russia has no intention giving Trump what he wants in Syria. It's what THEY WANT that should make us nervous.

As for China, why would they want to thwart Kim Jong Un? On July 5, 2017 Trump tweeted, *"Trade between China and North Korea grew almost 40% in the first quarter. So much for China working with us - but we had to give it a try!"* This tweet came right before the dealer was ready to split the deck and Trump farted at the table.

After not restating the commitment to Article 5 at the NATO meetings, why would the G20 nations think that Trump can be trusted? Yes, he finally said he would, but what a dud not uniting the NATO group when they were all face-to-face.

When a bully is being attacked by another bigger bully from another playground, why does the home bully think that he can rally the tormented to help him thump the invader? Merkel wants to make sure the EU is protected, and that means keeping Russia in its own borders and off line. Russia wants to disrupt America. China wants to make sure Trump thinks he's in charge. And the other kids on the playground just want to make sure that a global unity helps them maintain stability in their own homes.

What Donald Trump thought he needed to say to get elected has isolated him from those who really listen and want America to be successful. Trump sacrificed his credibility with the players around the table with lies, exaggerations and ludicrous statements about how things work.

When everyone else shows their strong face cards, Trump will be left with the cards he pilfered from the deck before the other people arrived. Trump has continually played the isolation card and, sadly, he's been showing the Joker more than any other card at the world table. Someone needs to tell our great Orange Leader that the Joker has no value at this table.

75. "NOBODY REALLY KNOWS"
Trump Sows the Seed of Doubt
Posted: 7-6-2017

Donald Trump is an interesting speaker. After saying, *"Nobody really knows"* who hacked our 2016 national election," he says, *"And there's nothing wrong with that statement."* Much like salting his verbiage with the plea, *"Believe me,"* it serves to block or deny the interviewer the next question, "What is the truth, Mr. President." Clearly to Trump, the truth is what he says it is and, one thing for sure, he doesn't want anyone to question him.

Agent Orange says in his legal documents, which we call tweets, *"North Korea is behaving very badly. They have been "playing" the United States for years."* We see that he is irritated at how the US has handled that country in the past. There are times when I feel sorry for President Trump. He lives in a world where everybody that came before him is stupid, or incompetent. In his little, inexperienced mind, everybody else is not smart and surely the solution is simple. He asks, *"Why didn't they do something?"*

The reason I feel sorry for him is because the closer he gets to a problem, the more realizes it's complicated, like healthcare. Because he believes that only he knows a solution, he fails to comprehend that solutions weren't achieved previously because global problems are multifaceted. Does he understand that three out of the five things you could do would be a total disaster? The two other ideas are only good for us. And for how long?

When asked earlier about what he would do if North Korea launched an intercontinental ballistic missile targeting US soil, Trump tweeted, *"It won't happen!"* Well, I guess that was "Fake News" because, in fact, Kim Jong Un carried out a test of what most experts agree was an ICBM capable of reaching at least to Alaska and Sarah Palin's back porch.

In his unrelenting desire to denigrate the previous president, Trump cares not where he is or which audience is listening. He will do everything he can to put-down Obama. Does Trump realize that from Truman to Obama there were eleven presidents who had to deal with North Korea and nothing has changed? There have been eleven presidents before Trump since Israel was created and we still don't have peace in the Middle East. Nobody really knows if Trump understands this.

Trump was very critical about previous administrations declaring "red lines," whether they were in the sand, in the snow or on poorly drawn maps, but now that President Trump is confronted with less than adoring support from many of the other nations of the world, he will have to make his due with the devil. And who is the devil? The very man who many think, helped him get elected. Putin will want more than he gives.

We don't know if Donald Trump is smart enough to be President, but we do know that the people around him have little sway on what he thinks, what he does or what a new world order should be. His ping-ponging between sword rattling and attempting to outsource his problems to Russia or China have failed. Both world powers have no intention of carrying out any plan that would weaken their economies or statures on the world stage. Both Russia and China benefit from trade with North Korea. Russia loves to sell things to Cuba, Iran and Syria. Most likely, Japan and Germany will craft a trade deal that will hurt Detroit and Trump will be helpless to do anything about it. If only Trump was open to some free trade that would help America.

The Donald needs strong counseling about how his sowing doubt makes him sound unsure of himself. Why wouldn't you want the leader of the free world to know things? He claims he knows more than everyone else, but on certain things he is passive, clueless and uninvolved, perhaps posturing so that someone else can take the blame. A blamer always needs someone to blame.

Now, after saying he would be able to stop North Korean's leader from testing rockets and nukes, he has thrown out increasingly stern warnings. According to the Washington Post (July 6, 2017), *In Warsaw, Trump said the*

Nobody knows what that "something" could be. Perhaps, our great Donald is still formulating those ideas. It's clear to the world that if you want to stop someone from doing something, you either talk to them or punch them. Trump sure does a lot of talking, but he doesn't put his money where his mouth is. Perhaps he wants to use someone else's money to solve problems that won't go away.

With trade, climate and immigration on the table and discussions with the EU soured, Trump is all alone. When sitting with Russia, China, Japan and South Korea, our President should be prepared to listen as much as he talks.

Trump should work on knowing the issues and having answers. He should stop diluting his speeches with anti-press, anti-Obama and anti-trade tirades. Nobody knows why he does it, and nobody outside of the US cares about his fake fight with CNN. Focus, Donald, focus!

76. FAKE NEWS vs. REAL JOURNALISM
Trump's Attempt to Muddy the Waters
Posted: 7-7-2017

In February of 2017 Trump tweeted: *"The FAKE NEWS media (failing @nytimes, @NBCNews, @ABC, @CBS, @CNN) is not my enemy, it is the enemy of the American People!"* Then he deleted that tweet and posted something similar, but took ABC off his enemies list. Trump, obviously not a student of history, missed this fact, Vladimir Lenin and Joseph Stalin used the term *"enemy of the nation/people"* to refer to those who disagreed with the Bolshevik government. Did you write that one, Steve Bannon?

Trump went on a rant July 1, 2017, after receiving heavy criticism from both sides of the political spectrum due to his attacks on MSNBC talk show hosts, *"The FAKE & FRAUDULENT NEWS MEDIA is working hard to convince Republicans and others I should not use social media - but remember, I won the 2016 election with interviews, speeches and social media. I had to beat #FakeNews, and did. We will continue to WIN!"*

On that same day, Mr. President continued, *"My use of social media is not Presidential - it's MODERN DAY PRESIDENTIAL. Make America Great Again!"* Along with his jingoistic rhetoric, Donald Trump, like so many other power-hungry leaders around the world, wants to control the media. He attempts to distort whatever truth is left and brands his lies as official doctrine. And the phrase Modern Day conjures a vision of a *"Modern Day Prophet,"* for those following along in church.

Those of us who were schooled in the trade of journalism, take the responsibility of our craft seriously. The Fourth Estate is usually reserved for the printed press and credible broadcast news teams. The Fifth Estate, the newer term, stands for groupings of diverse viewpoints in contemporary society, such as bloggers and others publishing in social media other non-mainstream outlets. The people between right of center to the extreme Alt-

Right use the phrase "mainstream media" as a pejorative term, whereas, the Breitbart site represents what was called in the 1950s, 'Yellow Journalism.' Look it up, kids.

The 'fourth estate' flows from the European concept of three estates of the realm: the clergy, the nobility, and the commoners. The Press was supposed to hold the three other estates to a standard by information gathering, storytelling based on truth and distribution of the facts to everyone equally. Yes, the King should be able to learn that he has no pants.

We know that Donald Trump has struck a raw exposed nerve in the disadvantaged and struggling middle class. With much of America moving away from reading the newspaper and getting their news from the internet, the line of what is credible or legit has become blurred.

The price of entry into the newspaper business in most cities is so great that even large companies attempting to bring a new paper to market have an uphill, if not impossible, climb. With the internet providing more outlets than needles on a porcupine's back there are plenty of free opinions and micro-targeted sites that can sanction what consumers think and stick anyone with the press of a button.

This tendency to interpret new evidence as confirmation of one's existing beliefs or theories even has its own term, Confirmation Bias. It is so important to be "right" that many people spend hours every day watching a news channel that corroborates their baseline beliefs. Fox News leans to the right, while MSNBC leans to the left. Those are their branding positions and, depending on who is in power, their ratings will rise or fall accordingly.

CNN, the new Trump target, understands that there are **millions of people who don't like Trump** and his low approval ratings can be exploited for a larger audience. The sad part is that I haven't mentioned journalistic integrity or award-winning writing. Those are less important in this instant gratification world. Reporting Trump news produces ratings on both sides, those outlets that support him and the others that do not.

THE LATE SHOW with STEPHEN COLBERT on CBS-TV *has increased ratings almost 30%* according to TV News Desk (July 6, 2017), and you can easily correlate this growth with Colbert's direct aim at Trump. The Donald, whether he likes it or not, is easy to parody because of what he says and how his administration attempts to govern. Writing jokes and monologues about Trump has a built-in benefit. If you manage to get under his thin skin he mentions you or if he attacks you, all the better, your ratings will rise even higher.

I may be in the minority but I think the "news" that the President maligns is less news than fake. Yes, they are hardly ever fake, but they don't get straight A's in journalism. When our great Orange Leader is confronted with anything that makes fun of him, or puts him down, or (can I say this?) bullies him, he launches into an overly emotional rebuttal.

True investigative journalism is taking place in our newspapers. Think about it, every major break or leak has come from the newspapers. The Michael Flynn lies came from the newspapers. The Comey meetings with Trump came from the newspapers. And the ethics conflicts of Kushner and the Trumps all came from the print media.

The TV journalists at CNN are hampered by the burden of trying fit real journalism into a small box of endless talking heads and opinionated "experts" who, at times, do more harm than good. Stop and think about it, do we need Rick Santorum giving his opinion on what the news means? He's a failed neo-conservative right-winged politician, spewing nothing but RNC talking points. What about Sean Hannity? Well, he couldn't write a lead to a story to save his life. Then, of course, we know what happened to poor Brian Williams. These are the people most Americans would say represent the "news" business.? Really?

The one investigative reporter I want to hear from isn't a journalist at all. His name is Robert Mueller. I would like to hear his story, in fact, now that would be BREAKING NEWS!

77. SERIOUS TRUMP - GOOFY DONALD
Can We Have the Serious One?
Posted: 7-10-2017

Ruth Marcus of the Washington Post was on Meet the Press this week (July 9, 2017) using the term *"Teleprompter Trump."* She was describing our president who sometimes reads someone else's words when speaking in public and gets better grades for being presidential than the man known as *"Twitter Trump."*

May I also suggest there is a third person inside the human Cheeto? How about the *"Impromptu Trump?"* This persona appears when Trump goes on camera to make a point that everyone else in his administration has been making for the previous 24-hours, except he says something completely different than they did!

With our multi-personality president, we must divert the different streams of verbiage into the appropriate buckets. When POTUS spoke in Poland, we heard from *Teleprompter Trump.*

In that speech Trump said, *"We urge Russia to cease its destabilizing activities in Ukraine and elsewhere and its support for hostile regimes including Syria and Iran, and to instead join the community of responsible nations in our fight against common enemies and the defense of civilization itself."*

We live in a sound-bite/headline word. Out of the speech in Warsaw came the line questioning the west's will to survive, while a warning to Russia was buried in the rest of the lecture. The speech was a few days before Trump and Tillerson met with Putin and Russian Ambassador Kislyak. Right after that meeting, Kislyak produced more controversy with his statements.

Kislyak and Putin claimed in their press briefings at the G20 conference that, indeed, Trump brought up cyber meddling in the US election. They also said that Trump had accepted Putin's denial. Trump left town before doing a press briefing, therefore the story got out in front of him.

The administration thought Trump's tweet would soften the astonishment of those who thought he left the Russians off the hook. Trump wrote, *"Putin & I discussed forming an impenetrable Cyber Security unit so that election hacking, & many other negative things, will be guarded."*

Donald Trump has said that it's easy to be a critic. I, for one, don't have to try very hard to muster up some serious criticism about things that *Twitter Trump* types. But really, are we going to get together with the fox and talk about security at the hen house? Will dinner be served?

As Air Force One made its way back to Washington, a story broke in the New York Times reporting that Donald, Jr., Jared Kushner and Paul Manafort met with a Russian lawyer who offered "information" on Hillary Clinton. This meeting occurred right after the Donald won the Republican nomination in 2016.

As the weekend progressed, more and more "adjustments" were made to the story. Finally, we received the official word that, yes, the meeting took place, but the nominee, Donald Trump, was not at the meeting and knew nothing about it. Kushner and Manafort were working for the campaign at that time.

While the super hawks of the Senate, Lyndsey Graham and John McCain, were on the Sunday talk shows making fun of the suggestion of a cyber security unit with Russia, it wasn't long before our great Orange Leader was taking back his own words on Twitter, *"The fact that President Putin and I discussed a Cyber Security unit doesn't mean I think it can happen. It can't-but a ceasefire can, & did!"* (July 9, 2017) Unbelievable.

Now what would *Teleprompter Trump* say about this? We hardly ever get to see *Impromptu Trump,* so we probably won't be able to confront that personality on this issue, but, for sure, if Donald J. Trump was in front of cameras and asked about this he would start to defend himself and then make a quick turn to talk about the ceasefire that is taking place in small zones in

Syria, not the whole country. But then, *Twitter Trump* drives the narrative and thus action plan of this White House.

May I point out that what was once known as Multiple Personality Disorder is now called Dissociative Identity Disorder? It's a condition under which a person's mind is fragmented into two or more distinct personality states. It's said that people with this rare condition were often victims of severe abuse. Maybe the metal in the silver-spoon in Donald's mouth leeched into his tiny brain when he was young. Dissociative Identity Disorder is D.I.D., as in "Did I say that?"

Those who lie and exaggerate are often forced to retract, restate and reform the things they said. With Trump's tribe of surrogates on-call to course-correct our President's words, one could honestly ask whether Donald Trump has any talent for clarity. In fact, he continuously and clearly steps on his own proclamations. How can this be good for America?

Trump can restate his mantra of *"No Connection, No Collusion"* all he wants, but the intent of getting information on Clinton was the reason for the meeting with the Russian lawyer. Don, Jr. threw himself under the bus to protect the old man and now we have proof of a desire for dirt, thus a first step toward collusion.

Donald Trump should think about negotiating a cease-fire with the free press by giving them some real facts. Slowly, the conflict between *Teleprompter Trump, Twitter Trump* and *Impromptu Trump* will continue to plague this administration's ability to create a positive presidential presence for most Americans; you know, the Popular Vote.

Editor's Note: We borrowed the "Cheeto" moniker from SLIPKNOT and STONE SOUR singer Corey Taylor in his book: "America 51: A Probe Into The Realities That Are Hiding Inside 'The Greatest Country In The World'"

78. RUSSIA! RUSSIA! RUSSIA!
Shameful Abuse of Stupid
Posted: 7-12-2017

"The apple doesn't fall far from the tree," was my first thought when I read the emails that were sent to Donald Trump, Jr. He believed they were from a Russian government lawyer who was willing to give him dirt on the Clinton campaign. A weekend of misdirects from Don Jr. finally turned out to be his release of the emails the New York Times was citing on the affair. By the way, his release came only minutes before the Times divulged the emails. Coincidence?

Another fact that whooshed through my brain was the old P.T. Barnum line, *"There's no such thing as bad publicity."* This is true in business and, I guess, the circus, but in politics and governance that is only a semi-fact. Trump has always fed fact fragments and partial truths to the press, believing that they are stupid enough to print it. Worse, the Donald believes that citizens are gullible and unaware, and, therefore, will believe anything he says.

This news of a meeting in the Trump Tower between Don Jr., Jared Kushner and Paul Manafort, was documented in an email that the New York Times craftily obtained. This revelation was clearly bad news for the Trump White House, because they contended there was never a meeting with Russians. Well, *the cat is now out of the bag* and a conspiracy has been revealed. Even with Don Jr. protecting his Dad, this stinks like *a dead skunk on a country road.*

Maybe Donald Trump and his extended DNA believe that only children and fools tell the truth, but when you become President of the United States, you are expected to be honest. The oath that the President elect takes, says, *"I do solemnly swear that I will faithfully execute the Office of President of the United States, and will to the best of my ability, preserve, protect and defend the Constitution of the United States."*

I might be accused of being presumptuous here, but I do believe the framers were assuming that the President would always tell the truth. Right?

The defense of little Don-Don is quite fantastic. Lawyers are paid to spin, deny and deliver a positive verdict for their clients, but wait, why do they all have different attorneys? Oh my, does this mean, they are agreeing that something is there? Are they afraid of individually being in legal jeopardy? Clearly, the release of Don Jr's. own emails can be called *"transparent"* by his father but, in fact, the son of the POTUS released the missives to get out in front of the Times story. This is much like James Comey releasing his notes to the New York Times before the President claimed something different was said at their meetings.

The legal team's disguise was constructed on the basis that Don Jr didn't know who he was meeting with and the event was so insignificant that he never told his father, then the candidate for President. In fact, Jared Kushner also "forgot" to include the meeting in his security clearance form. It has been said that he amended that form which started the press inquiries into what was discussed at that meeting.

The President's plausible deniability will be based on Kushner, Manafort and Don Jr never telling him about the meeting, but is there a way to find that out? They all need to be put under oath.

The meeting with the Russian operative was thought to have some meat, thus the CC to Manafort and Kushner. All three men attended the meeting. At least Donald Jr and Jared Kushner can make sure they have their story straight, but Paul Manafort, a person who received millions of dollars from a Kremlin backed candidate in the Ukraine, surely has his own lawyer and perhaps a different recollection of the meeting.

The government could very easily "turn" Manafort and Michael Flynn against the President himself if they squeeze the vice tightly and make it clear there could be jail time. Let's see if I am reading the Logan Act correctly, *"Any citizen of the United States, wherever he may be, who, without authority of the United States, directly or indirectly commences or carries on any correspondence or intercourse with any foreign government or any officer or agent thereof, with intent to influence the measures or conduct of any foreign government or of any officer or agent thereof, in relation to any disputes or controversies with the United States, or to defeat the measures of the United States, shall be fined under this title or imprisoned not more than three years, or both."* Surely, Manafort and Flynn have discussed sanctions with the "agent thereof," the Russian government. Would protecting the President be worth three years in jail?

I know that the Trump Teams will defend this "little" twenty-minute meeting by saying nothing of value was exchanged. Even though the content of the emails clearly shows Don Jr's delight at the prospect of getting what they called "opposition research" from this Russian lawyer. Time will tell if that was the only meeting, or were there a series of other meetings or communications? Indeed, the "so-called" research ended up at the doorsteps of Wikileaks and was published, so we do know something happened in the late summer timeline that Don Jr desired in writing.

Today (July 12, 2017) Donald Trump tweeted, *"My son Donald did a good job last night. He was open, transparent and innocent. This is the greatest Witch Hunt in political history. Sad!"* The President was referring to an appearance on the Fox News channel where he admitted to Sean Hannity, a known Trump operative, *"In retrospect, I probably would have done things a little differently."* Good boy, good boy, sit, roll over, good little Donnie. Here's a little treat, now go back to your office and shut up. So much for *"Witch Hunt"* Mr. President. You cannot escape from the truth with flashy jargon.

I find it immensely irritating when our President and all his men and women defend lies by talking about the past. It's like a child getting caught and then, responding straight from an over-grown amygdala, *"Bobby did it first Mommy."* Even Donald Trump, the father, cannot stop this repetitive invective for things, *"Why aren't the same standards placed on the Democrats? Look what Hillary Clinton may have gotten away with. Disgraceful!"*

The only change of tone was the use of the phrase *"may have gotten away with,"* which psychologists say is one typically used when threatened with the truth. It's an attempt to throw doubt on someone else. In this case, however, Trump seems to be less cavalier and a bit more legalistic with his words saying, *"may have."*

The word Russia is being said more and more each week as the forces claw their way closer to the truth. We may have to step on some "stupid" to get the facts, but we will get there eventually. And as we close in, more and more Republicans will realize that their party has been hijacked and they will surely start positioning to take it back.

Republicans are tired of hearing the chant of Russia, Russia, Russia and the American people will settle for a President Pence to put this behind us.

79. TRUMP GOT PLAYED BY PUTIN
Rookie President, Rookie Mistakes
Posted: 7-13-2017

We are starting to see things the way they really are. The President of the United States, Donald J. Trump, has a way of throwing things to the side with short little bursts of belligerence and denials. Trump is not an experienced politician. He's a decent marketer and silly entertainer but, like many famous people, he lacks basic common sense on many levels.

When he recently (July 12, 2017) recorded an interview with televangelist Pat Robertson, Trump talked about his *"very great"* meeting with Vladimir Putin. Trump said claims that Russia wanted to help him win the election is an illogical conclusion. Really?

The Donald said that Putin would have been happier with Hillary Clinton in the White House. He bases this opinion on the Trump administration's buildup of the military and attempts to become a player in exporting energy. He speculated that *"competition"* with Russia makes Putin uneasy and Hillary would not have taken such steps

The more we hear from this president, the more we realize that he has no fib filter. How can we possibly believe Trump's words about his meeting with Putin? Did they discuss sanctions? We don't know. Did they talk about what could happen in Syria if Assad is dethroned? We don't know. There is no transparency with our beloved Mr. Trump.

Experts warned Trump that Putin would deny any wrong doing in the 2016 US election. They also said that Putin would agree with Trump about cyber-security being a major issue and would they create a joint task force to work on the problem together. Our great Orange Leader fell for that hook, line and sinker. He proudly announced it, until he heard loudly from thoughtful and fearless Senators that it was a colossally stupid idea. Then, he retreated with a tweet.

The mystery underlying this whole Russian interference fiasco is a disconnect from reality. When did evangelicals, hardworking middle-class Americans and classic Republicans decide that Russia was our friend? We don't sell Russian cars here in America. We don't back Russian aggression in eastern Europe and we certainly don't like that Russia's allies are Iran and Syria. So, in what world do these people live?

The Russian Supreme Court firmly recognizes only the Russian Orthodox Church and has banned Jehovah's Witnesses by labeling them an extremist group. They have criminalized preaching, praying and evangelization outside of registered religious sites. Why wouldn't Trump bring this issue up with Putin when he had his grand meeting? He didn't. He didn't talk about human rights at all. I guess it's a lower priority for a guy who slams journalists while talking with another guy who kills journalists.

We can now read and study the emails between Donald Trump, Jr. and what was presented as *"opposition research"* from a foreign adversary. Little Donald said, *"If it is what you say, I love it!"* and now his old man says that anyone would have taken that meeting.

While the President was defending his son, the Senate was examining Christopher Wray in a hearing for his approval as the next FBI director. The senior Senator from South Carolina, Lindsey Graham, made sure Wray knew his position on the meetings with known Russian operatives, *"You want to be director of the FBI, pal. So, here's what I want you to tell every politician: If you get a call from somebody suggesting that a foreign government wants to help you by disparaging your opponent, tell us all to call the FBI."* Graham, a Republican, was very clear what someone should do when something like this happens in the future. Was that a teachable moment or what?

Putin probably pulled the strings and suggested his people get in touch with Trump's people and, of course, the best avenue to Trump and his associates would be through a business partner. Donald Trump has lied about not having any business in Russia and he keeps that fabrication alive by doing all he can to discredit the investigation of Russia's possible manipulation of our election. In short, Donald, Sr. is acting like a guilty person and Donald Jr. is showing the world that he is an inept fool.

Some say that Don Jr's mistake was simply that of a rookie. His actions were certainly naïve and probably driven by a need to please his father. Many believe that he told his father about the meeting before or shortly after it happened. Only one Donald will have to admit that under oath. Surely, Don Jr. will take the Fifth.

It's not so much that Don Jr. was a rookie, or that Jared Kushner left the meeting early, or that Paul Manafort's experience might have been dulled by his rude cellphone addiction during the meeting, but more so that the candidate in the campaign did not properly manage the situation.

Donald Trump can't fire his son. This presents a dilemma of epic proportions to our President. He can say only that his son is innocent. Sad!

The real winner in all this is Putin. We must watch Trump carefully now. Four months after Donald Trump fired Preet Bharara, who was then Manhattan US Attorney, a money-laundering suit was settled for nearly 6 million dollars against a Russian owned Cyprus-based company. Some in the know say that the amount paid was nothing compared to what could have been retrieved in court. Did Trump and Sessions pull strings for Russia?

Trump was played by Putin and this will continually be a shadow on our president's term in office. As a player on the opposing team once said of Putin's preference for president, *"Well, that's because he'd rather have a puppet as president of the United States."*

People are asking if Don Jr. could have been that naïve. I ask, can Donald J. Trump be that stupid?

80. THE WHITE HOUSE IS NOT A FAMILY BUSINESS
Whatever Happened to Nepotism Rules?
Posted: 7-14-20176

Nepotism is a practice among those in power of favoring relatives or friends, especially by giving them jobs. The law is clear in our government and it applies to anyone hired in the executive, legislative or judicial branch: *"A public official may not appoint, employ, promote, advance, or advocate for appointment, employment, promotion, or advancement, in or to a civilian position in the agency in which he is serving or over which he exercises jurisdiction or control any individual who is a relative of the public official."*

This isn't "Fake News", it's 5 US Code § 3110 - Employment of relatives; restrictions. I don't believe that the absence of a paycheck negates this rule. It says, *"appoint to a civilian position."* The appointment alone is not allowed.

Why does Ivanka Trump, the President's daughter, have an office in the White House? Why is her husband, Jared Kushner, a top adviser and *"employee"* of the White House? They said they put their companies in a trust, although many ethics experts say that they haven't done enough. Trump, the President himself, is benefiting from money flowing from foreign governments through his properties, but the issue and violation of the Emoluments Clause, will be covered later.

Let's focus on nepotism for this article. Why is this important? Why is there a rule that prohibits this? One problem that can arise is the government advertising an opening at one of its agencies, interviewing applicants and then hiring a less qualified relative of a power broker to serve in the position. It's a shoddy business practice to hire the less qualified person.

Another possible issue can occur if someone is passed over, and then claims they didn't get the job because of something other than their talent and qualifications. That could trigger a lawsuit based on the Civil Rights Act of 1964, which, of course, bars discrimination because of race, color, sex, religion or national origin. You may not be able to prove the intent, but the embarrassment of a court battle would cost the country money and time.

A further problem can result when a senior male or female employee marries a lower ranking female or male member of the team. Who must then leave the agency? This brings about a possible legal problem of sexual discrimination. In the case of Ivanka and Jared, we don't have that problem, but we do see the complications when family members are given responsibilities.

The situation with Donald Trump, Jr. and his meeting with a Russian attorney has another negative side. It's the very real possibility that Trump will lie to protect his kids, just as easily as he lies about so many other things.

If Don Jr. was a mere employee of the campaign, like Paul Manafort, Daddy Trump would have thrown him under the bus. Parents don't usually do the right thing **with** their kids, instead they do the right thing **for** their kids. Think about what Trump Sr. said about his son, *"He's a good boy."* He's almost 40-years-old Mr. President, but you see him as a *"boy?"* And the praise for all his transparency was so father-like, while today (July 14, 2017) we learned that there were two other people in the room during the meeting. This is previously undisclosed information. What are they hiding? Wait, more than that; eight people in the room?

Experts say that nepotism causes problems or at least complications and discomfort 60% of the time. So, why are we, the people, allowing Donald Trump to instate less qualified people in positions around him without anyone charging forward and waving 5 US Code § 3110 in his face? Who checks the White House on the matter of employment?

We broke away from a King and a kingdom in 1776. Part of what the rebels here in the 13 States wanted to avoid was an unelected king operating freely and unchecked above the law. Their solution was to create a revolution and break away from the tyranny of Kings. Royalty is based on bloodlines and the children of Kings and Queens get to take over when the parent expires. Does the US now live in that world?

Why are any of Trump's kids involved in this administration? Perhaps the president needs the "blankie" of his children blindly supporting him and telling him he's right, but problems can result. Don Jr. and the exposure of his emails is one example of why there is a rule about hiring your kids. Also, one might ask, "What does Ivanka do? What is her job description?" As a tax payer, can you answer that? NEPOTISM is bad for business and worse for the United States.

I find it remarkable that seven months into this administration we hear the words, *"innocent"*, *"unethical"*, *"illegal"* and *"hoax"* more often than would be heard in a normal White House. We can only hope that the Democrats find some believable messenger between now and 2020. The king has no pants and not a lot of regard for the law.

81. PROOFLESS PRESIDENT
Poor Donald the Victim
Posted: 7-17-2017

Missouri has a great nickname, *"The Show Me State."* They say that people from Missouri have a devotion to simple, common sense. In 1899, Representative Willard D. Vandiver said, *"Frothy eloquence neither convinces nor satisfies me. I'm from Missouri."*

When Donald Trump and his father, Fred, were accused of violating the Fair Housing Act in New York in the early 1970s, the Human Rights Commission claimed that Trump rental agents had used a code on applications to note if the applicant was African-American or Hispanic so they could prevent them from renting a Trump property. The company was sued by the DOJ in 1973. The case was settled out of court and, although Trump claimed he did nothing wrong, he presented no proof of his innocence.

He then created the Trump Foundation which, according to public records, has raised 9.3 million dollars from outside sources. For what it's worth, Trump hasn't put any money into the Foundation since 2008. The organization never registered the charity with the state of New York. Vince and Linda McMahon, the wrestling people, gave the Foundation a bunch of money, and now Linda runs the Small Business Administration, a political appointment. Was that a long-term pay-to-play scenario?

It has been alleged that Trump diverted taxable incomes, both personal and business, into the Foundation by urging people who owed him money to pay it back directly into the foundation. Without tax returns from Donald J. Trump, we cannot disprove that the Foundation was laundering money. Again, no proof of innocence.

According to the very well-written book, *The Case for Impeachment* by Allan J. Lichtman, Donald Trump and his organization broke laws by trying to place a casino in Cuba when there was a total embargo on that country. They spent $68,000 in Cuba to explore investment opportunities. The embargo disallowed money to be spent in Cuba. Was Trump changing the rules on travel to Cuba meant to hurt the Marriott corporation's current efforts to build hotels there? Again, no proof of innocence.

Lichtman also points out that *"Trump was fined $200,000 by New Jersey regulators for removing African-American and female employees from the crap tables at the request of a high roller."* Again, no proof of innocence.

We all know about Trump University turned out to be a scam to defraud hopeful students out of their hard-earned money for nothing of real value or opportunities in real estate. Trump claimed no wrongdoing, but settled out of court. Again, no proof of innocence.

Trump building projects have exploited undocumented workers. Look no further than the Polish undocumented laborers who were employed on the demolition project for the buildings removed to construct Trump Tower. According to Time magazine: *"The men were putting in 12-hour shifts with inadequate safety equipment at subpar wages that their contractor paid sporadically, if at all. A lawyer for many of the Poles demanded that the workers be paid or else he would serve Trump with a lien on the property. One Polish worker even went to Trump's office to ask him for money in person, according to sworn testimony and a deposition filed under oath in a court case."* Again, no proof of innocence.

For years Donald J. Trump claimed that President Barack Obama was not born in America and he began a crusade to delegitimize the 44th President. Trump asserted that he hired investigators who went to Hawaii and then had the audacity to call it victory when Obama finally released a copy of his birth certificate. Trump never apologized for his unproven farce, but his statement on the issue had no empathy or comprehension of the damage his charges caused. He simply said, *"President Barack Obama was born in the United States. Period."* Again, no proof of innocence.

This brings us to his biggest cover-up of all. His public denials that no one in his administration met with any Russians during his campaign or transition to the presidency. He lied, or if you want to give him the benefit of the doubt, he had no idea what his comrades were doing while he wasn't in the room. Really? I thought he was on top of everything.

He keeps tweeting that this *"Russia-Trump story"* is a *"hoax"* and he uses language like, *"With all of its phony unnamed sources & highly slanted & even fraudulent reporting, #Fake News is DISTORTING DEMOCRACY in our country!"* (July 16, 2017)

When reading the Don Jr. emails, I keep asking myself, did they make this up? It's so revealing and stupid that it feels like "FAKE NEWS," but it's not and this proves that Donald Trump is not the victim here. If Jared Kushner didn't tell candidate Trump about that meeting, he should be fired. Again, no proof of innocence.

There is not much "frothy eloquence" from those in power right now, but they need to step up and show us something. They must prove they had nothing to do with the possible desecration of our election process. Hey, Trump, the longer you wait to explain what really happened the more your lies collide with each other in the ether of history. So far, I have seen no proof of your innocence.

82. MADE IN AMERICA
Fair Trade vs. Free Trade
Posted: 7-18-2017

One of the things you can say about Donald J. Trump is that he's consistent, but he's hardly ever right. For example, he thinks he knows a lot about money. The logic runs something like this, *"I made a billion dollars, so I know how to fix things."*

It would be different if the stock market wasn't at an all-time high. It would be different if the unemployment rate was in the toilet. But as the administration rolled out fire trucks and back hoes on the front lawn of the White House to promote their America First dogma, the headline in the Washington Post was: *"Trump's 'Made in America' week is a hypocritical joke."*

None of Donald and Ivanka Trump products are made in America. Ivanka's shoes, handbags, blouses, dresses, jeans and shirts are made in Bangladesh, Indonesia, Vietnam and China. Donald's ties and suits are made in China, Bangladesh and Mexico. When confronted with this fact, the two moguls say, *"Everybody else does it."* Really?

Why does the press keep slapping this man? It seems like everything our President touches turns into a controversy at least and a bag of flaming crap at worst. Our very own Don "Quixote" Trump is not only fighting windmills, he is attempting to stop Niagara Falls with his bare hands. Our brave hero.

The aftermath of the World Wars is a lesson that escapes Donald Trump. The first war led the losers to disastrous economic plights which turned people inward and paved the way for them to place people like Hitler and Mussolini into high offices.

The nations of victors in WWII knew that they had to help the economies of many countries to ensure a lasting peace. The United States made Japan a special project. We airlifted in experts and technologies to teach the Japanese how to make many products.

The hard-working Japanese culture, and South Korean's post conflict manufacturing, produced some of the finest electronics for the world, and still do. The Donald was busy being rich in the 1950s and doesn't remember how America was flooded with cheap products, like transistor radios, that were labeled *Made in Japan.*

As more and more American companies realized that they could get cheap parts for their products, the floodgates opened. Our automotive industry needed more and more computer technologies, thus the need to import more parts from other countries. We also created giant discount box-stores that sold everything from TVs to T-Shirts at rock bottom prices. Why did we do this? We bought products from other countries that had a cost advantage because were made by low wage workers.

While the United States began to see that our workers and factories here were being phased out, we had a belief we could move those workforces to other industries. That happened only when a worker saw the writing on the wall early and either had or acquired the skills needed in another field.

Training was essential to complete the migration from the agricultural age to the manufacturing age. Did we forget about this? Logic follows that it would take the re-education of millions of workers to pull off the job migration. Some people just didn't want to change.

Now, our great Orange Leader wants to brand all our products with "Made in America." I get that, but it's just a Band-Aid. Incidentally, the Band-Aid was invented in 1920 by Thomas Anderson and Johnson & Johnson employee Earle Dickson in Highland Park, New Jersey. Not all bandages are made in America, but they are a great example of an American invention that the world now uses. There are countless other examples. We design things well but we cannot make them at reasonable prices because Americans demand a fair wage to match our prosperous economy. It's a double-edged sword.

When the North American Free-Trade Agreement (NAFTA) was signed, products moved from Canada and Mexico into the US without tariff. We also sold tons of stuff to those two countries.

According to the United States of America Trade Representative (an office of the President): "The US goods and services trade deficit with Mexico was $55.6 billion in 2016. Mexico is currently our 3rd largest goods trading partner with $525.1 billion in total (two way) goods trade during 2016. Goods exports totaled $231.0 billion; goods imports totaled $294.2 billion."

Their figures on Canada are similar: US goods and services trade with Canada totaled an estimated $627.8 billion in 2016. Exports were $320.1 billion; imports were $307.6 billion. The US goods and services trade surplus with Canada was $12.5 billion in 2016. Canada is currently our second largest goods trading partner with $544.0 billion in total (two way) goods trade during 2016.

As you can see, this cry-baby tantrum about "fair trade" is foolish rhetoric by the President considering the benefits of NAFTA. It's a different question with respect to China and other Pacific Rim countries, but best not to ask it too loudly. With the amount of US debt that Chinese banks hold, and our need for China to control North Korea, we might want to carefully plan what we say. It would be best not to Tweet.

Why does Trump keep complaining about trade? He skillfully convinced those workers who have been displaced by global trade to vote for him. He must keep them in the hypnotic trance under which he promises to magically carry them back to a "better time."

The mantra of *"Jobs, Jobs, Jobs"* means something only if the great one can create them. Focusing on coal mining is convoluted logic. Coal has been displaced by natural gas and, the good news, the US pumps lots of that resource. The symbolism might be rich, but Trump is regressive in his thinking. Why did China just take the lead on producing solar energy products? Did we miss that?

Trump believes that eliminating regulations will magically grow plants and jobs. Rules don't keep people from being successful, global markets do.

Even if we got rid of every regulation, we would still have to produce steel at a price that competes.

"Globals" will always be able to make things cheaper and while we could tax the imports that would increase the price here. Why make the America consumer pay for Trump's trade myopia?

What Agent Orange doesn't understand is that he's a President for 1959, not a president for 2017. It's too late to stop the windmills of the world from turning. If they don't sell to America, they will sell to someone else. The water will keep coming over the falls, because that is how nature works.

Trump's one man fight against globalization might make him look like Captain America, but he's just another American businessman taking advantage of Free Trade for his own benefit. Buy one of his ties and see where it was made.

83. OBAMACARE vs. TRUMPCARE
Trump Alone Can Fix It, Except Healthcare
Posted: 7-19-2017

Well, here we are again. The Democrats gave the country the gift of healthcare and, like an addict, we do not want the Republicans to take it away. After seven-years of complaining about Obamacare, the elephants in the room forgot to author an alternative bill. No one was working on a rewrite of the plan?

The blame sits in the lap of the 45th President of the United States. Donald Trump has brought nothing to the debate and his actions are embarrassingly superficial and valueless. His language about how the plan will be *"beautiful"* and *"really great"* are terms he could have used for one of his beauty pageant contestants. His lack of understanding of healthcare was exposed when he admitted that it was *"complicated."*

If all those great and *"really smart"* people that Trump brought into his cabinet and administration were truly intelligent and great, they would have revised the 906-page Affordable Healthcare Act and made it a better law

As we watch this drama and dysfunctional relationship between Congress and the White House play out, we learn how little influence Donald Trump has on the process. The Congress must stand behind their work while getting an earful from their constituents when they hold town meetings. Some say that people are being bused in from outside of their districts to lodge these protests, but we are talking about a national bill, right? Why would it matter where the people came from if they are against a healthcare act that will affect all Americans?

This healthcare episode has vividly exposed the great divide between Republicans. We hear little about those snarly Tea Party people, but they are still around and they are against anything the government might do that has any hint of helping people. We are also seeing the imaginary line between "normal"

GOP members and the neo-conservatives. I use the 'neo' prefix is because they aren't old line conservatives like Ronald Reagan, who never walked away from a tax increase that could fix a problem. These new conservatives, like Rand Paul, seem to have some deep-seated reason to not like a good idea. Might Rand be a plant in the Senate for doctors?

Trump should be listening to the CBO scores because the organizations and lobbyists that are paid to protect groups like kids and retired people use the data to send emails to millions of people.

Scare headlines like: "Pregnancy to cost 425% more under Donald Trump's health plan compared to Obamacare," are being splashed on the front pages of newspapers all over the world. Why? Because most other countries have a single-payer system and they find Trump's battle with healthcare to be rather humorous. See, they have already solved that problem.

The Donald has once again showed his lack of understanding about how government works and how Congress moves like a turtle. If he was wiser he would have gone right into rebuilding US infrastructure, moving forward with a plan that would have helped commerce in our country. Most products move on rail, road or runway and if they are in disrepair the economy suffers. Healthcare, in its present state, keeps people at work and that helps the country. Why kill it?

How can the President of the United States sit by and let this happen? It's as if he is powerless and has no ability to fix what is there now. Perhaps he simply doesn't care. His words, *"Let Obamacare fail. It'll be a lot easier, and I think we're probably in that position where we'll just let Obamacare fail. We're not going to own it. I'm not going to own it. I can tell you the Republicans are not going to own it."*

Once again, it's blame the other guy and let the people suffer. The atrophy of this so-called leader is demoralizing.

This morning (July 18, 2017), USA Today ran a story asking if Trump will exercise: *"He's 71, holds down an incredibly stressful job, and is overweight. He doesn't exercise. His eating habits are less than ideal. And to top it off, he doesn't get enough sleep."*

The good news for Trump is that he doesn't smoke cigarettes or drink alcohol. But after rolling back nutritional standards on school lunches he's guilty of being part of the healthcare problem in more ways than one.

The anxiety and stress that Donald is feeling in his new job is the probably like the stress he has created for undocumented immigrants and citizens with pre-existing health conditions. Clearly, Donald J. Trump is bad for the health of America. Wait until we discover more lead in the drinking water somewhere in America. In short, Trump hasn't fixed healthcare for America, he's made it worse.

84. HEROES & VILLIANS
The Undisclosed Trump
Posted: 7-20-2017

Robert Mueller has a lot of work to do. The press is drilling to find their "deep throat." The drip, drip, drip of facts surrounding the presidency keep leading to more questions. We know that there is, indeed, a connection between the campaign and Russia, but we still don't have the complete story.

What Congress must do is pass a law that says anyone running for President, and every President in office, must disclose all their financial entanglements. The financial position and high international business profile of Donald Trump is unprecedented in the history of the US Presidency. Is it even possible that anyone with such ongoing enterprises would be free of conflicts of interest? We might be able to know if the tradition of releasing tax returns would become codified by a law.

Lawyers can argue that the President is above the normal conflicts rules, litigations and laws because we wouldn't want his every judgement to end up in the court. While that would be extremely distracting, we must hold the man in the White House to ethical standards. If not, then we need to rewrite the laws to make him or her more transparent than private companies or sole proprietors. The president's position is not a limited liability corporation. He's the leader of our country and we deserve to know his debtors and cash flow.

Donald Trump has pulled another con by saying that his sons will run his businesses, without a firm trust or sell off. He brought his daughter, who still has her own company, into the White House along with his son-in-law. Why? Was it so he could control them or protect them? Under this unique arrangement both Ivanka and Jared should release their complete income tax returns and financial entanglements as well.

I wouldn't be asking for this kind of information to be made public if I really trusted Trump. The President of the United States has said things on twitter, in public and in his proclamations and executive orders that beg the question, why did he say that? Why can't our great Orange Leader simply release all the material that proves that he was born in America, ah, I mean, that he has no connections to Russia.

Mr. President says that the, *"Russia thing with Trump is a hoax"* and *"This is the greatest Witch Hunt in political history."* Really? Why would this be "FAKE NEWS" when his own son put it on the front page by releasing his emails?

The Donald cannot get out in front of this story because he keeps throwing more wood on the fire. If he wants it to go away he should stop talking about it. Maybe Trump has a blood clot in his brain. That could explain his misuse of the bully pulpit. The truth is he's not getting anything done

We should be able to see the President's medical records for the safety of this country. For someone so important, we have a right to know if he is hiding any deep and dark medical secrets that could affect the way he governs. It's only fair that Americans understand as much as they can about the person holding their trust. And, of course, if he has some creeping disorder or disease, like Ronald Reagan endured, then we the people have a legal path to replace him: Section 4 of the 25th Admendment.

We know the amazing military record of a real American hero, John McCain. All his records are out there to see. Trump should release his medical records so we can understand what kept him out of military service.

Donald Trump never talks about his mother. This bothers me greatly. I have never respected a person who seems to have no connection to the lady that brought him to the dance. I wonder what this means? He should disclose his life experiences that gave him such distorted views of his wealth, his fame and his ego. He keeps too many secrets, which make him *"unpredictable."* Do we really want a fickle leader? If he made a capricious move with some of the bad guys in the world, he could get us into a war.

Donald Trump worships money. He has proven he will lie, cheat and steal to get more of it. He will sue his way out of any situation that damages his weak self-esteem. He will attack people, even if they are innocent, with all the fury of a madman. He is just what many say he is, unhinged.

Most people agree on one point, he is not forthcoming. He thinks that secrets have value and, maybe so, but there is a cost for keeping them.

TRUTH; the American people deserve honesty, openness and transparency from its President. The art of the lie might be making some people laugh, but for most citizens in the country Trump's lack of candor is slowing eroding trust, even within his base. People are now understanding that this President lies. Perhaps they feel okay with their guns and bibles right now, but in the end, they will be screwed just like the sub-contractors of a Trump building. Those who voted for Trump will come to the realization soon that Donald J. Trump is not Making America Great.

85. RATS LEAVING THE SHIP
Trump's Creeping Corruption
Posted: 7-21-2017

When Donald Trump ran for President he promised us he would *"drain the swamp,"* which was a terrific marketing slogan. Part of the 10-square miles that make up Washington, DC was built on swampland, so the language was colorful and meaningful. What Donald didn't expect was that once the water was gone he would face lots of angry alligators ready to take him down.

A Washington newcomer cannot quickly or easily push aside all the institutions, customs and traditions of our country. I've never thought of Donald Trump as anybody but a third-rate entertainer who is addicted to the roar of the crowd and the smell of the grease paint, or is that orange makeup? He takes nothing seriously until he doesn't get what he wants. Then he uses the claws of lawyers and influencers and pouts like a little spoiled brat.

As the clock ticks, we learn more and more about Donald Trump and his associates. Today (July 21, 2017) it was disclosed that Exxon Mobil violated sanctions by doing business with Russia. The company, which at the time had Rex Tillerson as its CEO, was fined 2 million dollars for this infraction. Immediately, Exxon Mobil announced that they would sue Steven Mnuchin and the Treasury Department, which Mnuchin heads. How can this be happening? During Tillerson's confirmation hearing he was asked about this. So much for extreme vetting. Under any other administration, the now Secretary of State would be asked to step down during this lawsuit. How can he testify against the very government that employs him?

Ties with Russia seem to be woven into Trump's words, actions and deeds. We have stopped sending arms to the rebels in Syria, which is what Putin wants us to do.

If the United States returns those two seized properties that were allegedly used for Russian intelligence, we will see that Trump truly is Putin's puppet. We were warned this would happen.

If Trump deletes the Magnitsky Act, which puts sanctions on Russia for Human Rights violations, it will be one more give-away to Putin by Trump.

The lack of transparency about Russia seems more like creeping corruption than good diplomacy. The first thing I would ask Trump is this. What are we getting out of it, Mr. Big-Shot-Dealmaker?

When Trump rambled on in his New York Times interview (July 20, 2017), he seemed to warn the Special Counsel that his companies, his family's and his own private finances were off-limits. The accused doesn't get to block the vision of the investigators seeking the truth.

Now we learn that Robert Mueller has sent a letter to the White House saying they must preserve all the documents, text messages, voice mails and correspondence pertaining to the 2016 meeting with Don, Jr., et. al. and Russians. The plot thickens.

And if Friday wasn't hot enough outside, inside the administration just got hotter. Sean Spicer, the White House press secretary, resigned. He told President Trump he vehemently disagreed with the appointment of New York financier Anthony Scaramucci to the position of Communications Director. Will we see more rats leaving the ship?

Whether true or not, it has been leaked, probably by Trump himself, that his team of lawyers are discussing how Presidential pardons work. Aren't they putting the cart in front of the horse? You don't talk about how to get out of jail before you are caught doing the crime.

Our great Orange Leader failed to understand the old yarn about not hanging out your dirty laundry when he disparaged his Attorney General in the interview with the Times. He is circling his wagons with more loyalists. Trump reciprocating that loyalty, however, is one royal LIE!

The routine has been heard before from the Donald. If a legal mind, or someone in the judiciary, decides against our 14-year-old leader, he wars against judges with his words. He is not fit to be President and something must be done.

The creeping corruption is slowing working its way to the very man who could end it all, just by telling the truth. Those who stay by his side will be dragged into this mess. Time to be a patriot and get away from this madman. Absolute corruption, corrupts absolutely.

86. "I LOVE THE PRESIDENT"
Respect is Not Enough for Trump
Posted: 7-24-2017

400 years before the birth of Jesus Christ, the Greek physician Hippocrates, incorporated four temperaments into his early practice: sanguine (enthusiastic, active, and social), choleric (short-tempered, fast, or irritable), melancholic (analytical, wise, and quiet), and phlegmatic (relaxed and peaceful). Of course, no one person stays in one zone all the time. We each have mixtures of these temperaments at any given time.

Our current president, seems to live in the sanguine and choleric areas much of the time. To stay on his team, one must broadcast their open "love" for him. With the appointment of Anthony Scaramucci to Communications Director, we learned his modus operandi early by witnessing the praise and proclamations of love lavished on his new boss.

Mr. Scaramucci has obviously consumed the whole jug of Kool-Aid and will be framing the argument for and massaging the defense of Trump with the skill of a Wall Street tycoon, which is what he is. But that doesn't change anything. Trump is still the President and his short-tempered, fast and irritating way of overreacting cannot be polished by a slick, well-dressed pitchman. Donald Trump is a high-risk investment.

The enthusiastic, active and highly social (sanguine) Trump is hardly ever positive. Our great Orange Leader uses rants and disrespect to intimidate his critics, while attempting to extort more love from his base. He's like an abusive parent giving a treat after the beating. He fronts each topic with how bad things are to make himself seem the savior.

Being loved should not be more important than facts, truth, honesty or transparency. Saying that his son's extremely incriminating email release was being transparent lacks logic, credibility and honesty. Does he love his son more than he says he loves America? Would he lie for his son?

Scaramucci might think he can turn the gray battleship around, but he's just a summer replacement player in the reality show known as the Donald J. Trump Presidency. Even Anthony S. said the President is 71-years-old and, *"You are not going to change him."* Perhaps, if we think a bit Freudian here, could Anthony Scaramucci be the kind of son the Donald wish he had? He obviously likes Jared Kushner like a son. Maybe his kids, other than Ivanka, aren't quite enough like him?

The new Communications Director, Slick Anthony, used the term *"mainstream media,"* which is code for anything negative about the president reported by any news outlet. They boxed up negative press as *"mainstream"* and are attempting to redefine it as *"Fake."*

Fox News, a major ratings mass media channel, isn't considered mainstream because they usually agree with Trump. Why is that? Please tell me the true definition of *"mainstream,"* and then explain to me how a website with a few million readers is more important than any mass media outlet.

Truth has a way of rising and breaking the layer of scum on the surface of the swamp. If the mainstream media is trying to convince the 32% of America that Donald Trump was a bad choice, they are wasting their time.

Trump may control the Supreme Court picks while he is in power, but he should be very careful about who he pardons or even thinks about awarding a get-out-of-jail card. That roll of the dice could be as bad as Trump's monumental failure at the Taj Mahal in Atlantic City. When the Republicans finally admit that Trump is politically bankrupt, they will prepare his impeachment to save their own jobs.

One would think the Supreme Court should have a duty to block an aggressive attempt to remodel executive power. Any move that would force

America into a constitutional crisis would verify to the other 68% of America that Donald Trump is not an honest human being. Trump will never win over those people.

The analytical, wise, and quiet people who toil every day to make the government work for all the people are still there. They are in the Justice Department, they file into the Treasury, they sit on the Supreme Court and some are even in Congress. They want to do their job and keep the machine running.

The silliness and departures from normal protocols show the world only one man's view about how things should be. There is no proof that what Trump is doing is good for America.

We never want a president to tell us what to believe. We never want a President to "explain" how things are as if they, and only they, know the truth. We expect him or her to listen to us and then make rational decisions that will benefit as many people as possible. Donald Trump wants everyone to love him, but doesn't understand that he must give love to get love.

When the man with the most power in the United States of America can be provoked by the least little criticism, we should worry. When the man who will be the President's voice says he loves the man more than a half-a-dozen times in his first press briefing, he shows us how things work with the Great Orange One.

He shows us why Putin is more important than protecting America from cyber-attacks from Russia. We saw Macron in France use the love offensive to charm his way right into Trump's small hands. I don't want to love the president; I want to respect him.

If someone says Trump is not always 100% right, they become the enemy and Trump automatically aligns against them. To all those people during the campaign who said that the Donald did not have the temperament to be president, you were right. He is 90% choleric (short-tempered, fast, or irritable) and that is why we judge all that he does through a negative lens. No one can trust what he says. Just ask the Carrier workers in Indiana.

Scaramucci's "new guy" enthusiasm is a nice change, but when he says, *"The American people love this guy"* I must stop him there. Anthony, you need to do some research. More than 50% of American's do not like this "guy;" your buddy. You need more than 50% to get a bill passed in Congress and we certainly ought to have a president who garners more respect and positive feedback than 32% of our citizens. Scaramucci's job is to make more Americans favor and support the President. Good luck, Anthony.

The standard comeback by the 1600 Pennsylvania Avenue talking heads when asked about low approval presidential ratings is that the President has higher ratings than the media or Congress. And they're bragging about that?

I'm looking forward to a relaxed and peaceful time when we aren't screaming at each other and the President of the United States has more than 50% approval rating and that his plans actually work. Right now, we have the wrong plans, the wrong message and the wrong president.

We must ask, *"What has gotten better?"* Insurance rates are sky-high, wages are NOT moving up fast enough and taxes are the same. The big infrastructure plan is frozen. For a guy who said we would be winning really, really fast, we are waiting, and waiting. Go for accomplishments Mr. President, not love.

87. DONALD J AND JARED
Trump's Circle of Trust
Posted: 7-25-2017

There is something not quite right about the relationship that President Donald Trump has with his family and his work. He cannot separate the two. While the mingling of business and family might be common in some royal families, in America it's viewed with skepticism.

There are those who didn't like John Kennedy appointing his brother, Robert, to Attorney General. And Harry Truman gave his wife, Bess, a job in the White House. She rose to Chairman of the Senate Special Committee to Investigate the National Defense Program, a position that gave her a paycheck but, according to biographers, not a position in which she actively participated.

Now, we have the President's son-in-law in a role of intense involvement and power, Senior Advisory to the President. There was stretch when Donald Trump was assigning young Jared a new job every other day, from bringing peace in the middle east to reorganizing the government to fixing the judicial system. Really?

Let's remember that Jared's blast into taking over the Kushner family business started when his father went to jail. And the person who helped put Charles Kushner behind bars was Chris Christie. You know the one who got passed over by the Donald.

Jared was forced into running the family's affairs at the age of 26 while his father was in federal prison convicted of illegal campaign contributions, tax evasion, and witness tampering.

I have just read the full six-pages of Jared Kushner's statement to the Congressional Committee. This well-written document seems rather honest and direct. He's 36 years old, but he seems to be traveling in a space way over his head. He forgets people, he doesn't recall meetings, and, worst of all, he didn't read all the email messages that Don Jr. sent him. Jared, you must learn to read from the bottom up. This is a problem with top-down rich kids. And come on, how could you forget the name of the Russian Ambassador to the US?

Jared doesn't remember meetings but clearly remembers getting an email from Guccifer400, huh? Then he admits asking the Russian Ambassador if there was an, *"existing communications channel at his (Russian) embassy"* and mere sentences later, says, *"I did not suggest a 'secret back channel.'"* He needs to get his own story straight.

His last paragraph raised some eyebrows, *"I have not relied on Russian funds to finance my business activities in the private sector."* This is one of those sentences written by a skilled attorney. *"I have not relied…"* doesn't mean, I have no Russian investors in my properties. It could simply mean *"I received financing but didn't rely on it"* In fact, many Russian investors have bought or rented space in Trump and Kushner properties. They are customers.

Mr. Kushner needs to be placed under oath and questioned about the meeting with the banker on December 13, 2016. The bank is a state-owned property and the banker, Sergey Gorkov, gave Jared presents from his grandparents' home in Belarus. Wait, the Kushners are from Belarus? Is that the same Belarus that was once part of Russia and became a founding member of the Union of Soviet Socialist Republics in 1922. Oh boy, this story can't get any richer.

So, Jared's grand parents came from a Soviet bloc country and Donald Trump's grand parents came from Germany. They are both second-generation immigrants. Of course, sons of different mothers, but this certainly makes the Trump anti-immigrant stance paradoxical.

Back to the President's son-in-law, why does Trump need his daughter and Jared in the White House? What amount of insecurity must we, the American public, endure with Trump? We need him to make clear, objective decisions. The advice of family members can be tainted if they are more eager to please rather than providing truthful feedback. Ivanka could go on every

Climate Change march and wear a skin-tight-fitting T-shirt that screamed Save the Planet and her father would ignore any action to help accomplish a better environment. How is she helping?

Jared, with his liberal views and democratic ways, is simply a "yes man" and the "doer" while the Donald can jet around and scream to crazy-cult crowds of supporters. We know that Jared has contributed zero to the healthcare bill. As he said in his statement to the Congressional Committee, he's so busy with thousands of emails, he doesn't have time to read them all. He's so busy, he doesn't have time to do his job.

I almost laughed at the explanation about why the SF-86 had to be amended so many times. Jared Kushner's excuse sounds like one of those *'dog ate my homework'* stories that so many parents and teachers have heard. Okay, you messed up kid, your assistant submitted a rough draft to the FBI. Wow, sure glad it wasn't some important document.

All of this vividly reveals that Donald J. Trump and his associates are unaware of the laws of governance and uninterested in proper documentation. They are flying by the seat of their pants, and those pants aren't even made in America.

In the movie *Meet the Parents*, Robert De Niro's character, Jack Byrnes, introduces Ben Stiller's persona, Greg Focker, to what Jack calls the *"Byrnes Circle of Trust."* There's this dialog: *"See if I can't trust you Greg, then I have no choice but to put you outside the circle. Once you're out, you're out. There's no coming back."*

The difference between Trump and Jack Byrnes is when Trump sends someone away that he has endorsed in the past, he doesn't send them out of the circle. He cannot admit he was wrong. He still speaks well of Michael Flynn, a person who could bring the Donald's presidency to its knees. He says nice things about Sean Spicer. And maybe that is why he uses his family members as tools. Poor Don Jr. is a *"good kid."*

It's easier to be loyal to your family members than to those outside the circle of trust. Everyone will give Trump a pass on sticking up for his kids, but it's getting harder to believe that Trump can shovel the same hackneyed phrases and conspiracy theories to the entire country without someone asking a couple of questions. Why do we want to be friends with Russia? Why is being friends with them so important to Trump and Jared? Are we worried more about protecting Belarus than the Ukrainian people from Russia? Hey, just asking.

88. THE AMERICAN ASSHOLE
No Leading, Just Tweeting
Posted: 7-25-2017

While Russia may be arming the Taliban in Afghanistan, our President sits on the toilet blasting tweets about what appears to be his main problem, the Attorney General? While most liberals have few common points with the 'law and order' appointed cabinet member, the public flogging of Jefferson B. Sessions III is disturbing on many levels. This was the headline in this morning's Guardian newspaper: *"Donald Trump denounces Jeff Sessions for being 'weak' on Hillary Clinton"*

We are sure that Trump didn't learn this management style while attending the University of Pennsylvania Wharton Business School. His wasteful and harsh tweets today (July 25, 2017) are a great example of his truly asinine style, *"Attorney General Jeff Sessions has taken a VERY weak position on Hillary Clinton crimes (where are E-mails & DNC server) & Intel leakers!"*

If the President of the United States really thinks he can bully the Attorney General into using the Department of Justice to force a political party to release their server, or go after the person who ran against him in the election, then we are no better than some banana republic or third-world country with a power-hungry dictator. We have already seen this movie. It was called McCarthyism. With each day in office, Donald J. Trump displays an unconscionable distortion of truth and justice.

Then Donald accuses an ally of collusion with the Democrats by this tweet, *"Ukrainian efforts to sabotage Trump campaign - "quietly working to boost Clinton. So where is the investigation A.G."*

Has Trump totally forgotten what Russia did in Crimea? The President polishes his shallow veneer with the cover-up that Russia's cyber-attack was a myth, a hoax, and the investigation is a 'witch hunt.' Does he really believe that reporters getting dirt on Paul Manafort and the money he received from a pro-Russian candidate in the Ukraine is a conspiracy by the DNC to hurt him? The facts speak for themselves. Manafort declared the income.

While Trump has tweeted Jeff Sessions onto his list of whipping boys, his spokespeople are saying that Sessions has the President's confidence. Why are they torturing this person? This is a point of law which Donald Trump doesn't respect. Our great Orange Leader thinks that Sessions' primary responsibility is to protect the president and be loyal to Trump himself. Above the law?

Trump embarrassed himself and our great country by giving a speech at the Boy Scout Jamboree filled with brash braggadocio and self-anointed political taunting. He even took this opportunity to deride former President Obama instead of promoting values, honor, country and loyalty, which the scout organization touts. The Jamboree felt the need to issue this note to the attendees: *"Chants of certain phrases heard during the campaign (e.g. 'build the wall', 'lock her up') are considered divisive by many members of our audience, and may cause unnecessary friction."* They also offered an apology after the rally for the President's remarks.

Now, we have this human anal opening posing as President of the United States without any respect for the law, without any awareness of the lack of appropriateness of his comments at gatherings of children and minors and, worst of all, without any admission that his need for loyalty is a one-way street.

He is not loyal to people he hires and he seems to have no loyalty to the laws of the land. Remember, he took a loyalty pledge with the American public: *"I do solemnly swear (or affirm) that I will faithfully execute the Office of President of the United States, and will to the best of my ability, preserve, protect and defend the Constitution of the United States."*

If we take Trump's tweets at face-value, we see he wants to lock up Hillary Clinton and that he wants Jeff Sessions to do what he demands rather than follow the procedure and protocols of the Department of Justice.

Donald J. Trump is no lawyer, although he has made many of them rich. He thinks he knows everything about everything, when, in fact, he has the emotional make-up of a 14-year old boy and the legal knowledge of maybe a half of a *Law and Order* episode. Why should we accept anything smart from someone who reads the National Inquirer?

During his presidential campaign Donald Trump said that John McCain was NOT a hero because he was captured, insulting every POW and their families. Now we get this tweet today: *"So great that John McCain is coming back to vote. Brave - American hero! Thank you, John."* When you need his vote, he's a hero. When the man was just told he has cancer, he's a hero. And that, Mr. President, makes you one large, gaping asshole.

89. ROUND UP ALL THE TRANSGENDERS
Trump Draws Rainbow Line in the Sand
Posted: 7-26-2017

Today on Twitter (July 26, 2017) the President of the United States proclaimed on that he has ruled on whether transgender people may serve their country. Here is what he said: *"After consultation with my generals and military experts, please be advised that the United States government will not accept or allow transgender individuals to serve in any capacity in the US military. Our military must be focused on decisive and overwhelming victory and cannot be burdened with the tremendous medical costs and disruption that transgender in the military would entail."*

Paul Callan, a legal analyst for CNN, has coined the term *"tweet-law"* for the President's phone blasts that greatly affect the laws and policies of the government. Right after the missive from our great Orange Leader was posted, some reporters said that the Pentagon, *"the Generals"* had no idea a decision of this magnitude had been made. When the President declares that transgender people are some great *"disruption"* to military life, he belittles them as being less human, less valuable and less a citizen of this great land.

Robert Sapolsky in his fabulous book, *"Behave: The Biology of Humans at Our Best and Worst"*, points out that when a high-status rat in a pack gets electric shocks that produce stress, he proceeds to attack lessor status rats by biting them. That seems to relieve their stress. Could the President's decree about transgender people serving in the military simply be his way of inflicting pain on a class of people he feels beneath him? According to his recent tweets, he is outwardly stressed. He's condemning his own team.

The President's new *'tweet-law'* will create the challenging task that will involve *"asking and telling"* an enlistee's sexual orientation. Then, if a soldier stands tall in his or her skin, they will be fired? Really? You are going to send them away without a pension, without pay or record because of their sexual orientation? Is that American?

It's not the cost of surgery that the president thinks government might have to pay, it's the idea that these people are disruptive in some way. Disruption in the military isn't allowed. What is this President thinking? Oh, yeah, forgot, he doesn't think.

This is all part of the Pence Effect driven by Mike's overzealous, religious "grounding" that is basically discrimination justified by Leviticus 18:22. It's tantamount to a suggestion that Sharia Law be used to create US law. Mike Pence and many evangelicals cannot deal with the reality that we should never discriminate against people, even if the bible tells you to.

We have laws that prohibit employers from discriminating against applicants and employees based on race, color, religion, sex, and national origin (including membership in a Native American tribe). It is true that around two dozen states still don't have anti-discrimination laws protecting individuals from being discriminated against based on their sexual orientation. But, the President just blew the candle out on this issue.

Perhaps Congress can step up and sort this out, but Trump will never get votes from the LGBTQ community again. On June 1, 2017 Ivanka Trump tweeted: *"I am proud to support my LGBTQ friends and the LGBTQ Americans who have made immense contributions to our society and economy."* It's all part of the plan to make the liberals have hope, while that great Beach Boys song comes to mind, *"And she'll have fun, fun, fun, 'til her daddy takes the T-bird away."*

Daddy is calculating everything for purposes of enriching himself, his image or his family rather than being the president for all people. He's a racist, a xenophobe, a homophobe and his transphobia was brightly exposed today with his mindless and insensitive tweet.

He's a bully, or to put this into the perspective of a neurobiologist, he's an alpha male rat who has been shocked by the lack of love from Congress, the Attorney General and the press. His teeth aren't as sharp as they were in business with his gang of lawyers and liars surrounding him. When he bites and people bleed and someone points out his insensitivity, he replies, *"I'm the President and you aren't!"*

What a shallow and intolerable person. Donald J. Trump is America's number one problem. I wonder who will solve him? He can keep his twitter account, but we want the White House back.

90. AN OPEN LETTER TO THE REPUBLICAN PARTY
Now What Are You Going to Do?
Posted: 7-27-2017

One should be proud to be a member of the party that freed the slaves. The President who Donald Trump most admires, Andrew Jackson, was a Democrat. No one seems to mention that. Grant and Lincoln were Republicans, and Teddy Roosevelt was a Republican, but his cousin FDR was a Democrat. JFK was a Democrat, while the disgraced Richard Nixon was a Republican. As times change, parties change, but people need to feel the party they support has a core set of values that warrants their vote.

The Republican party's platform supports American exceptionalism. Okay, USA, USA, USA, but then they say: *"This platform is optimistic because the American people are optimistic. This platform lays out — in clear language — the path to making America great and united again. For the past 8 years America has been led in the wrong direction."* So much for the optimism. I wonder how many people in any political party read its platform?

Research shows that there are many factors that make up the decision on affiliation to a party. Your family or where you grew up have a great influence over whether you follow the elephant or the donkey. Not sure why those images are used for the parties, but we also must remember we have other independent parties. Make no doubt about it, our government, from the Bill of Rights, to the Constitution and through the rules and traditions of the Legislative branch, works best with two parties.

Donald J. Trump changed from liberal New York Democrat to a nationalist Republican. The reason for this move, he claims, is because he changed his viewpoints on so many issues that he just morphed into a Republican. Huh? Most political experts know that Trump's move to another party was purely a political move with an eye on being elected.

Trump's public comments demonstrated his obvious hate of Barack Obama. The Donald was also critical of George W. Bush's governance, which didn't disqualify him as a Republican but created a wall between Trump and the Bush families. He even called George W. a liar during the debates. Nice guy, team player.

Donald Trump should have started his own party, but it was so much easier to hijack the Republican party and remodel it around his base of right-winged maniacs. There is some wisdom in putting down Washington and people of both parties, because many citizens already disliked our government in a generic way.

Here is my question to the Republicans who jumped on the band wagon, either early on or after nomination. What happened to your so-called moral bedrock? When Donald Trump came down that escalator and claimed that *"Mexicans are rapists"* you had your chance to pick up the phone and tell him that is not our message and we cannot have that in our party; but you were too busy trying to figure out how to win, rather than standing by your code of ethics.

You let Donald's guy, Paul Manafort, change a plank in the platform to give Russia a stronger hand in the Ukraine. Why did you allow that to happen? Was it because you wanted to win? And now what do you have, a President without roots in your party and with no respect for the history of this country. Actually, no knowledge of history.

The fact that Trump conned the evangelicals into backing him from the pulpits of their mega-churches and television churches is so unseemly that I would ask them, *"What does Jesus think?"* People like Jerry Falwell, Jr. have sided with the money changers outside of the temple. They will be judged by a higher power, but you shouldn't be fooled by these few money-hungry false prophets.

The Republican Party is now in deep conflict. You have deep-seated radical Tea Party people who will block most issues based on far-right initiatives (a minority in America) rather than what their constituents really want. You have half-baked neo-conservatives who pray to their Ronald Reagan photo every night but have little understanding of how Ron could get things done. Reagan governed, even with tax increases, using professional acting prowess and statesmanship. He was previously the president of a labor union. He understood both sides.

The Republican party has some great members. Lindsey Graham, the Senator from South Carolina, has always told it like it is. John McCain, the Senator from Arizona who's a bit old-fashioned, but understands how it all works and what government is supposed to do. Sure, he sides with his party, but he's not siding with the nonsense and the sabotage created by political whores like Newt Gingrich.

Winning is great, but you have a poor manager of government in the White House in the form of a godforsaken, lousy President. How did you let that happen? You have a president who doesn't care about law. Where were you during this process of nomination? You have a charismatic show man with his long red ties, creepy, massive hair and pancake makeup trying to be the leader of free world but doing a horrendous job. You slap his back and smile for the cameras, because he was the winner and you didn't want to lose. You have no balls.

The President and his new consigliere, Slick Anthony, use Twitter to shame and bully employees of the government. This is not only uncouth but may be against the law. They are employees of the Federal government. Is not harassment against the labor law?

You Republicans have damaged your own party, but I guess you can sleep at night, because you know how dysfunctional the other party is. In the end, however, you will have to make the biggest decision in 2020. Do you back the incumbent, or do you find someone else to proudly represent your party? You know, it would be a lot easier to just impeach him.

91. DISRUPTION COMBUSTION
The Unpeaceful Transfer of Power
Posted: 7-28-2017

There is some wisdom in the structure of the United States government. Having three branches gives some feeling of checks and balances, but we are entering the twilight zone with the current executive branch.

The July 27, 2017 interview with the new Communications Chief, Anthony Scaramucci, that appeared in The New Yorker magazine bared the visceral and raw nature of the people President Trump chooses to advise him. The little white lie that Trump hires only the best people was torn down in one fell swoop with Slick Anthony's trashing of the Trump team.

The airing of dirty laundry in public is one thing, but the use of locker room terminologies to decry the chief of staff and the senior advisor is far beneath what we expect from our White House. If the First Lady calls it *"boy talk"* I will throw up. Remember, she was the one who said her pet cause would be cyber-bullying. The whole family from son-in-law to daughter to daddy all seem to be the greatest cons and hypocrites of the century.

Such harassment of a fellow employee would never be allowed in business. Remember, Trump said he would use his successful businessman skills to fix the country while it appears that he cannot tie his shoes.

Although I have no respect for Priebus and Bannon, Scaramucci's vulgar, public flogging of them was childish, disturbing and disruptive. If you don't like them, fire them. Beyond the Bannon self-pleasuring and dime-store psychological analysis of Reince Priebus, Scaramucci has done nothing but make the situation worse. He's another egomaniacal, rich, white guy who thinks he can fix things, just like his boss.

The reason Anthony got the communications job is because he hit back against CNN and got two reporters fired. What the Donald doesn't understand is that Scaramucci was in the private sector when he targeted CNN.

Now he is part of the administration and the rules have changed. Every move he makes is under the microscope and the freedom of information act will not work in his favor. We do have the First Amendment when it comes to covering the White House, and maybe it's time to remind King Donald that, (a.) he's not a nice guy and, (b.) he works for the taxpayers of this great land.

If I hear one more self-anointed ass wipe say that he *"serves at the pleasure of the President"* I am going throw a sledgehammer through the TV screen. You serve the American public. You are nothing but a government employee. And if Anthony Scaramucci had used that vulgar language on the floor of the Congress, he would have been disciplined and censured. It's sad that Trump won't restrain Scaramucci, because he finds him to be funny and entertaining.

If Trump cares so much about ratings, he should look at his own. With only 36% approval, his TV show would have been canceled.

This administration's lack of clarity is due to the shoddy communication and the distractions that Trump himself drops into the punch bowl. We knew that he would be different and he reminds us every day that he is neither a statesman nor a smart politician. He shows us with his actions that he is an amateur at governance and not qualified to be the leader of a Cub Scout group much less the free world.

Bringing Scaramucci into the White House will prove to be a colossal error. His words and deeds so far remind me of the ineffective business guy who says, *"I'm going to fire one person every day until morale improves around this place."* That doesn't work and, in the end, finding the leaks will not be as important as finding out 'why' people are leaking.

Just to get this on the record, White House Communications chief Anthony Scaramucci said this about Reince, *"Priebus is a fucking paranoid schizophrenic, a paranoiac."* He also laid into the President's adviser, Steve Bannon, with, *"I'm not Steve Bannon, I'm not trying to suck my own cock. I'm not trying to build my own brand off the fucking strength of the President. I'm here to serve the country."* Let's see how long he really serves.

So, there you have it folks. We've entrusted our government and military to these people. Really? Thanks to The New Yorker magazine for their brilliant UNFAKE NEWS.

If I said those things about my co-workers using that language, I would have been hauled into HR. Does the White House even have a Human Resources office? Any of us using such uncouth and reprehensible language in the workplace would have, at least, received a memo urging enrollment in anger management classes with a copy of that memo placed in their personnel folder.

These people are nothing more than bush league bureaucrats. That is what happens when you elect the wrong person for the wrong reason. Time will tell, as the Donald said about Jeff Sessions, that what most thoughtful citizens of this country are saying is true. Time will tell how long it will take for people in America to wake up and realize they've made a drastic mistake, and then do something about it.

92. MCCAIN'S REVENGE
Trump's Unifying Bridge Burned
Posted: 7-28-2017

What makes people work together? You can talk about common goals, community or even sense of family, but what gets things done on the world stage is empathy and truth.

When Donald J. Trump was sworn in as the 45th President of the United States he had an opportunity, a chance, to unite all Americans around a more moderate approach rather than the antics of that bombastic clown campaign candidate. Some of the pundits and experts believed that there would be a substantial pivot to something more presidential. They were all wrong. What we saw, is what we got, a clown.

Even when veteran judges were asked to evaluate his *"Travel Ban"* they vocalized their desire to separate what candidate Trump said from what President Trump said and did. I'm not sure why the things Trump said during his presidential pitch would not be allowed as evidence in a court of law. When a seller of a product misrepresents what that product does in their marketing they can he held accountable. Why is pre-President Trump being forgotten?

Billionaire Mark Cuban was very direct in his 'Shark Tank-like' evaluation of Trump. Mark said that Trump would not just leave the campaign behind. Cuban believed the Donald would double-down on some of the campaign's aspects and even take them to more absurd levels. Mark was right.

Whenever someone says something is important, it's clear those words matter. Listen carefully a person's words and you can look right into their soul. People are not perfect and they reveal so much if you are open to the nuisances.

From the beginning of Donald Trump's rise in the public atmosphere of New York, he was at best a playboy, at worst a misogynic woman hater. He flaunted it and loved the spotlight that was aimed at him and the beautiful women on his arm. He cheated on his wives and he bragged about his conquests. The Access Hollywood tape and the women who came forward saying he touched them inappropriately, might have been forgotten by those confederate flag waving rednecks, but American women know how that attitude feels. It's learned from an early age and it's ugly.

When Trump was asked about John McCain during the campaign, he very cynically said that he didn't think McCain was a war hero because he was captured. Then he blasted from every auditorium microphone his plan to make sure every veteran would be treated better by the Veterans Administration. Was that simply his subconscious guilt for his McCain comment, or his fear of being exposed by his obvious scheme to get out of military service himself? As someone who has a bone-spur, I can tell you that with the right shoes you can do anything.

Trump thinks he can do everything better than Obama, who had very little interaction with members of the House and Senate. The great Orange Leader bombed with Congress because of too much contact. His little bribes and free White House luncheons showed his lack of knowledge on the legislation that was being considered. One Republican commented, *"He didn't seem to understand what we were trying to do with the bill."*

His big party on the lawn of the White House with Representatives to celebrate one step in the process of repealing and replacing Obamacare was his "Mission Accomplished" moment. He truly believes you can throw a beer bash and everyone in DC will get in line. Oh, how foolish and naïve this business person is.

In the early morning hours of July 28, 2017, with 49 voting in favor and 51 voting against what was known as the 'Skinny Bill', the Senate stopped repeal dead in its tracks. Three Republican senators, John McCain of Arizona, Lisa Murkowski of Alaska and Susan Collins of Maine voted no along with all 48 Democrats.

Why this should be very alarming to the administration comes in many different colored poison pills they must swallow. First, the obvious fact that

Trump has no real sway with the Senate. He has pockets of deeply loyal fans in the House, but you cannot get America to do anything without the Senate, and they know it.

Trump can hurl his psychological vomiting toward the players via Twitter, but deep down inside he's in a quandary about why this "extremely lovable playboy" cannot be taken seriously. One wouldn't turn to Hugh Hefner for marriage advice, so why is America depending on a tax-evading, draft dodging, pussy grabbing man-child to govern our country?

Let's put it more simply for the people moving their lips while reading this. Those who voted against all the bills promoted by Trump did so because of things he said in the past.

What do Murkowski and Collins have in common? They are both women and they are sensitive to women's issues. Planned Parenthood has 56 independent local affiliates that operate more than 600 health centers throughout the United States, providing high-quality services to women, men, and teens. This legislation would have, more, or less, closed those facilities. Rural hospitals are closing birthing rooms forcing mothers to drive two hours or more to give birth. Is that America? Why not give Planned Parenthood more money and let them expand?

The cookie Congress was throwing in for women's health was money for community health centers. To do what? You cannot deal with female issues without dealing with reproduction and diseases that affect their body parts. And of course, the whole world wasn't watching when 13 male Senators created this bill behind closed doors. No women allowed? Then, at the 11th hour, the administration threatened these women and see what it got them? A NO VOTE.

I am sure John McCain, who spent six-years as a prisoner of war in Vietnam, has all the patience of a saint. He brushed aside Trump's insult on the campaign trail and, I am sure, never expected an apology. But a prisoner of war learns a lesson that business cannot teach you: it's prudent to wait for the right moment.

When Trump asked McCain for his vote, he hailed him as a hero, but a funny thing happened on the way to the Senate. John McCain, recently diagnosed with brain cancer, got on a plane and with his first vote set in motion a series of very statesmenlike actions. First, he gave a speech about how Congress is getting nothing done and urged his fellow legislatures to return to what is called "regular order." He was asking them to do things right. As he was giving the speech, I found myself thinking, wow, he would have made a great President.

But what Trump and his band of not-so-merry-men in the West Wing found out is that it takes two to tango, and McCain was leading while the music played. From my perspective, he got his revenge for the mean and disruptive statements Trump has made. He waited his turn, played his card and voted *"NO!"*

John McCain already has a legacy much greater than most, but what he did in the dead of night was punch a little crack in the dam of ignorance that elected this demigod to the highest office in the land. The pressure will build behind the Republican dam and others will take their turn at making that crack a little bigger.

When the gate is opened, water from Capitol Hill will be released and will flow toward 1600 Pennsylvania Avenue. By then, surely the country will want the current occupants to be gone.

93. THE WORLD JUST GOT SERIOUS
Can Trump Follow Suit?
Posted: 7-31-2017

There is a big distance between rhetoric and action, but in Trump World, our leader thinks that if he says it, it is so. Or, even worse, he thinks that if he orders something, then it will automatically happen. This pompous, over-blown self-evaluation of his salesmanship prowess and imaginary ability to get things done is really embarrassing.

He keeps telling us how much he has completed and all we see are carcasses of the people he has fired along the way. If these people weren't good enough to go more than six months, then the guy who hired them clearly doesn't know what he is doing. Trump creates these "Mission Accomplished" moments every day, which then fade into the sea of bullshit on which he floats.

Congress may have boxed Trump in with the sanctions bill against Russia, but their actions were done for all to see. They are working on shoring up their reputations and getting reelected. They don't live in an electoral college world, they sink or swim according to a popular vote, therefore, they must be 'popular' with as many constituents as possible.

Trump downplayed Russia's evil agenda during the election for reasons we will hopefully understand better when all the dust clears from the handful of investigations currently underway. Trump focused his discontentment on China with his campaign rhetoric. He never accused Russia of currency manipulation, unfair trade practices or unfair treatment of the American worker. He dumped all that on China.

It was no surprise when our President tweeted away on July 29, 2017: *"I am very disappointed in China. Our foolish past leaders have allowed them to make hundreds of billions of dollars a year in trade, yet they do NOTHING for us with North Korea, just talk. We will no longer allow this to continue. China could easily solve this problem!"*

And while he thought he had this "great" relationship with China's President Xi Jinping, Trump can't be straightforward about Russia, who increased trade with North Korea by 40% since Trump took office. North Korea showed a 4% growth rate. What?

Doesn't the Donald know he is being played by this punk kid Kim Jong Un, the KGB spy Putin and the all-powerful Xi Jinping? The fact is, Russia and China do NOT want to see a united Korean peninsula. They will each do all they can to prop up North Korea and Kim Jong Un so that unification never happens. Why does the Donald think he can job-out the responsibility of reeling in Un to China?

Trump just went through an embarrassing week, vividly demonstrated by the vulgar language of his new buddy, "slick Anthony, the Mooch, Scaramucci." Little Tony, the "front stabber" revealed the infighting and destructive forces in the vortex of Trump's inner circle. I would even advance the notion here that Trump is being played by his son-in-law and daughter to get rid of all the people who they don't agree with. Do they think they are "protecting" the President? Well, the apples don't fall… you know the rest. To fix the general discontent and chaos in the White House, let's bring in a general. General Mills? General Motors? No, no, a real General.

The final act of this passion play opens with Steve Bannon left dangerously dangling outside of the circle of trust. On the next episode of Reality President, we will learn if Bannon will be sent on his merry way, or be given a seat at the grown-up's table.

Now that the new sheriff in town, John Kelly, the former General from Boston, is in command of the staff, he will not put up with the very thing he hated about Obama: intellectual engagement. Generals don't like thinkers such as Steve Bannon because they get in the way of marching. It won't take long for Kelly to lose patience with the lack of a chain of command. Those he can fire, he will. The kids, of course, are off limits. The very reason they should NOT be there.

North Korea has tested 14 missiles this year, that's almost one for every person already fired from the young Trump administration or the government. As the President preaches about law and order to a group of police officers urging them **not** to be nice to people they arrest, his little "joke" was not warmly welcomed by police federations and departments across this land.

The idea of letting the cops be the prejudger of whether someone arrested should be treated harshly during arrest ought to make all Americans nervous. Stop joking around Mr. President. What you suggested is why young Muslim girls get slashed by white supremacists and African-American men get gunned down by over-zealous and nervous cops.

In retaliation for Congress passing a stiff sanctions bill against Russia for meddling in our election, Putin has decided to expel 755 diplomats and foreign service workers from Moscow. Amazingly, Trump says he will sign the bill, which would be a smart and serious move on his part. If he were to veto this bill, he would rip the scab off the wound known as the Russia Investigation. As the investigation takes a break from the front pages, Trump will be wise to press forward and get serious about his role in the world.

Maybe Anthony Scaramucci did something productive when he showed the petty, uncomfortable, back biting working environment that exists inside the White House. This is Trump's fault. Even privately held corporations would come under scrutiny with this kind of public harassment of co-workers.

I still hear Trump voters say how the great Orange One is running the government like a company. Unfortunately for America, he's running the country like a Trump organization, and all those loyal Trump voters have never had a chance to work where H1B visa holding, non-Americans get jobs before they do. Boy, what a great boss, what a hypocrite. Check the employees at Mar-a-Lago.

Donald Trump might think he's doing a great job, but the healthcare fiasco is just one example of his miserable failure. He brags about the stock market as if he invented it. The stock market was already on an upward swing before he was elected. The job market started growing in the Spring of 2015, but Trump was too busy bashing Mexicans back then.

The stock market doesn't need Donald Trump to be successful. It was there before he was born. The New York Stock Exchange opened in March of 1817 and it will be there long after he is gone.

Just as Obama couldn't ever take full credit for the stock market, Donald Trump can't own the bump and then blame any future decease on someone else. If you say you own it, Donald, then you own it. If Trump was to be impeached and Mike Pence took office, the stock market wouldn't collapse. It might even go higher. The stock market loves certainty, not unpredictability.

There are many challenges, both domestically and globally, that Trump must confront and manage in a sober manner. He has already spent a lot of "serious leader currency" by saying stupid things about world events, organizations and treaties. Meanwhile, back at home, his hurtful attacks on his own people have made it appear to many that he prefers chaos over order. Conflict before country and family before law. This is not the person who will help America stay great.

94. THE MASTER MICROMANAGER
Trump's Midsummer Coarse Correction
Posted: 8-1-2017

We have all worked for people who were oppressive micromanagers. Their need to be involved in everything we did stole our souls and self-determination. Some micromanagers would tell you they simply wanted things to go smoothly and be done right, when, in fact, their need for control was greater than the workers mental well-being or feelings of empowerment.

Donald J. Trump is not a micromanager and he's also a lazy worker. Rather than spending his valuable time studying the security reports and detailed analysis from seasoned professionals, he watches TV for his information. Much of what Trump seeks on his TiVo and cable is what people are saying about him. Trump isn't entirely wrong when saying lots of fake news is being pumped out daily, but he doesn't have the wherewithal to ascertain which channels are abundantly fake.

The number of uninformed opinions and preposterous predictions that flow from the media can be dangerous for anyone and totally alarming for this President because he uses the information in decision making.

Retired General John Kelly was tapped for Chief of Staff and the Mooch was meat. Booting Scaramucci on the first day of the Kelly command is a classic, old school tactic. I was once told by a self-proclaimed expert on management that I should fire one person (the troublemaker) my first day on the job to gain the respect by the rest of those I would manage. I was told this by a master micromanager.

Bringing in Kelly was a clear indication that the head micromanager decided he was too close to the situation. But wait, Donald Trump is like an alcoholic who knows he shouldn't drink, but all his friends (his base) urge him to have one more shot, *"Ah, come on Donald, just one more tweet for the road."*

Can a micromanager be cured? Probably not. We must realize that Trump has only a limited number of people he can fire before everyone in the world realizes that it's Trump who's the problem. The old yarn about a given place being a revolving door was always a message to good people to, steer clear, dear.

The decision to hire Scaramucci was the President's and the President's alone. There are those surrogates who are already saying that Anthony served a purpose. Really? Exactly what purpose was that? Advancing the vocabulary of common speech?

History will forget that little foul-mouthed jerk because the real bully remains in power. What Trump doesn't understand is that micromanaging automatically sets one up to be responsible for everything, all the blame with no deniably. At least Scaramucci was sacked before he got a paycheck.

Last night's Washington Post (July 31, 2017) reported that Trump dictated his son's account of the meeting with the Russian lawyer in 2016, which would mean that, once again, our great Orange Leader **lied** about his involvement. It's not a crime to lie for your kids. All of us have probably done it, but that doesn't make it right. This spineless, controlling fool in our nation's highest office thinks he is smarter than his lawyers and does whatever he wants, classic micromanager.

South Carolina Senator Lindsey Graham said on NBC's Today show (August 1, 2017) that *all the chaos in the White House is created by the President himself,* and the cracks in the Republican dam are beginning to resonate with others in the party.

Jeff Flake, the ultra-conservative Senator from Arizona said, "…*his party is in 'denial' about President Donald Trump.* "Flake goes on to say, in a Politico op-ed, some very honest things, *"It was we conservatives who, upon Obama's election, stated that our number-one priority was not advancing a conservative policy agenda but making Obama a one-term president — the corollary to this binary thinking being that his failure would be our success and the fortunes of the citizenry would presumably be sorted out in the meantime."* Trump has pledged 10 million dollars to defeat Flake in the 2018 election. What a fine Republican the Donald turned out to be; breaking Ronald Reagan's golden rule, *never say anything bad about a party member.*

Donald Trump is not a Democrat, not a Republican and not a Conservative. He is a Reactionary who opposes any political or social liberalization or reform. He isn't changing Washington. He is attempting to micromanage every detail of America while making tons of money for his companies and kids. Why did Congress pass such a tough sanctions bill on Russia? **They don't trust Trump.**

Managing the White House staff won't be a difficult task for John Kelly, but handling the 14-year-old in the Oval Office will be a full-time job. While the Donald nervously awaits the evidence that Robert Mueller will bring to the table, I imagine he feels he has been dealt a bad hand from a soiled deck of cards. Nothing is ever his fault.

When someone lies, the energy and time it takes to micromanage the fabrications by creating even more deceptions keeps them from getting things done. It was reported in the Washington Post that President Trump worked on the flight back from the G20 meeting structuring untruthful statements outlining how Donald Trump Jr. would respond to questions about his meeting with the Russians. The good news is Trump Sr. wasn't watching TV. The bad news is he was investing time on a lie, which ended up biting him on his bulbous buttocks.

As we approach his 200th day in office, it is clear to this writer that the President of the United States is a seriously flawed human being with neither the talent nor the patience needed for his job. Perhaps his ascent to the Presidency started as a mean joke to annoy Obama, or maybe a need to micromanage the world, but we now have a man in office who hates his job, hates his critics, hates the press and hates the arcane political processes of our country. And, slowly but surely, we are seeing that Donald Trump even hates the people he picks to help him govern. To use his word, "Sad!"

95. A WARTIME PRESIDENT
Can Trump Be Trusted?
Posted: 8-2-2017

While television is saturated with the stories about Trump writing the Don Jr cover-up statement and the White House being implicated in a law suit concerning a FAKE Fox News story linking a murdered campaign worker to leaked emails from the DNC, there is another story beckoning our attention. War is on the horizon. You certainly would never want to be in a war or escalated conflict anywhere in the world, and the very last thing we need right now is an amateur in the White House to deal with this incendiary situation.

North Korea is a powder keg. Syria is a problem that we have given to Russia, while we fight on in Afghanistan, the forgotten war. For 16 years, the United States has been in that country with no peace in sight. Obama did everything he could to keep America out of war, deploying strategic drone strikes with limited US military casualties. After more than 14 missiles being launched by North Korea's Kim Jong Un, we decided to launch our own test missile from California. (August 1, 2017) More sword rattling.

While Donald Trump domestically treads water in the deeper, darker end of the swamp, the world is watching his next move with North Korea. As we get to the first day of August 2017, the White House is in chaos. The press is hitting Trump and family very hard about their lies and misrepresentations. At the same time, North Korea is becoming a huge problem. If Donald Trump doesn't draw a red line in the sand with Kim Jong Un, he could well become the chess player who freezes and cannot make the next move. If you do nothing but maintain your unpredictability, you will get nothing accomplished.

What is the next move? Has Rex Tillerson really done anything to defuse the potential situation by establishing a diplomatic dialogue? This dance of the mighty with blasting rockets by both parties, is a waste of fuel. When Un propels an ICBM into the sky, we fly our fighters near the boundary of North

Korea. If this seems a bit childish and over-reactionary, you must remember that the players. are two boy-bullies on the playground.

One positive consequence of having lots of generals on the administration payroll is the added layer of stability to an otherwise chaotic White House. There are those who would fear having lots of generals around, but Trump thinks they might protect him from a military coup. Funny how conspiracy oriented the Donald is. Silly man.

There is a political theory that Presidents have always done well with re-election when they are in the middle of a war. We trust that the generals would never conspire with Trump to pull off a popular war to aid Trump, but think about this. If the White House would stoop so low as to use a murder to cover up collusion with Russia, where is their moral compass?

One of the things that the Trump team says when they are bailing out our leader after he offends or misspeaks is, *"Oh, he was just joking."* When you are the President of the United States and dealing with risky regimes and rogue rulers, you must be careful not to drop a bad joke. Trump isn't as funny as he thinks, but in front of an adoring audience he gets carried away. This is the guy who has the nuclear codes? God save us.

Donald J. Trump thinks he knows everything. He reminds me of a rich guy who likes to watch baseball and decides he knows enough to buy a baseball team. He says, *"I will show them how to win."* After a few years in the league and millions of dollars lost, he becomes frustrated that winning on the professional level is so difficult. What most people don't realize is that just because you can watch something on TV doesn't make you an expert.

Recall that our Orange Leader said, *"Who knew healthcare was so complicated?"* Well everyone but you knew it's complicated, airhead. And guess what, Donald? Foreign affairs, political planning and domestic programs are nothing compared to war. Is our President qualified to be the Commander-in-Chief? We think not.

With Trump's inability to quell what he calls a "witch-hunt" how can he possibly deal with actual witches? Yes, war is a witch, the evilest, most terrible sorceress, who drains our sons and daughter's blood, rips the gold from our coffers and stains any presidency. There is no dry-cleaner in historical analysis.

While we all watch North Korea develop a nuclear weapons program, Trump will soon be seen for the fake that he is. And if he gets talked into striking first, he won't be bragging about our great stock market. Just look at a list of the products that come out of Japan, South Korea and China. War is a long, dark winter and if this President takes that step, then we are economically doomed.

96. ALL TIME LOWS
Trump Sinks and Blames
Posted: 8-3-2017

When the latest polls were released today (August 3,2017), we could feel a shiver move through the Republican party. The 2018 elections are approaching and those running for reelection now worry that the political depression from the big guy might rain on their parade.

The latest Quinnipiac poll demonstrates that there is another leak the President should be watching; the leak of his popularity. The headline out of the latest stats is Trump's approval rating is now only 33%. Wow, that isn't very popular. I wonder why the administration isn't trying to figure out what to do about that, or is it too late?

The poll surveyed 1,125 voters around the country from July 27 to August 1, 2017. It has a margin of error of plus/minus 3.4 points.

- 54% said they were embarrassed to have him as president

- 57% said they he was abusing the powers of his office

- 71% said Trump was not levelheaded

- 62% said Trump was not honest

- 63% said Trump did not have good leadership skills

- 59% said he did not care about average Americans

- 63% said he did not share their values

The number that jumps out most for me is the 62% of the people surveyed said that the 45th President of the United States is not honest. The other number that really stuns me is the 59% who said that Trump doesn't care about average Americans. Sad!

As these numbers hit the press today, Trump was back on Twitter with his latest whine: *"Our relationship with Russia is at an all-time & very dangerous low. You can thank Congress, the same people that can't even give us HCare!"* [sic]

We can always count on the Donald to deflect blame and to attempt to position himself far away from the kitchen of governance. Now the military is starting to get a taste of his modus operandi, served up with a side of naiveté.

He pissed off *"his generals"* in the Situation Room by complaining about not winning in Afghanistan. Really? The great Orange Leader should pick up the phone and call his friend in Russia and learn how well they did in Afghanistan. They spent 10 years in the country and the only accomplishment was empowering Osama bin Laden, a terrorist.

Trump's lack of historical knowledge is astounding and his pathological way of shifting blame away from himself is not only disturbing, it's counterproductive. Our relationship with Russia is bad is because we caught them trying to hack our election and pushing propaganda to help Trump get elected. Congress was just doing their job, finally.

When 71% of those surveyed said that you are not levelheaded Mr. Trump, you should be thinking about how to manage the damage that has been done, rather than casting blame toward the Legislative branch.

This is all part of the things we have covered on this blog over that last eight months. We can keep doing the same thing repeatedly, but the more we experience of this White House, the more those stats from Quinnipiac seem correct.

Trump always took pride in his ability to manipulate the press and handle his own PR, but when he's finally put under the microscope by the American public, they see the little germs and viruses in his current sample of leadership.

Trump will get on the taxpayer-funded jet airplane tonight and fly to West Virginia to get feedback from a select group of rabid fans. He will once again get love from some people who believe he was the right choice. But as time goes on, and things don't get better, that 33% approval rating will drop lower. And the truth is, Trump has only himself to blame.

97. MY FINAL ARGUMENT
Time to Save the Republic

When I started my blog I never imagined there would be enough material to fill a book. I also didn't think I would write more than one post a week, but the Trump administration had different plans for me. Every morning I would read through a few articles in either the Washington Post or the New York Times and then watch the morning TV shows to see what was happening.

It wasn't more than an hour each day before I was sitting at my keyboard with a cup of coffee and hundreds of words flowing out of my fingers. Sure, it was merely psychological vomiting, but I had to get my passion and frustrations down on paper or, better yet, posted to my web site www.WhyWait4Years.com.

As the President himself said, *"It's easy to be a critic."* He was right and I, for one, have had no problem finding the many flaws and fallacies of this guy. My feelings are based on my love for America, but that love is not unconditional. These daily diatribes were a way to ask questions. What is America? What do Americans in any political party want from their government? I also have no problem sticking up for the Constitution and speaking up when I think things are going terribly wrong.

Growing up in the American 50s and 60s, I saw the country change dramatically. I realized that believing in what people say on TV or in press conferences as the truth, without researching the facts, is folly. Between reading the newspaper every day, to going to college and being part of the movement to question the then president's actions in Vietnam, I was immersed in the process. And because I have lived almost half of my life in the north and half in the south, I understand some of the fundamental cultural viewpoints that make up this great country.

I have experienced these American presidents; a general, a blueblood Bostonian statesman who was assassinated, a crude true Texan politician, a corrupt little California lawyer, a Grand Rapids civil servant, a well-meaning southern peanut farmer, a bigger-than-life movie actor, a New Englander turned Texan oil millionaire, a slick-talkin' southern Rhodes scholar, the son of the Texas politician and a neighborhood organizer from Hawaii via Chicago, who also happened to be African-American. I observed that anyone could become President of the United States. This time around, we have elected a person with all the answers and all the solutions and to put it his way, he will, *"Make America Great Again."* So, I ask, when did America get "un-great" and how are you going to fix it?

When Donald J. Trump was elected the 45th President, I was eager to see if the campaign clown and agitator persona would remain intact after he was sworn in, or if he would become moderate and bring the country together. The latter didn't happen. The former is solidly in place.

Through the arcane method of protecting the country from a lunatic, we got a lunatic. The electoral college was won by the Trump team and Hillary Clinton snagged the popular vote by almost three million people. To be exact, the final numbers were Clinton with 65,844,610 votes, or 48.2% of the total vote, and Trump with 62,979,636 votes, or 46.1% of the total vote. That's a difference of 2.86 million votes. Hardly a mandate for Trump, but the system once again has provided us with a leader from the game and not from the total number of votes. We could change that system, but would that be a fair way to elect the next president?

One of the things I hope to accomplish with this book is to help you work through the current events of the first 200 days in almost in real-time. The multiple personalities that emerged from Donald Trump showed a vast difference between formal presentations and wild early morning tweets and leaks. This book is simply a record of those days, with my opinions and perspectives added.

We have learned so much about this president and his administration and the facts are more and more disturbing with each passing day. As the magician holds your attention with totally false or unimportant gimmicks, there are things happening behind the scenes that should disturb citizens of any party. As a matter of fact, I wonder where all the hard-core Libertarians stand on these issues?

Many comments in this book might seem harsh or mean, but I stand by everything I wrote. I am not going to dilute my feelings. My emotions are no less important than the opinions expressed in our president's collection of diatribes.

Much like a young boy with his toy soldiers, it seems as if this President is playing a game, a game where **his winning** is the only positive result. I do believe that Donald J. Trump thinks that if he wins, America wins. He truly carries the burden of his statement that only he can solve problems, and he continually and harshly expresses his view of how terrible things are in the United States to play on the fears of Americans. In some cases, he's invented things to be afraid of and constantly reminds us how much we are in trouble, then he turns on a dime and tells everyone how great he is doing. He's like an over-critical parent who abuses the child and then reminds her of how great she has it with him as her dad. What is this man doing?

Trump is not a builder, he is a turmoil enabler. He likes to construct, initiate and watch conflict, because, as any screenwriter will tell you, *"You cannot have drama without conflict."*

Let's look at the conflicts Donald Trump has created:

- Pitting his political base against the majority of America.
- Enabling hate and bigotry instead of inclusiveness and progress.
- Pushing fear and a bullying method rather than fair, mature leadership.
- Employing hyperbole and lies without truth and facts.

- Selling domestic supremacy against global leadership.
- Demolishing rules for business at the expense of the environment and allowing fraud.
- Defunding education so that we can over-spend on military.
- Grabbing excessive executive power and creating a Constitutional crisis.
- Being unpredictable rather than consistent.

And now this writer will do his job and examine each of these perceptions and explain why every one of them is bad for America.

Political base against the majority

One thing that Richard Nixon and Donald Trump mislabelled was the notion of a silent majority. They are a loud minority who have always had chips on their shoulders and complaints about the many things that came up wrong in their lives. That harsh negativism should be tempered by positive, clear leader.

If you believe deep in your soul that the color of a person's skin determines their trustworthiness, then you are in that group. If you are a person who thinks that immigrants are taking the jobs from "real" citizens, then you are on the Trump train. If you want to put a confederate "stars and bars" flag on your pickup truck to claim you are honoring all those brave people who tried to overthrow the United States, then you have a lifetime membership in the club. These attitudes can be scientifically tested and verified, just like your DNA.

There is another part of Trump's base populated by folks who believe they are NOT like the people I described in the previous paragraph and foster this feeling that Democrats are elitists. People who give away all the tax dollars to people who don't work very hard and for some reason don't deserve those benefits. Not sure why poor people never merit a break?

There are people with what I call the Republican gene that says you cannot trust the government or its judgement on everything from God, to guns to abortions and land use. We must all remember that governments are just people doing their jobs. And when they fail to work for us, we should boot them out.

If you respond to the verbal complaint, *"Things aren't fair,"* you probably are in the Trump camp. But let's focus on some facts.

The Trump people I described above are not **most Americans** (SEE VOTE TOTALS). People who didn't vote for Trump aren't just those who live in the cities and coastal towns of this great country, as most propagandists would have you believe. There were millions of people who didn't vote for Trump in every county in the country. They are Americans too and they have a voice, even though they didn't have a candidate they really loved in 2016.

Trump is a neophyte governmental leader with lots of people whispering in his ear. These loyalists know they must keep the crabby, portly, old rich man happy. They work to make sure he hears people cheering for him. If you could get Donald Trump into a room where 40,000 people booed him, the President would come back to the White House and fire everyone—except his kids.

If we held the election today, and Donald Trump ran against anyone other than Hillary Clinton, he would lose the election. You could pit Billy Bush against the Donald and Billy would win. That would be good news for Billy, who lost his job due to Trump's big mouth.

Hate and bigotry against inclusiveness

Now there are lots of people who know Donald Trump personally who claim he is not a bigot, sexist, racist, anti-Semitic, or xenophobic, but this man is not a modern man. Some of his attitudes and comments would have fit nicely into the 1950s.

Our great Orange Leader decries the concept of political correctness and has created a more open and aggressive verbal society. I'm not sure he should be proud of that. He wants to be able to say anything, but when other people exercise their First Amendment right, Trump is there to put them down. Hypocrite.

Trump threatened withholding federal grants to universities that canceled speakers he felt were saying things he would've presented. His march toward saying whatever he wants has promoted lots of people to be downright racist and rude out loud.

And when we say something he doesn't want to hear, he calls it *"Fake News,"* or he uses a hackneyed Nixon/Agnew response that the media is *"the enemy of the people."* Who's your daddy Trump, Adolf Hitler or Joseph Stalin? He doesn't even realize they used that phrase.

Let the record show that when you are endorsed by a white supremacy group, and you don't take a very vocal stand against them, you just might be a racist. If you have an increase in violence and hate crimes against Jews and Muslims after you made some outlandish statement, you just might be part of the problem. When you push for a complete ban against Muslims entering the United States until the government can figure out *"what the hell is going on,"* you just might be culpable. If you never apologize for anything you say or do, you can never get off the hook for your transgressions. You said it, you own it.

The President has done nothing to unite the country. He likes to compare himself to Abraham Lincoln, when good old honest Abe wouldn't even let him pick up his axe.

Historians have written much about Lincoln. Some have suggested that he was gay, some have said he was really a racist, but the question the 45th President should ask is this, *"What will historians write about him?"*

His hate will stand out, from urging violence at rallies to banning transgenders from the military to not calling out racists to lashing out at the press, there seems to be hate on many sides, many sides. Donald Trump has lots of hate to go around and it really does get in the way of uniting our country. It's what divides us.

Fear mongering and bullying instead of mature leadership

When I read an article recently about high school bullies castigating and harassing young Muslim girls who, by the way, were born in America, with chants urging them to leave our country, I saw Trump's work in action. There will be no fireside chats from our great Orange Leader to calm the hate of the young people who think he's funny and great.

Sure, I get it. A 14-year-old boy would think Trump is cool, because Trump is a 14-year-old boy. I would like to talk to those boys and find out if they truly are Trump supporters. Today, they are just using words to hurt others. Tomorrow they will be picking up guns and knives. The President has done nothing to quell this hate, rather he has incited it. He thinks he's being funny when he "jokes" about police brutality in front of a group of law enforcement officers. Mr. Trump, I dare you to go to Harlem and address civic leaders with that same speech!

The Donald's method is simple, he attacks anyone who says anything negative about him. Anyone who disagrees with him must be personally disgraced and professionally disparaged. I wonder what book Donald Trump read that said you can be a better salesperson by making people dislike you before you even start your pitch. Why would I buy anything from a person I don't want to be around? Why would any leader from another country trust him?

Trump will never realize that some people who are voting against him in Congress are doing so simply because they don't like him. The bully pulpit has turned into a bully bulldozer. This destructive "take no prisoners" attitude will cause Trump's downfall. He can be the bull in the china shop, but he should realize that the American taxpayers will eventually have to pay for his destructiveness.

When the vote for healthcare came down to one person, and that one person voted against Trump, he should have taken note. That one vote could cause the end his presidency during an impeachment hearing.

Hyperbole and lies against truth

Let's put this in perspective. If I elect someone to be my President, I want that person, above all else, to be honest. Now, I know that part of good salesmanship is adding hype and creative suggestions to motivate buyers. As someone with a marketing background, I admit that I have taken liberty with language to create a positive pitch for a product. However, while bending the language, I was careful to never lie. A lie, even if made by mistake, can cause lost business and profits.

This subject could fill an entire book, but truth in governance has always been a challenge. Lyndon Johnson lied about where the bombs were dropping in southeast Asia and he was caught. Nixon lied and much was revealed about his vile administration. Bill Clinton lied about having sexual relations with *"that woman."* George W. Bush lied about weapons of mass destruction and Obama lied about keeping your doctor.

So, the bar has been set pretty low, and maybe it's time to change that, to start telling us the truth. Why do we have to wait for some whistle-blower like Edward Snowden to show us what is really happening?

All campaigns lie and the American public allows it to happen. Are the citizens of our country so stupid that they don't hold any of these goofballs accountable for their statements? One of the recent headlines in the Washington Post (July 26, 2017) read: *"26 hours, 29 Trumpian false or misleading claims"* The current numbers are worse. Trump's outright lies number in the hundreds nearing one thousand. WHY?

What angers me the most is the absence of desire to get things right. Trump watches Fox News, reads far right web sites and digests the National Inquirer and believes what they disseminate is fact. With all the people who work for the President of the United States, you would think someone would be assigned the job of verifying the truthfulness of Trump's next tweet storm. It's as if no one in the administration cares if our leader speaks truth or lies. As Senator Bernie Sanders put it, *"Trump is a pathological liar."* And that is the truth.

I don't want a president who lies. Is that too much to ask? In the final paragraph of this book, I will disclose how lying will bring this President down.

Domestic supremacy against global leadership

This topic is also multifaced and it too could fill a library of books, but let me simplify the subject. America has never been isolated from the rest of the world. Even from the first day of this nation it was in part created by cooperation with another nation. Thanks, France.

Oh, there have been those people who believed that Harry Truman was crazy when he introduced the Marshall Plan. It essentially said that if a problem somewhere in the world had the least bit of a chance of blowing up into a world war, we would fund the problem away. It started with Turkey and now we give aid to many, many countries.

There were people who thought Woodrow Wilson was right about not wanting to get involved in Europe's first great war of the 1900s. They were wrong. The way that war was ended and how peace was negotiated by too many cooks in the kitchen set up the Second World War. But there is one truism, the United States must be involved in global affairs or bad things happen, repeatedly.

Trump is not a student of anything but the Donald Trump story, and even he doesn't know how that story will end. He barely reads, yet he thinks he has everything figured out. When you elect a president, and give him the keys to the car, you expect him to drive carefully and not crash. Trump wants to drive at 200 mph, while most of the world travels at much safer speeds.

China didn't just wake up one day with massive industrial and currency power. Richard Nixon, oh yeah, that one, went to China and set it all in motion.

The trade deals we live by today were orchestrated by Nixon, and those arrangements did indeed help destroy the American factory and its workers. From car parts, to light bulbs, to Donald Trump's suits and ties, other countries can make things cheaper.

Europe saw what was happening and merged their economic fates in the European Union. They did this to compete. And now let's reveal the real winner here, capitalism. Yes, even the Russians know that if you sell oil and gas to other countries you can make tons of money. Screw communism, never worked, never will.

We have this biased "capitalist" in the White House who thinks that the deals made by all those bright CEOs, he keeps saying he loves, were involved in some great greedy conspiracy. In fact, he is guilty of that very infraction. Trump claims that there aren't American companies that can do the work to produce his and Ivanka's branded products. Boy, where is the *"buy and hire American"* slogan when it really counts? Hypocrite.

I love it when people like Steve Mnuchin, who makes a ton of money producing movies, claims that we will pay for all the Trump tax breaks with *"growth."* Trump has been sucked into trickle-down, voodoo economics that have never worked and will probably never work. Making rich people richer has never helped the middle class. Nobody in Michigan, Ohio or Pennsylvania got richer when Donald Trump amassed wealth. Why have they fallen for this false prophecy?

Wow, these guys are like used cars salesmen, *"Sure, she was only driven each Sunday for 240 years, but she runs like a dream, but only when a Republican is behind the wheel."* Really?

We have always embraced commerce and enriched ourselves through trade with other countries. Some countries make products we like to buy, just as they like to buy our machinery, electronics, vehicles, aircraft, plastics, minerals, optical and medical apparatus and of course, pharmaceuticals. All these guys have powerful lobbyists.

If the original Trump premise is that the world is beating up the United States, **why are we doing so well?** Can the Donald build new plants to make his ties and trousers in time for re-election? And will Trump pay those workers fair wages, or con them into working at sub-standard wages so that *"America can complete"* with other countries? Patriotism doesn't pay for the food that's put on the table each night.

The answer to all this is the city that Trump talked about in his big dismantling of the Paris Accord speech: Pittsburgh. Full disclosure, I am from Pittsburgh and I was very proud when Mayor, Bill Peduto, took Trump to task on his misuse of the city's name.

Pittsburgh is an example of how an industry was ripped from its heart and how the place reset to become a city of the future. Sure, there's still old money and lots of headquarters located in the 'burgh, but the city didn't just stick its head in the sand. No, they figured out where America was headed and got there like a hockey player skating to where he knew the puck would be.

Along the area adjacent to Pittsburgh's Monongahela River, where I worked in a steel mill during college, now sits an industrial park with companies that manufacture high-tech products like hard-drives. Gee, I guess they were thinking globally and acting locally.

Trump wants to bring back the past and amass power. If he was smart, he would spend more time talking to the mayors of successful cities instead of wasting his breath telling us how bad our cities are. I would be talking to the leaders of municipalities that are adding jobs in renewable energy, like the solar and wind sectors. Those cities know what they are doing.

Demolishing rules and the environment

When the New England Patriots and Tom Brady were accused of deflating footballs so that Tom's small hands could get a better grip, I laughed. Really? Did people believe that having special balls for this veteran superstar would make a difference in a football game? Not really, but it mattered because there are rules.

When someone breaks the law, they should be punished. That is what Jeff Sessions and Donald Trump claimed was meant by being the *"Law and Order"* candidate. The result will be more people in for-profit prisons and an endless amount of money that won't be spent on useful programs will be given to prison corporations that made mega donations to the Trump campaign.

I suggest that there are other, equally dangerous people in the White House, but they don't wear orange outfits. If the administration doesn't like a rule, they just change it. They have even suggested breaking the law to destroy Obamacare only because they don't like it. Hospitals and insurance companies might have to sue the administration just to get paid for services already rendered.

If some industrialist wants to dump his waste in the river, change the law. Oh, you want to drill for oil on federal lands, sure, go ahead and do it. You want to frack the shit out of Oklahoma and let insurance companies NOT cover earthquake damage, let her rip.

Tom Brady was guilty and we all know it. Remember that he destroyed his cell phone to get rid of evidence. Did he *"bleach his emails"* and text messages too? Donald Trump stonewalls the American public by not releasing his tax returns. I am sure that any evidence of Trump's personal Russian involvement has been deleted.

The world and our country must be protected with thoughtful policies and environmental rules that make sense. When the children of Syria were poisoned by a dictator, Trump dropped 59 tomahawk missiles on an airfield. Sadly, he didn't take the whole facility out. The airbase was up and running a few days later. Trump might have felt like a big man, but he didn't inflict much damage as he ate his huge chocolate cake. In the future, when US kids get poisoned by their drinking water, what will you say to the American public?

Trump has already relaxed the rules on dumping pollutants in their water supply. How can we live with such hypocrisy?

As the President says when he's confronted with some problem he can't fix at that moment, *"Time will tell."* He's right, but the environment and public health and safety isn't a *"let's wait and see what happens"* situation.

Trump fails to understand how science works. He's like most deniers. When he gets seriously sick he will hire the smartest doctor to cure him. But he fails to listen to the smartest doctors when it concerns anyone else's life. If you just look at the floods, the fires and the destructive force of the weather in the summer of 2017, and you don't equate it to the hottest days on record, you are a fool.

There are ramifications to things like global warming, climate change and massive amounts of pollutants in our atmosphere. We go back to the Robert Sapolsky book, *Behave: The biology of humans at our best and worst.* As he points out, for every three degrees of increase in temperature, there is a four percent increase in interpersonal violence and a 14 percent rise in group violence. Donald Trump can say all he wants about the Paris Climate Accord being a *"bad deal"* for the United States, but the real question is this: What planet does Donald Trump live on?

He wants to reduce crime and violence, but Trump's actions from healthcare to education to environment will produce the opposite effect. If he doesn't believe in what everybody else says is real, he labels it as *"fake"* or a *"hoax."* I am sure the polar bears know it's real and when our great Orange Leader's Florida golf club and fortress Mar-a-Lago is under water, his kids can tell his grandkids, *"Yeah, too bad, your grandfather was wrong."* Where does it say that the whole country, and maybe the world, will collapse because of some ill-informed lunatic who thinks he's king of the weather?

Defund education, over-spend on military

The bad news for America is that Donald Trump spent his formative years in a military school. We are not sure why his mother and father sent him there, but it's clear it gave him a bogus feeling that he knows something about the military. He is the tin soldier who dictates rather than leads.

No one can argue against having a strong Army, Navy, Air Force and Marines to keep the homeland safe. You can add the Coast Guard in that mix because they are doing some good work curbing illegal immigration and illicit drug and human trafficking. Then why did Trump cut millions out of the Coast Guard in his first budget? The one force that guards our borders got the shaft.

His lack of understanding of how the military works is due to not only his lack of experience in that arena, but also because he thinks power will overcome any roadblock. He might have a heart, but his trigger finger is a bit too quick and unplanned to be effective.

Let's assume that we have a great military force and that we can keep building and buying our way to the top of a stack where we have always dominated. I get it, we want to be stronger to deter other countries from having a second thought. However, you can't deter crazy people like Putin and Un. They are not impressed with how much we have, they are jealous of how much we have.

That brings us to the talk, the talk we must have with this President about the future. Tomorrow is not going to wait for some bird-brained egomaniac to figure out what matters. It will creep up on us until it may be too late to fix. The fact is, that if you want to make America great, you must first make America smart again.

Let's face the truth. We are not educating our next generation very well. Some will say we shouldn't pour money into broken down public schools, but the Trump-DeVos plan to isolate kids in private schools with vouchers will create a class-bound society. The result will be a wretched cycle of poor kids from the wrong zip codes getting less of a chance to succeed. Little success, lots of crime.

We need to rebuild public schools. There is no proof that a Catholic education is somehow better than instruction at a good public school. In fact, many children have been harmed for life by a Catholic education, but that is another book.

There is proof that segregating children by race and class promotes a kind of racism or, at least, imposes a reduction of equality and diversity. Why is that good? America isn't getting whiter, Mr. Trump.

The Donald picked Betsy DeVos, and it's her crazy idea that we can walk away from public education. Further, nowhere in the Trump agenda is there a plan to get more kids into college. It's almost as if Trump doesn't care about college, or he wants to do the opposite of whatever Bernie Sanders proposed.

The poorer our schools are, the fewer kids will get a good education and better jobs, which will lead to higher crime rates. We see what this did in the Middle East, and Trump is letting this happen in America. What a farce!

Grabbing excessive power = Constitutional crisis

We all should have seen this coming. During the campaign, I said to hard-core Trump people, *"Watch out, your candidate may one day figure out that crime with guns can be lowered by taking away the guns."* No one listened. One day the Donald might wake-up and figure out that the way to end gun violence in Chicago is to take all the guns away. We aren't there yet, but Trump has taken a direct approach maligning the Congress, the courts and the press. It's clear that he plans to do whatever he wants.

It makes me laugh to hear how *"illegal"* those Obama executive orders were. Executive orders were only illegal to Donald Trump when he disagreed with them. In his first 100 days in office, Trump signed 30 executive orders. As of May 1, 2017, he had signed 77 orders. Some of them more symbolic than real, while one was extremely troublesome and involved the Supreme Court having to pass judgement on it twice.

He might think he is getting things done, but he is only play-acting his presidency for the media. He signs things because that is what you do when you run big companies, but he's failed to explain why any of these orders are good for most Americans. They all seem to fix one small group's demand or implement some campaign promise he made. He simply doesn't consider the 48 percent of America that didn't vote for him.

Much like Obama's pledge to close the Guantanamo Bay detention camp, not all campaign promises happen. Trump's wall will probably never happen, but that won't stop him from signing something that says, *"Build that Wall."* The Freedom Caucus and hard-core conservatives will never let Trump waste that much money.

The person we should all be watching through this period of power struggle is the Attorney General. Some of the moves his department made have already taken away the rights of people. The tough *"law and order"* former Senator and judge, Jeff Sessions, although occasionally a punching bag for Trump, truly does get things done. In a way, his actions could give the President more power. Little mentioned was the law suit the DOJ launched trying to say that being fired because of your sexual orientation is not protected under discrimination laws. Now we hear that the DOJ will fight to protect White Americans from discrimination by the admissions offices at colleges. Really? White people need help?

It might not be long before some of the DOJ's actions will be challenged and taken up by the Supreme Court. Will the court grant Trump these powers, or will they protect the constitution? The next appointed member of the Supreme Court will determine how much power Trump and every future president will have. The only hope is a diligent Senate.

This is one critical reason to remove Trump from office soon and get on with the business of moderate governance. A country doesn't do well when its president has too much power. Look at what happened in Iraq and, for the older readers, Germany.

Unpredictable rather than Consistent

Donald Trump brags about being unpredictable. There are times when he uses that to answer a question, much like a protective screen.

For example, in one of his tweets Trump stated that North Korea will never get an intercontinental ballistic missile. When the North Korean missiles became a threat to the United States, Trump said he would handle it. However, when pressed, he rebuked the question with a stern reminder that he isn't going to say what he's going to do. He wants to be unpredictable. Great, but now that North Korea has ICBM weaponry, what is your answer again, Mr. President?

Trump constantly scolds Obama and admonishes all former Presidents for not stopping North Korea, but what has he done? What is his plan? Kim Jong Un keeps moving forward and nothing has stopped them. That's exactly how Pakistan got the atomic bomb. Every nation told them not to do it, and they did it anyway. How is North Korea different?

One must think about the opposite of unpredictable. Words that come to mind are: certain, definite, reliable, stable, steady, sure, unchanging, constant and of course, predictable.

We do not have a steady and stable president. The writing is on the wall, and it's not a wall keeping people out, it's the wall that Trump has built around himself. He has never been an inclusive person and his blurry foreign policies make other nations nervous.

He is truly the kind of northeast elitist that the far-right fights against. He is the enemy of the middle-class and a useless blow-hard for the poor. He is a money-hungry, Godless old, fat fool who really believes he, and he alone, can fix the problem.

Okay, you can sit back and put this book on the shelf and say, what an imprudent ideolog spouting negatives about someone who he didn't vote for.

And you would be correct. I have witnessed the first 200 days of a president who I don't want, don't like and indeed, didn't vote for, but please answer a few questions for me before we are finished.

Did Donald J. Trump bring America together? Did your paycheck increase? Did your medical bills lessen? Did violence go down in the inner cities? Did Congress get more productive? Did America become the tiniest bit greater?

What comes to mind is the horrible scene of Charlie Sheen streaming online his pointless monologue, smoking cigarettes and talking about winning. The movie and TV star babbled about how the whole world was going to miss him. And in the end, it wasn't the winning he got, it was the pain of realizing that the mistakes he made his whole life had come back to haunt him.

Donald Trump wants America to win, I get that. I don't doubt that when he first started thinking about being president he had a strong, genuine desire to make things better. What he didn't realize is that running the United States of America isn't like managing a business. You cannot cook the books, float a rumor or play a joke on someone without lots of people noticing. It's too bad that Trump never ran a public company, he would have seen what it is like to have a board of directors suck the life out of your ego.

My daily diatribes do sound like the thoughts of a delusional blogger, but I had to write this stuff. If the election was held today, Donald Trump would not win. I am sure someone else could do a better job, even Mike Pence, but it will take a lot of people standing up and saying Number 45 must go.

The best Christmas present for America this year would be Donald Trump finally figuring out that this is not the right job for him. I hope that when he leaves he addresses not only his base but the whole nation. He doesn't need to say he is sorry, but he should at least tell us that he tried his best and that it just didn't work out. He cannot admit that he was never qualified for the job in the first place. That would be much too honest for America's most powerful liar.

And that brings me to the most important thing I will say in this book. We talked in the beginning about what it would take to impeach a president. The President can be removed from office with a finding and conviction in the Senate for treason, bribery, or other high crimes and misdemeanors.

What we have in the first 200 days is a collection of what may appear as small things, but they start to multiply and build into not only less credibility for this President, but a real question of lack of transparency and truthful execution. The lies that were used to get elected, one might look beyond those tricks in the campaign game, but they were lies. They misled the American people. We do know that Russian hackers got to into the DNC server and leaked emails and documents through Wikileaks, an activity that candidate Trump endorsed. He has done nothing as President to press that investigation or speak out against Russian interference with the election. Why?

He openly admitted that he fired James Comey, a key person in the investigation of Russian interference, because the Russian matter was giving him too much pressure. He waited for weeks before firing Michael Flynn, even after the last President, the DOJ and others gave him advice that Flynn was a bad actor. Yet, Trump didn't fire him until he was forced to when the facts of Flynn's meetings and discussions with Russian agents where disclosed by the Washington Post. The reason Trump gave for firing Flynn was the fact that he lied to Vice President Pence. But then, Trump added this, *"He didn't have to do that (resign), because what he did wasn't wrong."* Was he trying to say that lying is okay, as long as it doesn't embarrass someone in the administration? Why?

When the Flynn controversy flared-up, Trump attacked the press and called the investigation a "witch-hunt." The President's actions are clearly the application of intimidation and use of his office in order to obstruct justice. He took the uncouth steps to use his public forum, Twitter, to harass the Attorney General for recusing himself. The highest-ranking officer of the Department of Justice was directly rebuked in pubic for his lawful and appropriate action. This was in a sense, asking a member of his cabinet to look the other way on a law and procedure baked into our system to help maintain the credibility and impartiality of those in Justice.

In public view, Donald J. Trump attempted to answer the question about his or his campaign's involvement with Russia said, *"Nobody that I know of. How many times do I have to answer this question? Russia is a ruse. I have nothing to do with Russia. Haven't made a phone call to Russia in years. I own nothing in Russia, I have no loans in Russia, I don't have any deals in Russia. Russia is fake news."*

At the press conference with the President of Colombia, Trump said, *"... there is no collusion between certainly myself and my campaign, but I can always speak for myself -- and the Russians: zero. Because, believe me, there's no collusion. Russia is fine. But whether it's Russia or anybody else, my total priority, believe me, is the United States of America."*

We only had to wait a few months later when it was admitted that not only Flynn had met with and communicated with Russians, but Paul Manafort, Jared Kushner, Jeff Sessions and Trump's own son, Don, Jr. had significant meetings with Russians. While the President may focus his defense on the legal term, "collusion" as if that's the silver bullet to bring down his presidency, he fails his office when he defends the lies with more lies. It just doesn't work like that when you are President. You can't just say that *"anyone would have taken that meeting to get opposition information."* When people operate legally, they don't go to the Russian dirt meeting without the FBI being notified.

There are lots of hot spots in the world, like Syria, Russian encroachment in eastern Europe and of course, North Korea. Trump is being challenged on domestic issues and feels the need to over-sell himself in light of these criticisms, but he keeps telling lies. He keeps exaggerating in an attempt to make people like him, while his obvious thin-skin shows the real man inside the veneer. He's a born liar and that is his worst sin. The risk we are taking is that America will be less great when he is done and that will mean that all his promises were lies.

There are legal scholars who can debate the finer points of what it takes to remove the President from office, but I would like to propose something that I haven't heard elsewhere. Someone on TV recently said that a possible misdemeanor, and even a felony in certain settings, occurs when someone lies under oath.

When the President stood before America, and said: *"I do solemnly swear that I will faithfully execute the Office of President of the United States, and will to the best of my ability, preserve, protect and defend the Constitution of the United States,"* he took an oath. That oath doesn't go away. The President is under that oath every day of his life as President.

The phrase, *"faithfully execute"* is the most powerful part of the oath. Taking the word *"faithfully,"* we see that it has two meanings. The first is proceeding in *a loyal manner*, while the second meaning says, *in a manner that is true to the facts* or the original.

The person being sworn in is stating that they will *execute*, carry out or put into effect, their office in a *loyal manner* and in a manner, that is *true to the facts* or the original.

I assume in this situation; the original would be George Washington. And of course, he could never tell a lie; he confessed to cutting down the cherry tree. So, the oath is demanding that the President carry out his duties *in a manner that is true to the facts*. By taking the oath, the President is agreeing not to lie to the citizens of the United States.

And with the best of that person's ability, they must *preserve, protect and defend the Constitution of the United States*. This means that any of their actions that would destroy, lessen or deface the words in that sacred document would be breaking their oath, and, I believe, breaking the law.

This man has lied under oath and should be removed from office. I assume we all agree that the oath to become the President of the United States is important. Only the importance of the Republic is greater. Therefore, Donald Trump should be repealed, replaced and impeached.

THANK YOU

First, I would like to say thanks all those people who haven't unfriended me on Facebook and Twitter and have enjoyed my daily posts and opinions.

Next, I would like to thank my college buddy of 50 years ago, Kenny Lee, for his brilliant pagination and formatting of the text for this book and his many hours of editing my work. He was there every day for me.

Once again, Aimee Lim brought home a great book cover design for this work and I thank her for everything she has done for me. I owe her a cookie.

Thanks to my partner and girlfriend Roxy Myzal for actually wanting to live with a writer who spends most of his day glued to a computer screen.

Also, thanks to the owners, publishers and writers of the great newspapers of the United States for telling the truth and doing their jobs uncovering the facts and fighting each day to combat the "Fake News" from the White House and those outliner web sites who think they are journalists.

And finally, thanks to Donald J. Trump for providing the material for this book. Always be yourself Donald and we will always speak truth to power.

ABOUT THE AUTHOR

Dwight C. Douglas was born in Pittsburgh, PA and attended Point Park University where he studied Journalism and Communication. He worked on the PBS TV show *Mister Rogers Neighborhood* as a film-telecine technician and worked at the American Broadcasting Companies as they were developing their FM properties.

Douglas moved to Atlanta to join the largest radio consulting firm in the world, Burkhart-Abrams & Associates, where he later became president and worked with media companies around the world. During that 25-year period, he was instrumental in recruiting and coaching high-profile radio morning shows, including Howard Stern.

He moved to New York in 2000 to be the vice president of marketing for a worldwide software company. In that same time, he produced a comedy web site. Throughout his career, he has written numerous screenplays, magazine articles and is the author of several books.

In 2017, Dwight Douglas retired from his marketing job so he could write full-time. He splits his time between the Adirondacks in upstate New York and Florida's Gold Coast; depending on the air temperature.

OTHER BOOKS BY THE AUTHOR

If God Could Talk... The Diary of a TV Journalist

A cable TV talk show host is approached by a friend who offers a guest for his show who has never been on TV before. The Diary of a TV Journalist is the story about the host of the show and his executive producer vetting the guest and attempting to determine If God Could Talk... Available at Amazon.com, GoodReads.com, Barnesandnoble.com

If God Could Cry – The True Meaning of Mercy

The famous cable TV talk show host, Jonas Bronck, leaves New York on his quest to find truth. He finds himself in the middle of terror and personal torment in the name of journalism. He once again asks, If God Could Cry, would he be crying for us, or with us?   Available at Amazon.com, GoodReads.com, Barnesandnoble.com